PSYCHOANALYSIS AND DEVELOPMENT

PSYCHOANALYTIC CROSSCURRENTS

General Editor: Leo Goldberger

SELF AND OTHER: OBJECT RELATIONS IN PSYCHOANALYSIS AND
LITERATURE
by Robert Rogers

THE IDEA OF THE PAST: HISTORY, SCIENCE, AND PRACTICE
IN AMERICAN PSYCHOANALYSIS
by Leonard Jonathan Lamm

SUBJECT AND AGENCY IN PSYCHOANALYSIS: WHICH IS
TO BE MASTER?
by Frances M. Moran

JACQUES LACAN'S RETURN TO FREUD: THE REAL,
THE SYMBOLIC, AND THE IMAGINARY
by Philippe Julien

FREUD'S TRUTH: THE ENCOUNTER WITH THE REAL
by M. Guy Thompson

PSYCHOANALYSIS AND DEVELOPMENT: REPRESENTATIONS
AND NARRATIVES
edited by Massimo Ammaniti and Daniel N. Stern

PSYCHOANALYSIS AND DEVELOPMENT

Representations and Narratives

Edited by Massimo Ammaniti
and Daniel N. Stern

NEW YORK UNIVERSITY PRESS
New York and London

NEW YORK UNIVERSITY PRESS
New York and London

Copyright © 1994 by New York University

Library of Congress Cataloging-in-Publication Data
Rappresentazioni e narrazioni. English.
Psychoanalysis and development : representations and narratives /
edited by Massimo Ammaniti and Daniel N. Stern.
p.   cm. — (Psychoanalytic crosscurrents)
Includes bibliographical references and index.
ISBN 0-8147-0616-9 (alk paper) :
1. Representation (Psychoanalysis)   2. Narration (Rhetoric)—
Psychological aspects.   3. Psychology—Biographical methods.
I. Ammaniti, Massimo, 1941–   . II. Stern, Daniel N.   III. Title.
IV. Series.
BF175.5.R43R3613   1994   94-14618
150.19′5—dc20   CIP

New York University Press books are printed on acid-free paper,
and their binding materials are chosen for strength and durability.

Manufactured in the United States of America

10   9   8   7   6   5   4   3   2   1

Contents

Part III: Representations and Narratives in Clinical Work

Foreword

The *Psychoanalytic Crosscurrents* series presents selected books and monographs that reveal the growing intellectual ferment within and across the boundaries of psychoanalysis.

Freud's theories and grand-scale speculative leaps have been found wanting, if not disturbing, from the very beginning and have led to a succession of derisive attacks, shifts in emphasis, revisions, modifications, and extensions. Despite the chronic and, at times, fierce debate that has characterized psychoanalysis, not only as a movement but also as a science, Freud's genius and transformational impact on the twentieth century have never been seriously questioned. Recent psychoanalytic thought has been subjected to dramatic reassessments under the sway of contemporary currents in the history of ideas, philosophy of science, epistemology, structuralism, critical theory, semantics, and semiology as well as in sociobiology, theology, and neurocognitive science. Not only is Freud's place in intellectual history being meticulously scrutinized; his texts, too, are being carefully read, explicated, and debated within a variety of conceptual frameworks and sociopolitical contexts.

The legacy of Freud is perhaps most notably evident within the narrow confines of psychoanalysis itself, the "impossible profession" that has served as the central platform for the promulgation of official orthodoxy. But Freud's contributions—his original radical thrust—reach far beyond the parochial concerns of the psychoanalyst as clinician. His writings touch on a wealth of issues, crossing traditional boundaries—be they situated in the biological, social, or humanistic spheres—that have profoundly altered our conception of the individual and society.

A rich and flowering literature, falling under the rubric of "applied psychoanalysis," came into being, reached its zenith many decades ago, and then almost vanished. Early contributors to this literature, in addition to Freud himself, came from a wide range of backgrounds both within and outside the medical/psychiatric field, many later becoming psychoanalysts themselves. These early efforts were characteristically reductionistic in their attempt to extrapolate from psychoanalytic theory (often the purely clinical theory) to explanations of phenomena lying at some distance from the clinical. Over the years, academic psychologists, educators, anthropologists, sociologists, political scientists, philosophers, jurists, literary critics, art historians, artists, and writers, among others (with or without formal psychoanalytic training), have joined in the proliferation of this literature.

The intent of the *Psychoanalytic Crosscurrents* series is to apply psychoanalytic ideas to topics that may lie beyond the narrowly clinical, but its essential conception and scope are quite different. The present series eschews the reductionistic tendency to be found in much traditional "applied psychoanalysis." It acknowledges not only the complexity of psychological phenomena but also the way in which they are embedded in social and scientific contexts that are constantly changing. It calls for a dialectical relationship to earlier theoretical views and conceptions rather than a mechanical repetition of Freud's dated thoughts. The series affirms the fact that contributions to and about psychoanalysis have come from many directions. It is designed as a forum for the multidisciplinary studies that intersect with psychoanalytic thought but without the requirement that psychoanalysis necessarily be the starting point or, indeed, the center focus. The criteria for inclusion in the series are that the work be significantly informed by psychoanalytic thought or that it be aimed at furthering our understanding of psychoanalysis in its broadest meaning as theory, practice, and social phenomenon; that it be of current topical interest and that it provide the critical reader with contemporary insights; and, above all, that it be high-quality scholarship, free of absolute dogma, banalization, and empty jargon. The author's professional identity and particular theoretical orientation matters only to the extent that such facts may serve to frame the work for the reader, alerting him or her to inevitable biases of the author.

The *Psychoanalytic Crosscurrents* series presents an array of works from the multidisciplinary domain in an attempt to capture the ferment of scholarly activities at the core as well as the boundaries of psychoanalysis.

The books and monographs are from a variety of sources: authors will be psychoanalysts—traditional, neo- and post-Freudian, existential, object relational, Kohutian, Lacanian, etc.—social scientists with quantitative or qualitative orientations to psychoanalytic data, and scholars from the vast diversity of approaches and interests that make up the humanities. The series entertains works on critical comparisons of psychoanalytic theories and concepts as well as philosophical examinations of fundamental assumptions and epistemic claims that furnish the base for psychoanalytic hypotheses. It includes studies of psychoanalysis as literature (discourse and narrative theory) as well as the application of psychoanalytic studies of creativity and the arts. Works in the cognitive and neurosciences will be included to the extent that they address some fundamental psychoanalytic tenet, such as the role of dreaming and other forms of unconscious mental processes.

It should be obvious that an exhaustive enumeration of the types of works that might fit into the *Psychoanalytic Crosscurrents* series is pointless. The studies comprise a lively and growing literature as a unique domain; books of this sort are frequently difficult to classify or catalog. Suffice it to say that the overriding aim of the editor of this series is to serve as a conduit for the identification of the outstanding yield of that emergent literature and to foster its further unhampered growth.

LEO GOLDBERGER
New York University

Contributors

MASSIMO AMMANITI is a psychoanalyst and Professor of Childhood Psychopathology at the University of Rome.

CHRISTOPHER BOLLAS is a psychoanalyst of the British Psychoanalytical Society.

JEROME BRUNER is Research Professor of Psychology and Senior Research Fellow in Law at New York University. He has studied the nature and growth of cognitive processes for many years. He is now at work on the forms of narrative thought and how these become institutionalized in literature and law.

ADELE NUNZIANTE CESARO is a psychotherapist and Professor at the University of Naples.

FRANCESCO CORRAO is a psychoanalyst of the Italian Psychoanalytical Society.

ROBERT N. EMDE is a psychoanalyst and Professor at the University of Colorado Medical School.

CAROL FLEISHER FELDMAN is a Senior Research Scientist in the Department of Psychology at New York University. She is interested in the various relations between language and thought. Recently she has been investigating forms of interpretative thinking that are supported by literary language—language that transcends the adaptive necessities of everyday life.

ENZO FUNARI is a psychoanalyst and Professor at the University of Milan.

ANNA MARIA GALDO is a psychoanalyst and Professor at the University of Naples.

CELESTINO GENOVESE is a psychoanalyst and Research Fellow at the University of Naples.

MAURO MANCIA is a psychoanalyst and Professor at the University of Milan.

CLOTILDE PONTECORVO is a psychopedagogist and Professor at the University of Rome.

JOSEPH SANDLER is Freud Memorial Professor of Psychoanalysis at the University of London and President of the International Psychoanalytical Association.

DANIEL N. STERN is a psychoanalyst and Professor of Psychology at the University of Geneva and Adjunct Professor of Psychiatry at Cornell University, New York.

Introduction

Massimo Ammaniti and
Daniel N. Stern

The concept of representation has played a key role in the development of psychoanalysis, clinical research, and theoretical speculation. This is already clear in the early writings of Freud, who had been influenced by German philosophical thought (see Funari's contribution). However, we find a far more complete explanation of this theoretical concept years later, in what is now considered a classic work by Sandler and Rosenblatt (1962). Sandler, author of one of the contributions to this volume, states that the term "representation" implies two separate concepts: a stable internal organization, an internal map which collects and integrates all mental images and relational dispositions between the self and others and, secondly, the contents and the cognitive-affective characteristics of these images, which dwell within each personal experience. A more controversial aspect is the way in which the process of internalization takes place. This involves the building up of an internal mental world quite separate from external reality and which allows us to give a meaning to our own experiences, make predictions, and make decisions about future behaviors. In the formation of representation it is difficult to establish the weight to be given to experiences directly connected to reality compared with unconscious phantasies. Examples of extreme positions are Melanie Klein's theories, according to which unconscious phantasies play a decisive role in the building of images of parental figures, and John Bowlby's theories, which, on the contrary, emphasize the role of real interactions which take place with attachment figures.

The concept of narration has a very different history; it has become influential in the field of psychoanalysis only during the last fifteen years. It should be remembered, however, that in Freud too the notion that personal experience might take on the character of a narrative construction is implied in his essay *Screen Memories* (1899). After speaking of the "peculiarity of infant scenes," Freud concluded that

> the recognition of this fact must diminish the distinction we have drawn between screen memories and other memories derived from our childhood. It may indeed be questioned whether we have any memories at all *from* our childhood: memories *relating* to our childhood may be all we possess. Our childhood memories show us our earliest years not as they were but as they appeared at the later periods when the memories were elicited. In these periods of "recall," the childhood memories did not, as people are accustomed to say, emerge, rather they were formed at that time. And a number of factors, with no concern for historical accuracy, had a part in forming them, as well as in the selection or the memories themselves. (322)

In Freud's opinion, the "raw material of memory" remains unknown in its original form, but according to a later rereading by Schafer (1989), in an analytical process it may find a psychic relevance through a narrative form.

A reference point on this subject is Roy Schafer's 1976 work "A New Language for Psychoanalysis," in which he suggests the concept of action language. The scene is set in the United States in the mid-seventies, Freudian metapsychology was going through an irreversible crisis; the theoretical construction of mental functioning which Rapaport had tried to organize, at the end of the fifties, in an effort to confer upon psychoanalysis a stable scientific status which might justify its entrance into the temple of science, was at an end. But just at the time when this sound theoretical explanation was put forward, radical criticism of the concept of psychic energy, which is central to psychoanalytical theory, was developing. Several American psychoanalysts who had participated in Rapaport's undertaking, such as George Klein, and Schafer himself, accused metapsychology of being too far removed from the subjective experience of the patient. Metapsychological language, with its lexicon made up of terms such as drives, forces, cathexis, and decathexis, appeared too distant from the everyday language of the patient, and every translation of this language ran the risk of betraying the meaning of personal experience.

While there is general agreement with the criticism of the abstractness of metapsychology, the same can not be said regarding the remedy proposed by Schafer. Returning to Wittgenstein's formulations, Schafer suggests that nouns should no longer be used to indicate objects, as they would give rise to reifications leading to a theoretical horizon composed of entities in no way correspondent to the real world. It would be more profitable to use verbs which may be qualified by adverbs: we would no longer refer to a patient as a narcissist, but rather we would speak of a patient who behaves narcissistically. Having entered the world of language, Schafer pursued this perspective further.

In "The Psychoanalytic Attitude" (1983) he states that we are forever telling ourselves stories about ourselves and in so doing and in telling them also to others for various reasons, we are doing something which might be defined as a narrative action. The direction provided by Schafer led inevitably toward hermeneutics and in particular toward narrative interpretations. In Schafer's more recent writings the legitimacy of this narrative paradigm receives further confirmation, as he introduces the idea of multiple stories: the patient has not one but a set of stories which he tells himself. A scenario is built up between the patient and his analyst which gathers together the memories and phantasies forming the network of personal and interpersonal meanings which in due time are revised and transformed into a narrative structure—this concept is developed by Corrao in this volume.

As Schafer added in a recent article (1989) "the introspecting subject extracts from the plenitude of potential experience what is wanted . . . and introspection does not encounter ready-made material. . . . [F]or these reasons developmental theories cannot avoid giving accounts of the different ways in which experience is constructed as advances take place in the child's and adult's cognitive and psychosexual functioning" (155). The thread of personal history, Schafer maintains, doesn't represent a concept which excludes self-representations, even though the former carries a wider meaning as it does not take into consideration single representations identified and analyzed as static and altogether disconnected mental contents. In this case the thread of personal history may be considered along a thematic perspective running throughout the network of representations.

Out of the psychoanalytical dialogue a story begins to take shape, a story told by both the protagonists: the psychoanalyst with his ability to integrate and retell the story, and the patient who, during the analytical process, becomes an increasingly open and reliable interlocutor.

Spence moves in the same direction in his "Narrative Truth and Historical Truth" (1982), even though his itinerary differs from that of Schafer both in his theoretical outlook and the theses he sustains. Spence's main concern was the same one that troubled Freud, especially in the last years of his life, as is evident from *Constructions in Analysis* (1937). In accordance with the well-known archaeological metaphor, in carrying out his work the analyst digs into the patient's personal history and reconstructs his childhood, this conception probably being borrowed from Charcot and from the conception of the childhood trauma which continues to linger, even though in a dissociated form, in the patient's mind. Nevertheless, in the last years of his life Freud began to realize that it was difficult to make reliable reconstructions, rather the analyst would create constructions which would be ratified during the course of the therapy on a purely emotional level. If we think of early childhood experiences, and in particular of the preverbal ones, to claim to reconstruct such early phases appears a rather difficult task for the reason that memory doesn't function statically like a filing cabinet from which memories can be brought to light when needed. Spence radicalizes this bipolarity: on the one hand there is historical truth, what actually happened to the patient, whilst on the other there is narrative truth which is constructed during the analytical process. On this subject Spence wrote (1982) that Freud has made us aware of the persuasive power of a coherent narration in particular of the way in which a suitably chosen reconstruction can fill the gap between two events which obviously don't correlate and in the course of a process can make sense of something which is apparently nonsensical. There is no doubt that a well constructed story possesses real and immediate narrative truth bearing a significance which is important for the process of therapeutic change.

In his most recent work, Spence (1990) has firmly opted for the field of rhetoric defined as "the art of using language for persuasion, in speaking or writing" (579). The use of metaphor, in Spence's opinion, is absolutely essential in scientific elaboration, above all in the clinical field where individual lived experiences can be better described by using anthropomorphic concepts. Spence (1990) goes further, affirming that psychoanalytical theory itself is still widely metaphorical and that the set of hypotheses and working models have been elaborated to such a small degree that to congeal them in definite theories would prove unhelpful. It's too early to try and talk of the "stuff" of the mind, while "the way we talk about the mind is probably just as important as the object being described" (595). On this point there is strong convergence with constructionism, which maintains that any effort to acquire knowledge about the mind by means of empirical verifications is mistaken. The rhetorical voice, however, would not, according to Spence, mask the voice of evidence, which is connected to the direct observation of phenomena. But the evidential voice is "only just beginning to be heard and—says Spence—this writing speaks only with a whisper" (599).

Clearly this option would mean betraying Freud's intention to make psychoanalysis a scientific discipline and would instead make it a historical hermeneutic discipline, on the same level as philology and exegesis. In abandoning all references to historical reality, narrativity becomes the only criterion for psychoanalytical validation. Sherwood defines narrativity as a full explanation unique to the history of the case and for a single patient; explaining has meaning for it reorganizes facts intelligibly so as to form a unique story. At this point the problem of proving the scientific validity of psychoanalysis fails completely and truth would be tied indissolubly to the history of the case.

This is not, however, the opinion of Ricoeur (1977), who maintains that "the narrative commitment" must proceed on a parallel with the "explanatory commitment," the latter being represented by its metapsychological theoretical level. If the ultimate truth claim—writes Ricoeur— "resides in the case histories, the means of proof reside in the articulation of the entire network: theory, hermeneutics, therapeutics, and narration" (863). The epistemological problems which open up are practically insoluble for the precise reason that we can't avoid the risk of circular thinking, or rather of a self-fulfilling prophesy. Schafer, while considering psychoanalytical validation to be limited exclusively to the therapeutic dyad, if it is coherent, organized, and endowed with common sense, nevertheless recognizes that some narrations about the self are stable in their organization and contents and thus indicate a psychic structure and a stable and coherent self.

This connection is particularly interesting in that it reveals the close and necessary relationship between representation and narration, implying that the latter has a place not only in the world of rhetoric but is linked to the organization of the mind. Ricoeur widens the horizon even further, maintaining that an external validation of psychoanalytical theory cannot be excluded: that is to say that there exist general hypotheses concerning the way in which the mind functions and develops, independently of the various narrations that can be construed. This is a point of view which would lead to intersections with other fields of research, represented, for example, by cognitivism and developmental psychology.

If we adopt a developmental outlook, we find ourselves faced with two epistemological meanings which appear irreconcilable, the equivalent of a "reconstructed clinical baby" (Stern 1985) and a "non-clinical directly observed baby." But the wall which divides the two may begin to crumble if we go back to the concept of narration and the studies about narrative competence. Clinical psychoanalytical data are based on autobiographical narrations told by the patient to his psychoanalyst as well as to himself, using the narrative forms of his own culture. In parallel, an enormous number of experimental studies are being carried out on children, who begin, after the age of three, to tell stories about themselves, making use of narrative forms suggested by culture and easily acquired at that age (Nelson 1989). It is doubtlessly true that there are differences between the psychoanalytical and the experimental setting, just as there are different motives for the autobiographical account, but these diversities no longer constitute an unbreachable epistemological gap. Through the study of narration, psychoanalysts and development psychologists find themselves studying basically similar data. Historically, a similar problem faced child psychoanalysis when it linked a child's symbolic play (which develops in the period in which narrative ability begins) with verbal production in adult patients. Studying these play activities, which have referents in experience, this objection was dropped. The question was no longer nonverbal play as opposed to associative verbal flow, but instead it was the symbolic play which became an almost independent aid which helped to clarify the basic data connected to the narration.

In the same way, the interchange between psychoanalysts and development psychologists represents an important opportunity for an exchange which may lead to new research instruments and converging concepts useful in reconstructing psychic reality. In terms of validation we can try to study how narration links up, from an evolutionary point of view, with the building up of a narrative Self, which, as Daniel Stern pointed out in 1985, constitutes an important developmental domain in a child's life, in as much as it involves the translation of personal experience into the narrative form.

Nonetheless it is likely that certain experiences remain fundamentally beyond words, like those pertaining to the body described by Nunziante Cesaro or, in a wider sense, prerepresentational, as Genovese writes, and can be translated only via other communication channels. Although the analytical stage is fundamentally verbal, there does exist a communicative link based on affective exchanges and unconscious processes of projective identification, as discussed by Bollas, Galdo, and Mancia in their contributions to this book. The dynamics of transference allow the unconscious representations to take shape and also the patient's "internal speech" which goes beyond what can be spoken. Also, the analyst's countertransference contributes to the constructing and reconstructing of the patient's story, since the patient's narration enters the analyst's world. This area has been defined by Cardona (1990) as "preformed and a-linguistic" and different from the area that is "formed and linguistic." In fact, with language "man enters into rational behavior which is controlled and social and so he casts off his instinctive behaviors" (363).

Validations in the field of development psychology find further interesting confirmation in recent research about the intergenerational transmission of styles of attachment started by Main and Goldwyn (1985), an example of which one of us supplies in his contribution to this volume, a research application beginning with narration during pregnancy.

These studies concerning intergenerational transmission permit an examination of the dynamics by means of which the internal working models, that is to say the parental mental representations, influence the child's style of attachment and finally his own way of representing himself and other significative figures. The internal working model finds a narrative expression in telling the story of childhood experiences, and this may be more or less coherent in character depending on the degree of integration of one's internal images. In the case of a coherent account, the flow of the story proceeds comprehensibly, with thoughts and feelings connected to the past and the episodes and experiences which marked it being consistent with each other. As Grice pointed out (1975), an account must comply with some rules of conversation which concern the quality (be truthful and be based on the evidence of what is said); the quantity (be succinct and at the same time complete); the relation (be relevant and comprehensible); and finally the style (be clear and ordered). On the basis of these conversational criteria Main and Goldwyn have elaborated an interesting classification of internal working models of Self and others, which constitute dynamic mental representations which are kept partially or completely outside our consciousness. As Bowlby wrote in 1980: "every situation in our lives is interpreted by the representational models that we have of the world about us and of ourselves. The information which reaches our sense organs is selected and interpreted on the basis of these models, their significance for us and those we care for is always evaluated on the basis of these models and plans of action are conceived and carried out with these models in mind" (229). These internal models are not only filters for our experiences, they also tend to actively recreate experiences which are consistent with our own relational history, and this constitutes a particularly relevant aspect of human behavior. Given the influence which internal working models have on our personal behavior and the way in which they govern our affects, a significant correspondence has been observed between mothers who have a sufficiently balanced representation of themselves and others and a secure attachment pattern on the part of a child aged one year. In these women a positive internalization of attachment figures and childhood experiences has taken place without their having been altered by idealization. There is an adequate evaluation of personal relationships, tolerance of imperfections, and the story flows coherently and convincingly. In their relationship with the child, these mothers demonstrate sensitivity to the affective signals given out by the child, they tolerate negative ones like pain or rage because they are able to see them in a relational context, which recognizes and accepts the child's needs. In this relational sphere the child will in turn build up the image of an attentive and caring parent, above all in times of personal suffering.

Regarding the motivational systems of attachment, the narration takes up a particular plot which focuses on and emphasizes the characteristics of the relationship with important figures, responses to separations, losses, reactions to stress, and trust in figures of attachment. However, even the formal structure of the story is influenced by it; this will happen whether it be a coherent narration where the relationship with the interlocutor is kept up and encouraged, whether the relationship is maintained at a distance, or whether it gets caught up in an enmeshed relationship, confirming once again the connection between relational style and manner of narrating and conversing with others. In other words, the way in which we represent our relationship with others is reflected in the way we narrate. What is true for the relationship between representation and narrations about attachment, is likely to be true for representation and narration concerning other motivational systems in this vein, Robert Emde reveals in his contribution that the Oedipus drama assumes different meanings depending on how its narration is punctuated and what is emphasized. Narrations in clinical work and research are not mythical stories which reside outside demonstration, instead they have important connections with the different human motivational system. Narrations, like human motivations, can change both at various points in an individual's life, and during the different phases of a life cycle, so that whilst during adolescence sexuality may be dominant as a motivational system, during middle age motivations pertaining to self-realization can assume greater value. Equally, in analytical work the character of the same narration can change, becoming enriched and accepting new points of view and a deeper affective meaning. There are also interesting convergences with cognitivism and psycholinguistics, which we can read about in the contributions to this book made by Bruner, Feldman, and Pontecorvo. Alongside a paradigmatic or logical-scientific thought which "carries on the ideal of a system which is descriptive and explanatory, formal and mathematical" (Bruner 1986), there exists a narrative-thought, whose rules are less well known to us. This way of thinking produces good stories, fascinating pictures, and historical outlines, which correspond not to the criterion of truth but to that of verisimilitude. Whilst the paradigmatic thought must provide proof and demonstration, the narrative thought endeavours to convince by presenting a coherent story, analogies, and metaphors, or by means of interpretations—as Carol Feldman writes in her essay—which describes the human world in terms of intentions. Just as scientific explanations are subject to rules, so are interpretative or narrative explanations, which can correspond to different mental models which are constructed during the course of childhood and adolescence. Mental models (Johnson-Laird 1983) don't ever portray the state of things as they are in reality, but rather show up what is useful or interesting at that time. This conception of mental models tends to relativize a representation for there exists no single optimal image; each individual lives in a different way from others, even though in a general context largely speaking common to all people.

The change from one point of view to another is in fact dramatic. In the field of history, as in other disciplines, there has been a move from a more objective conception to a perspectivistic type of conception, to quote Nietzsche. As Duby the historian states in his book *The Dream of History,* interest is moving away from the history of great events to phenomena more entwined in a perspective of daily life. From the moment in which even science no longer sets out for objectivity of knowledge but recognizes the relativistic character of the visions of the world, psychoanalysis can create—and this is the opinion of the American philosopher Nelson Goodman—a bridge between science and art, in as much as we would be dealing with different visions of the world, the scientific one being more impersonal and objective and the artistic one being more personal and subjective.

In this clash between objectivity and subjectivity from which there is no way out, it may be useful to quote Calvino from *Six Memos for the Next Millennium.* At the point in the chapter dedicated to Visibility he writes, "Science interests me just because of its efforts to escape from anthropomorphic knowledge, I am nonetheless convinced that our imagination cannot be anything *but* anthropomorphic. This is the reason for my anthropomorphic treatment of a universe in which man has never existed, and I would add that it seems extremely unlikely that man could ever exist in such a universe" (90).

REFERENCES

Ammaniti, M., ed. 1989. *La nascita del S__*. Rome: Laterza.

Ammaniti, M., and Dazzi, N., eds. 1990. *Affetti.* Rome: Laterza.

Bowlby, J. 1980. *Attachment and loss.* Vol. 3, *Loss: Sadness and depression.* London: Hogarth Press.

Bruner, J. 1986. *Actual minds, possible world.* Cambridge: Harvard University Press.

———. 1990. *Acts of meaning.* Cambridge: Harvard University Press.

Calvino, I. 1988. *Six memos for the next millennium.* Cambridge: Harvard University Press.

Cardona, G. R. 1990. *I linguaggi del sapere.* Rome: Laterza.

Freud, S. 1899. *Screen memories. S. E.* Vol. 3. London: Hogarth Press.

———. 1937. *Constructions in analysis. S. E.* Vol. 23. London: Hogarth Press.

Goodman, N. 1978. *Ways of worldmaking.* Indianapolis: Hackett.

Grice, H. P. 1975. Logic and conversation. In *Syntax and semantics III: Speech acts,* edited by P. Cole and J. L. Moran. New York: Academic Press.

Johnson-Laird, P. N. 1983. *Mental models: Towards a cognitive science of language, inference, and consciousness.* Cambridge: Cambridge University Press.

Main, M., et al. 1985. Security of attachment in infancy, childhood, and adulthood: A move to the level of representation. In *Growing points of attachment theory and research,* edited by I. Bretherton and E. Waters. Chicago: University of Chicago Press.

Nelson, K., ed. 1989. *Narratives from the crib.* Cambridge: Harvard University Press.

Ricoeur, P. 1977. The question of proof in Freud's psychoanalytic writings. *J. Am. Psychoanal. Assn.* 25:835–71.

Sandler, J., and Rosenblatt, B. 1962. The concept of the representational world. *Psychoanal. Study of the Child* 17: 128–45.

Schafer, R. 1976. *A new language for psychoanalysis.* New Haven: Yale University Press.

———. 1983. *The Psychoanalytic attitude.* New York: Basic Books.

———. 1989. Narratives of the self. In *Psychoanalysis toward the second century,* edited by A. M. Cooper, O. F. Kernberg, and E. S. Person. New Haven: Yale University Press.

Spence, D. P. 1982. *Narrative truth and historical truth.* New York: Norton.

———. 1990. The rhetorical voice of psychoanalysis, *J. Am. Psychoanal. Assn.* 38: 579–604.

Stern, D. N. 1985. *The interpersonal world of the infant.* New York: Basic Books.

———. 1989. The representation of relational patterns: Developmental considerations. In *Relationship disturbances in early childhood,* edited by A. J. Sameroff and R. N. Emde. New York: Basic Books.

Vygotsky, L. 1962. *Thought and language.* New York: Wiley.

Werner, H., and Kaplan, B. 1963. *Symbol formation: An organismic-developmental approach to language and expression of thought.* New York: Wiley.

I

THEORETICAL DIMENSIONS

1

The Narrative Construction of "Reality"

Jerome Bruner

Surely since the Enlightenment, if not before, study of mind has centered principally upon how man achieves a "true" knowledge of the world. Emphasis in this pursuit has varied, of course: empiricists have concentrated upon the mind's interplay with an external world of nature, hoping to find the key in the association of sensations and ideas, while rationalists have looked inward to the powers of mind itself for the principles of right reason. The objective, in either case, has been to discover how we achieve "reality," that is to say, how we get a reliable "fix" on the world, a world that is, as it were, assumed to be immutable and, as it were, "there to be observed."

This quest has, of course, had a profound effect on the development of psychology, and the empiricist and rationalist traditions have dominated our conceptions of how the mind grows and how it gets its grasp on the "real world." Indeed, at mid-century, Gestalt theory represented the rationalist wing of this enterprise and American learning theory the empiricist. Both gave accounts of mental development as proceeding in some more or less linear and uniform fashion from an initial incompetence in the grasp of reality to a final competence, in one case attributing it to the working out of internal processes or mental organization, and in the other to some unspecified principle of reflection by which—whether through reinforcement, association, or conditioning—we came to respond to the world "as it is." There have always been dissidents who challenged these views, but conjectures about human mental development have been in-

fluenced far more by majoritarian rationalism and empiricism than by
these dissident voices.

In more recent times, it was Piaget who became the spokesman for the
classic rationalist tradition by arguing the universality of a series of invariant developmental stages, each with its own set of inherent logical operations that successively and inexorably led the child to construct a mental
representation of the real world akin to that of the detached, dispassionate
scientist. While he did not quite drive the empiricist learning theorists
from the field (they have begun to take new life again through the
formulation of "connectionist" computer-simulations of learning), his
views surely dominated psychology in the three decades following the
Second World War.

Now there is mounting criticism of his views. The growth of knowledge of "reality" or of the mental powers that enable this growth to occur,
the critics argue, is neither unilinear, strictly derivational in a logical sense,
nor is it, as it were, "across the board." Mastery of one task does not
assure mastery of other tasks that, in a formal sense, are governed by the
same principles. Knowledge and skill, rather, are domain specific and,
consequently, uneven in their accretion. Principles and procedures learned
in one domain do not automatically transfer to other domains. Such
findings were not simply a "failure to confirm" Piaget or the rational
premise generally.[1] Rather, if the acquisition of knowledge and of mental
powers is indeed domain specific and not automatically transferable, this
surely implies that a domain, so called, is a set of principles and procedures, rather like a prosthetic device, that permits intelligence to be used
in certain ways, but not in others. Each particular way of using intelligence develops an integrity of its own—a kind of knowledge-plus-skill-
plus-tool integrity—that fits it to a particular range of applicability. It is a
little "reality" of its own that is constituted by the principles and procedures that we use within it.

These domains, looked at in another way, constitute something like a
culture's treasury of tool kits. Few people ever master the whole range of
tool kits: we grow clever in certain spheres, and remain incompetent in
others in which, as it were, we do not become "hitched" to the relevant
tool kit. Indeed, one can go even further and argue, as some have, that
such cultural tool kits (if I may so designate the principles and procedures
involved in domain-specific growth) may in fact have exerted selection
pressures on the evolution of human capacities. It may be, for example,

that the several forms of intelligence proposed by Howard Gardner (which he attempts to validate by the joint evidence of neuropathology, genius, and cultural specialization) may be outcomes of such evolutionary selection.[2] The attraction of this view is, of course, that it links man and his knowledge-gaining and knowledge-using capabilities to the culture of which he and his ancestors were active members. But it brings deeply into question not only the universality of knowledge from one domain to another, but the universal translatability of knowledge from one culture to another. For in this dispensation, knowledge is never "point-of-viewless."

This outlook is very compatible with another trend that has arisen in the analysis of human intelligence and of "reality construction." It is not a new view, but it has taken new life in a new guise. Originally introduced by Vygotsky, and championed by his widening circle of admirers, the new position is that cultural products, like language and other symbolic systems, mediate thought and place their stamp on our representations of reality.[3] In its latest version, it takes the name, after Seely-Brown, Collins, and Duguid of *distributed intelligence*.[4] An individual's working intelligence is never "solo." It cannot be understood without taking into account his or her reference books, notes, computer programs, and data bases, or most important of all, the network of friends, colleagues, or mentors on whom one leans for help and advice. Your chance of winning a Nobel Prize increases immeasurably if you have worked in the laboratory of somebody who has already won one, not because of pull but because of access to the ideas and criticisms of those who know better.[5]

Once one takes such views as seriously as they deserve, there are some interesting and nonobvious consequences. The first is that there are probably a fair number of important domains supported by cultural tool kits and distributional networks. A second is that the domains are probably differentially integrated in different cultures, as anthropologists have been insisting for some years now.[6] And a third is that many domains are not organized by logical principles or associative connections, particularly those that have to do with man's knowledge of himself, his social world, his culture. Indeed, most of our knowledge about human knowledge-getting and reality-constructing is drawn from studies of how people come to know the natural or physical world rather than the human or symbolic world. For many historical reasons, including the practical power inherent in the use of logic, mathematics, and empirical science, we have concentrated upon the child's growth as "little scientist," "little logician," "little mathematician." These are typically Enlightenment-inspired studies. It is curious how little effort has gone into discovering how man comes to construct the social world and the things that transpire therein. Surely, such challenging recent works as E. E. Jones's magisterial *Interpersonal Perception* make it clear that we do not achieve our mastery of social reality by growing up as "little scientists," "little logicians," or "little mathematicians."[7] So while we have learned a very great deal indeed about how we come eventually to construct and "explain" a world of nature in terms of causes, probabilities, space-time manifolds, etc., we know altogether too little about how we go about constructing and representing the rich and messy domain of human interaction.

It is with just this domain that I want now to concern myself. Like the domains of logical-scientific reality construction, it is well buttressed by principles and procedures. It has an available cultural tool kit or tradition on which its procedures are modeled, and its distributional reach is as wide and as active as gossip itself. Its form is so familiar and ubiquitous that it is likely to be overlooked, in much the same way as we suppose that the fish will be the last to discover water. As I have argued extensively elsewhere, we organize our experience and our memory of human happenings mainly in the form of narrative—stories, excuses, myths, reasons for doing and not doing, and so on. Narrative is a conventional form, transmitted culturally and constrained by each individual's level of mastery and by his conglomerate of prosthetic devices, colleagues, and mentors. Unlike the constructions generated by logical and scientific procedures which can be weeded out by falsification, narrative constructions can only achieve "verisimilitude." Narratives, then, are a version of reality whose acceptability is governed by convention and "narrative necessity" rather than by empirical verification and logical requiredness, although ironically, we have no compunction about calling stories true or false.[8]

I propose now to sketch out ten features of narrative, rather in the spirit of constructing an armature upon which a more systematic account might be constructed. As with all accounts of forms of representation of the world, I shall have a great difficulty in distinguishing what may be called the narrative mode of *thought* from the forms of narrative *discourse*. As with all prosthetic devices, each enables and gives form to the other, just as the structure of language and the structure of thought eventually become inextricable. Eventually it becomes a vain enterprise to say which is the more basic—the mental processes or the discourse form that expresses it—for, just as our experience of the natural world tends to imitate the categories of familiar science, so our experience of human affairs comes to take the form of the narratives we use in telling about them.

Much of what I have to say will not be at all new to those who have been working in the vineyards of narratology or who have concerned themselves with critical studies of narrative forms. Indeed, the ancestry of many of the ideas that will concern me can be traced back directly to the debates that have been going on among literary theorists over the last decade or two. My comments are echoes of those debates now reverberating in the last human sciences—not only in psychology, anthropology, and linguistics, but also in the philosophy of language. For once the "Cognitive Revolution" in the human sciences brought to the fore the issue of how "reality" is represented in the act of knowing, it became apparent that it did not suffice to equate representations with images, with propositions, with lexical networks, or even with such more temporally extended vehicles as sentences. It was perhaps a decade ago that psychologists became alive to the possibility of narrative as a form not only of representing but of constituting reality, a matter on which I shall have more to say presently. It was at this point that cognitively inclined psychologists and anthropologists began to discover that their colleagues in literary theory and historiography were deeply immersed in asking comparable questions about textually situated narrative. I think one can even date the "paradigm shift" to the appearance of a collection of essays in 1981—*On Narrative*.[9]

If some of what I have to say about the features of narrative, then, seems "old hat" to the literary theorist, let him or her bear in mind that the object is different. The central concern is not how narrative as text is constructed, but rather how it operates as an instrument of mind in the construction of reality. And now to the ten features of the narrative.

1. Narrative diachronicity. A narrative is an account of events occurring over time. It is irreducibly durative. It may be characterizable in seemingly nontemporal terms (as a "tragedy" or a "farce") but such terms only summarize what are quintessentially patterns of events occurring over time. The time involved, moreover, as Ricoeur has noted, is "human time" rather than abstract or "clock" time.[10] It is time whose significance is given by the meaning assigned to events within its compass. William

Labov, one of the greatest students of narrative, also regards temporal sequence as essential to narrative but he locates this temporality in the meaning-preserving sequence of clauses in narrative *discourse* itself.[11] While this is a useful aid to linguistic analysis, it nonetheless obscures an important aspect of narrative representation. For there are many conventionalized ways of expressing the sequenced durativity of narrative even in discourse, like flashbacks and flashforwards, temporal synecdoche, and so on. As Nelson Goodman warns, narrative comprises an ensemble of ways of constructing and representing the sequential, diachronic order of human events, of which the sequencing of clauses in spoken or written "stories" is only one device.[12] Even nonverbal media have conventions of narrative diachronicity, as in the "left-to-right" and "up-to-down" conventions of cartoon strips and cathedral windows. What underlies all conventionalized forms for representing narrative is a "mental model" that has its unique pattern of events over time that gives it its defining property. And to that we shall come presently.

2. Particularity. Narratives take as their ostensive reference particular happenings. But this is, as it were, their vehicle rather than their destination. For stories plainly fall into more general types; they are about boy-woos-girl, bully-gets-his-comeuppance, etc. In this sense the particulars of narratives are tokens of broader types. Where the boy-woos-girl script calls for the giving of a gift, for example, the gift can equally well be flowers, perfume, or even an endless golden thread. Any of these may serve as an appropriate token or emblem of a gift. Particularity achieves its emblematic status by its embeddedness in a story that is in some sense generic. And, indeed, it is by virtue of this embeddedness in genre, to look ahead, that narrative particulars can be "filled in" when they are missing from an account. The "suggestiveness" of a story lies, then, in the emblematic nature of its particulars, its relevance to a more inclusive narrative type. But for all that, a narrative cannot be realized save through particular embodiment.

3. Intentional state entailment. Narratives about people acting in a setting, and the happenings that befall them must be relevant to their intentional states while so engaged—to their beliefs, desires, theories, values, etc. When animals or nonagentive objects are cast as narrative protagonists, they must be endowed with intentional states for the purpose, like the

Little Red Engine in the children's story. Physical events play a role in stories chiefly by affecting the intentional states of their protagonists. As Baudelaire put it, "The first business of an artist is to substitute man for nature."

But intentional states in narrative never fully determine the course of events, since a character with a particular intentional state might end up *doing* practically anything. For some measure of agency is always present in narrative, and agency presupposes choice—some element of "freedom." If people can predict anything from a character's intentional states, it is only how he will feel or how he will have perceived the situation. The loose link between intentional states and subsequent action is the reason why narrative accounts cannot provide causal explanations. What they supply instead is the basis for *interpreting* why a character acted as he or she did. Interpretation is concerned with "reasons" for things happening, rather than strictly with their "causes," a matter to which we turn next.

4. Hermeneutic composability. A preliminary word of explanation is need here. The word *hermeneutic* implies that there is a text or a text analogue *through* which somebody has been trying to express a meaning and *from* which somebody is trying to extract a meaning. This in turn implies that there is a difference between what is *expressed* in the text and what the text might *mean*, and furthermore that there is no unique solution to the task of determining *the* meaning for *this* expression. Such hermeneutic interpretation is required when there is neither a *rational* method of assuring the "truth" of a meaning assigned to the text as a whole, nor an *empirical* method for determining the verifiability of the constituent elements that make up the text. In effect, the best hope of hermeneutic analysis is to provide an intuitively convincing account of the meaning of the text as a whole in the light of the constituent parts that make it up. This leads to the dilemma of the so-called "hermeneutic circle"—in which we try to justify the "rightness" of one reading of a text in terms of other readings rather than by, say, rational deduction or empirical proof. The most concrete way of explicating this dilemma or "circle" is by reference to the relations between the meanings assigned the whole of a text (say a story) and its constituent parts. As Charles Taylor puts it, "we are trying to establish a reading for the whole text, and for this we appeal to readings of its partial expressions; and yet because we are dealing with meaning, with making sense, where expressions only make sense or not in relation to others, the readings of partial expressions depend on those of others, and ultimately of the whole."[13]

This is probably nowhere better illustrated than in narrative. The accounts of protagonists and events that constitute a narrative are selected and shaped in terms of a putative story or plot that then "contains" them. At the same time, the "whole" (the mentally represented putative story) is dependent for its formation upon a supply of constituent candidate parts. In this sense, as we have already noted, parts and wholes in a narrative rely upon each other for their viability.[14] In Vladimir Propp's terms, the parts of a narrative serve as "functions" of the narrative structure as a whole.[15] But the whole cannot be constructed without appropriate parts. This puzzling part-whole interdependence in narrative is, of course, the defining property of what is called the "hermeneutic circle." For a story can only be "realized" when parts and whole can, as it were, be made to live together.

This hermeneutic property marks narrative both in its construction and in its comprehension. For narratives do not exist, as it were, in some real world, waiting there patiently and eternally to be veridically mirrored in a text. The act of constructing a narrative, moreover, is considerably more complicated than "selecting" events either from real life, from memory, or from fantasy and then placing them in an appropriate order. The events themselves need to be *constituted* in the light of the overall narrative—in Propp's terms, to be made "functions" of the story. This is a matter to which we will return later.

Now let me return to "hermeneutic composability." The telling of a story and its comprehension *as* a story depend upon the human capacity to process knowledge in this interpretive way. It is a way of processing that has, in the main, been grossly neglected by students of mind raised either in the rationalist or empiricist traditions. The former have been concerned with mind as an instrument of right reasoning, with the means we employ for establishing the necessary truth inherent in a set of connected propositions. Piaget was a striking example of this rational tradition. Empiricists, for their part, rested their claims upon a mind capable of verifying the constituent "atomic propositions" that comprised a text. But neither of these procedures, right reason or verification, suffice for explicating how a narrative is either put together by a speaker or interpreted by a hearer. This is the more surprising since there is compelling evidence to indicate that narrative comprehension is among the earliest powers of the mind to appear in the young child and among the most widely used forms of organizing human experience.[16]

Many literary theorists and philosophers of the mind have argued that the act of interpreting is forced upon us only when a text of the world to which it presumes to refer is in some way "confused, incomplete, cloudy. . . ."[17] Doubtless we are more aware of our interpretive efforts when faced with textual or referential ambiguities. But I would take strong exception to the general claim that interpretation is forced upon us only by a surfeit of ambiguity. The illusion created by a skillful narrative that this is not the case, that a story "is as it is" and needs no interpretation, is produced by two quite different processes. The first should probably be called "narrative seduction." Great storytellers have the artifices of narrative reality construction so well mastered that their telling preempts the possibility of any but a single interpretation—however conventionally bizarre it may be. The famous episode of a Martian invasion in the broadcast of Orson Welles's *War of the Worlds* provides a striking example.[18] Its brilliant exploitation of the devices of text, context, and *mise-en-scène* predisposed its hearers to one and only one interpretation, however bizarre it seemed to them in retrospect. It created "narrative necessity," a matter we understand much less well than its logical counterpart, logical necessity. The other route to making a story seem self-evident and not in need of interpretation is via "narrative banalization." It is when we take a narrative as so socially conventional, so well known, so in keeping with the canon, that we can assign it to some well-rehearsed and virtually automatic interpretive routine. These constitute what Roland Barthes called "readerly" texts in contrast to "writerly" ones that challenge the listener or reader into unrehearsed interpretive activity.[19]

In a word, then, it is not textual or referential ambiguity that compels interpretive activity in narrative comprehension, but narrative itself. Narrative seduction or narrative banalization may produce restricted or routine interpretive activity, but this does not alter the point. "Readerly" story interpretation or "hack" story constructions can be altered by surprisingly little instruction.[20] And the moment a hearer is made suspicious of the "facts" of a story or the ulterior motives of a narrator, he or she immediately becomes hermeneutically alert. If I may use an outrageous metaphor, automatized interpretations of narratives are comparable to the "default settings" of a computer: an economical, time- and effort-saving way of dealing with knowledge—or, as it has been called, a form of "mindlessness."[21]

Interpretation has a long history in biblical exegesis and in jurisprudence. It is studded with problems that will become more familiar shortly, problems that have to do more with context than text, with the conditions on telling rather than with what is told. Let me tag two of them with labels better to identify them for subsequent discussion. The first is the issue of *intention:* "why" the story is told how and when it is, and interpreted as it is by interlocutors caught in different intentional stances themselves. Narratives are not, to use Roy Harris's felicitous phrase, "unsponsored texts" to be taken as existing unintentionally as if cast by fate upon a printed page.[22] Even when the reader takes them in the most "readerly" way, he usually attributes them (following convention) as emanating from an omniscient narrator. But this condition is itself not to be overlooked as uninteresting. It probably derives from a set of social conditions that gave special status to the written word in a society where literacy was a minority prerogative.

A second contextual issue is the question of *background knowledge*—of both the storyteller and the listener, and how each interprets the background knowledge of the other. The philosopher Hilary Putnam, in a quite different context, proposes two principles: the first is a Principle of Benefit of Doubt, the second a Principle of Reasonable Ignorance: the first "forbids us to assume that . . . experts are factually omniscient," the second that "any speakers are philosophically omniscient (even unconsciously)."[23] We judge their accounts accordingly. At the other extreme, we are charitable toward ignorance and forgive children and neophytes their incomplete knowledge, "filling in" for them as necessary. Or Sperber and Wilson, in their well-known discussion of "relevance," argue that in dialogue we typically presuppose that what an interlocutor says in replying to us is topic-relevant and that accordingly we most often assign an interpretation to it in order to make it so, thereby easing our task in understanding Other Minds.[24] We also take for granted, indeed we institutionalize situations in which it is taken for granted that the "knowledge register" in which a story is told is different from the one in which it is taken up, as when the client tells the lawyer his story in "life talk" and is listened to in "law talk" so that the lawyer can advise about litigation (rather than life). The analyst and the analysand in therapy are comparable to the lawyer and client in legal consultation.[25]

Both these contextual domains, intention attribution and background knowledge, provide not only bases for interpretation but, or course, important grounds for negotiating how a story shall be taken—or, indeed, how it should be told, a matter being reserved for later.

5. Canonicality and breach. To begin with, not every sequence of events constitutes a narrative, even when it is diachronic, particular, and organized around intentional states. Some happenings do not warrant telling about and accounts of them are said to be "pointless" rather than storylike. A Schank-Abelson script is one such case: it is a prescription for canonical behavior in a culturally defined situation—how to behave in a restaurant, say.[26] Narratives require such scripts as necessary background, but they do not constitute narrativity itself. For to be worth telling, a tale must be about how an implicit canonical script has been breached, violated, or deviated from in a manner to do violence to what Hayden White calls the "legitimacy" of the canonical script.[27] This usually involves what Labov calls a "precipitating event," a concept that Barbara Herrnstein-Smith puts to good use in her exploration of literary narrative.[28]

Breaches of the canonical, like the scripts breached, are often highly conventional and are strongly influenced by narrative traditions. Such breaches are readily recognizable as familiar human plights—the betrayed wife, the cuckolded husband, the fleeced innocent, etc. Again, they are conventional plights of "readerly" narratives. But both scripts and their breaches also provide rich grounds for innovation—as witness the contemporary literary-journalistic invention of the "yuppy" script or the formulation of the white-collar criminal's breach. And this is, perhaps, what makes the innovative storyteller such a powerful figure in a culture. He may go beyond the conventional scripts, leading people to see human happenings in a fresh way, indeed, in a way they had never before "noticed" or even dreamed. The shift from Hesiod to Homer, the advent of "inner adventure" in Laurence Sterne's *Tristram Shandy,* the advent of Flaubert's perspectivalism, or Joyce's epiphanizing of banalities—these are all innovations that probably shaped our narrative versions of everyday reality as well as changing the course of literary history, the two perhaps being not that different.

It is to William Labov's great credit to have recognized and provided a linguistic account of narrative structure in terms of two components—what happened and why it is worth telling.[29] It was for the first of these that he proposed his notion of irreducible causal sequences. The second captures the element of breach in canonicality, and involves the use of what he calls *evaluation* for warranting a story's tellability as evidencing something unusual. From initial orientation to final coda, the language of evaluation is made to contrast with the language of clausal sequence—in tense, aspect, or other marking. It has even been remarked that in sign languages, the signing of sequence and of evaluation are done in different places in the course of telling a story, the former at the center of the body, the latter off to the side.

The "breach" component of a narrative can be created by linguistic means as well as by the use of a putatively delegitimizing precipitating even in the plot. Let me explain. The Russian Formalists distinguished between the "plot" of a narrative, its *fabula,* and its mode of telling, what they called its *sjuzet.* Just as there are linearization problems in converting a thought into a sentence, so there are problems in, so to speak, representing a *fabula* in its enabling *sjuzet.*[30] The literary linguist Tzvetan Todorov, whose ideas we shall visit again later, argues that the function of inventive narrative is not so much to "fabulate" new plots as to render previously familiar ones uncertain or problematical, challenging a reader into fresh interpretive activity—echoing Roman Jakobson's famous definition of the writer's task, "to make the ordinary strange."[31]

6. *Referentiality.* The acceptability of a narrative obviously cannot depend upon its correctly referring to reality, else there would be no fiction. Realism in fiction must then indeed be a literary convention rather than a matter of correct reference. Narrative "truth" is judged by it verisimilitude rather than its verifiability. There seems indeed to be some sense in which narrative, rather than referring to "reality," may in fact create or constitute it, as when "fiction" creates a "world" of its own—Joyce's "Dublin" where places like St. Stephen's Green or Grafton Street, for all that they bear familiar labels, are no less real or imaginary than the characters he invents to inhabit them. In a perhaps deeper sense, indeed, it may be that the plights and the intentional states depicted in "successful" fiction sensitize us to experience our own lives in ways to match. Which suggests, of course, that the distinction between narrative fiction and narrative truth

is nowhere nearly as obvious as common sense and usage would have us believe. *Why* common sense insists practically upon such a sharp distinction being drawn is quite another problem, perhaps related to the requirement of "bearing witness." But that lies beyond the scope of this chapter.

What does concern us, rather, is why the distinction is intrinsically difficult to make and sustain. Surely one reason lies in what I earlier called the hermeneutic composability of narrative itself. For such composability creates problems for the conventional distinction between "sense" and "reference." That is, the "sense" of a story as a whole may alter the reference and even the referentiality of its component parts. For a story's components, insofar as they become its "functions" or captives, lose their status as singular and definite referring expressions. St. Stephen's Green becomes, as it were, a type rather than a token, a class of locales including the locus so named in Dublin. It is an invented referent not entirely free of the meanings imparted by the real place, just as a story that requires a "betrayal" as one of its constituent functions, can convert the recounting of an ordinarily mundane event recounted into something that seems compellingly like a betrayal. And this, of course, is what makes circumstantial evidence so deadly and so often inadmissible in courts of law. Given hermeneutic composability, referring expressions within narrative are always problematic, never free of the narrative as a whole. What is meant by the "narrative as a whole"? This leads us to the so-called "law of genres," to which we turn next.

7. *Genericness.* We all know that there are recognizable "kinds" of narrative: farce, black comedy, tragedy, the *Bildungsroman,* romance, satire, travel saga, etc. But as Alastair Fowler so nicely put it, "genre is much less a pigeonhole than a pigeon."[32] That is to say, we can speak of genre both as a property of a text or as a way of comprehending narrative. Mary McCarthy wrote short stories in several literary genres. She later gathered some of them together in order of the increasing age of the chief female protagonist, added some interstitial "evaluation" sections, and published the lot as an autobiography entitled *Memories of a Catholic Girlhood.* Thereafter (and doubtless to her dismay) readers interpreted her new stories as further installments of autobiography. Genres seem to provide both writer and reader with commodious and conventional "models" for limiting the hermeneutic task of making sense of human happenings— ones we narrate to ourselves as well as ones we hear others tell.

What are genres, viewed psychologically? Merely conventionalized representations of human plights? There are surely such plights in all human cultures: conflicts of family loyalty, the vagaries of human trust, the vicissitudes of romance, etc. And it might even seem that they are universal, given that the classics can be done in "modern dress" and the tales of exotic peoples be locally translated. But I think that emphasis upon plights and upon their putative universality may obscure a deeper issue. For plight is only the plot form of a genre, its *fabula*. But genre is also a form of telling, its *sjuzet*. Even if genres specialize in conventionalized human plights, they achieve their effects by using language in a particular way. And to translate the "way of telling" of a genre into another language or culture where it does not exist requires a fresh literary-linguistic invention.[33] The invention may, of course, be culturally out of reach. Language, after all, is contained within its uses. It is not just a syntax and a lexicon. The so-called "inward turn of narrative" in Western literature, for example, may have depended upon the rise of silent reading, which is a rather recent invention. If the reflectiveness produced by silent reading was then intensified by the creation of new genres—the so-called modern and postmodern novels—we might well expect that such genres would not be easily accessible to the Western nonreader and even less so to a member of a nonliterate culture.

While genres, thus, may indeed be loose but conventional ways of representing human plights, they are also ways of telling that predispose us to use our minds and sensibilities in particular ways. In a word, while they may be representations of social ontology, they are also invitations to a particular style of epistemology. As such, they may have quite as powerful an influence in shaping our modes of thought as they have in creating the realities that their plots depict.[34] So, for example, we celebrate innovations in genre as changing not only the content of imagination but its modus operandi: Flaubert for introducing a perspectival relativism that dethroned both the omniscient narrator and the singular "true" story, Joyce for slyly substituting free association to break the constraint of semantic and even syntactic conventionalism, Beckett for shredding the narrative continuities we had come to take for granted in storytelling, Calvino for converting postmodern antifoundationalism into classic mythic forms, and so on.

Narrative genre, in this dispensation, can be thought of not only as a way of constructing human plights, but as providing a guide for using the mind, insofar as use of the mind is guided by use of an enabling language.

8. Normativeness. Because its "tellability" as a form of discourse rests upon a breach of conventional expectation, narrative is necessarily normative. A breach presupposes a norm. It is this founding condition of narrative that has led students of the subject, from Hayden White and Victor Turner to Paul Ricoeur, to propose that narrative is centrally concerned with cultural legitimacy.[35] A new generation of legal scholars, not surprisingly, has even begun to explore the implicit norms inherent in legal testimony, which, of course, is principally narrative in form.[36]

While everybody from Aristotle to the so-called narrative grammarians agrees that a story pivots on a breach in legitimacy, the differences in how the notion of breach is conceived are themselves revealing of differing cultural emphases. Take Kenneth Burke's celebrated account of the dramatic "pentad." The pentad consists of an Agent, and Action, a Scene, a Goal, and an Instrument, the appropriate balance between these elements being defined as a "ratio" determined by cultural convention. When this "ratio" becomes unbalanced, when conventional expectation is breached, Trouble ensues. And it is Trouble that provides the engine of the drama, Trouble as an imbalance between any and all of the five elements of the pentad: Nora in *A Doll's House,* for example, is a rebellious Agent in an inappropriately bourgeois Scene, etc. Precipitating events are, as it were, emblems of the imbalance. Burke's principal emphasis is on plight, *fabula.* It is, as it were, concerned ontologically with the cultural world and its arrangements, with norms as they "exist."

In the second half of our century, as the apparatus of skepticism comes to be applied not only to doubting the legitimacy of received social realities but also to questioning the very ways in which we come to know or construct reality, the normative program of narrative (both literary and popular) changes with it. "Trouble" becomes epistemic: Julian Barnes writes a stunning narrative on the *episteme* of Flaubert's perspectivalism, *Flaubert's Parrot;* or Italo Calvino produces a novel, *If on a Winter's Night a Traveler,* in which the issue is what is text and what context; and theories of poetics change accordingly. They too take an "epistemic turn." And so the linguist Tzvetvan Todorov sees the poetics of narrative as inhering in its very language, in a reliance on the use of linguistic transfor-

mations that render any and all accounts of human action more subjunc-
tive, less certain, and subject withal to doubt about their construal. It is
not simply that "text" becomes dominant but that the world to which it
putatively refers is, as it were, the creature of the text.[37]

The normativeness of narrative, in a word, is not historically or culturally "once and for all." Its form changes with the preoccupations of the
age and the circumstances surrounding its production. Nor is it required
of narrative, by the way, that the Trouble with which it deals be resolved.
Narrative, I believe, is designed to contain uncanniness rather than to
resolve it. It does not have to come out on the "right side." What Frank
Kermode calls the "consolation of narrative" is not the comfort of a
happy ending, but the comprehension of plight that, by being made
understandable, becomes bearable.[38]

9. Context sensitivity and negotiability. This is a topic whose complexities
we have already visited in an earlier discussion of "hermeneutic composability" and the interpretability of narrative. In considering context, the
familiar issues of narrative intention and of background knowledge arise
again. With respect to the first of these, much of literary theory has
abandoned Coleridge's dictum that the reader should suspend disbelief
and stand, as it were, naked before the text. Today we have "reader-
response" theory and books entitled *The Reader in the Text*.[39] Indeed, the
prevailing view is that the notion of totally suspending disbelief is at best
an idealization of the reader and, at worst, a distortion of what the
process of narrative comprehension involves. Inevitably, we assimilate
narrative on our own terms, however much (in Wolfgang Iser's account)
we treat the occasion of a narrative recital as a specialized speech act.[40]
We inevitably take the teller's intentions into account, and do so in
terms of our background knowledge (and, indeed, in the light of our
presuppositions about the teller's background knowledge).

I have a strong hunch, which may at first seem counterintuitive, that it
is this very context of sensitivity that makes narrative discourse in everyday life such a viable instrument for cultural negotiation. You tell your
version, I tell mine, and we rarely need legal confrontation to settle the
difference. Principles of charity and forgiveness prevail, balanced against
principles of sufficient ignorance and sufficient doubt to a degree one
would not expect where criteria of consistency and verification prevailed.
We seem to be able to take competing story versions with a perspectival

grain of salt, much more so than in the case of arguments or proofs. Judy Dunn's remarkable book on the beginning of social understanding in children makes it plain that this type of negotiation of different narrative versions starts early and is deeply imbedded in such practical social actions as the offering of excuses, not merely in storytelling per se.[41] I think it is precisely this interplay of perspectives in arriving at "narrative truth" that has led philosophers like Richard Rorty to abandon univocally verificationist views of truth in favor of pragmatic ones.[42] Nor is it surprising that not only anthropologists have increasingly turned away from positivist descriptions of cultures toward an interpretive one in which not objective categories but "meanings" are sought for, not meaning imposed *ex hypothesi* by an outsider, the anthropologist, but ones arrived at by indigenous participants immersed in the culture's own processes for negotiating meaning.[43]

On this view, it is the very context dependence of narrative accounts that permits cultural negotiation which, when successful, makes possible such coherence and interdependence as a culture can achieve.

10. Narrative accrual. How do we cobble stories together to make them into a whole of some sort? Sciences achieve their accrual by derivation from general principles, by relating particular findings to central paradigms, by couching empirical findings in a form that makes them subsumable under altering paradigms, and by countless other procedures for making science, as the saying goes, "cumulative." This is vastly aided, of course, by procedures for assuring verification though, as we know, verificationist criteria have limited applicability where human intentional states are concerned, which leaves psychology rather on the fringe.

Narrative accrual is not foundational in the scientist's sense. Yet narratives do accrue and, as anthropologists insist, the accruals eventually create something variously called a "culture" or a "history" or, more loosely, a "tradition." Even our own homely accounts of happenings in our own lives are eventually converted into more or less coherent autobiographies centered around a self acting more or less purposefully in a social world.[44] Families similarly create a corpus of connected and shared tales and Elinor Ochs's studies in progress on family dinner-table talk begin to shed light on how this is accomplished.[45] Institutions too, as we know from the innovative work of Eric Hobsbawm, "invent" traditions out of previously ordinary happenings and then endow them with privileged status.[46] And there are principles of jurisprudence, like the *state decisis,* that guarantee a tradition by assuring that once a "case" has been interpreted in one way, future cases that are "similar" shall be interpreted and decided equivalently. Insofar as the law insists upon such accrual of cases as "precedents," and insofar as "cases" are narratives, the legal system imposes an orderly process of narrative accrual.

There has been surprisingly little work done on this fascinating subject, although there are stirrings among anthropologists (influenced principally by Clifford Geertz) and among historiographers (prodded by Michel Foucault's ground-breaking *Archaeology of Knowledge*).[47] What kinds of strategies might guide the accrual of narratives into larger-scale cultures or traditions or "world versions?" Surely one of them must be through the imposition of bogus *historical-causal entailment:* for example, the assassination of Archduke Ferdinand is seen as "causing" the outbreak of the First World War, or Pope Leo III's coronation of Charlemagne as Holy Roman emperor on Christmas Day in 800 is offered as "a first step on the way toward" or as a precursor of the enactment of the European Community in 1992. There is a vast literature of caution against such simplicities by both philosophers and historians, but it has not in the least diminished our passion for converting *post hoc* into *propter hoc.*

Another strategy might be called, for lack of a better expression, *coherence by contemporaneity:* the belief that things happening at the same time must be connected. I made the wry discovery, writing my own intellectual autobiography several years ago, that once I had discovered in the *New York Times Index* what else had been happening at the time of some personal event, I could scarcely resist connecting the lot into one coherent whole—connecting, not subsuming, not creating historical-causal entailments, but winding it into story. My first scientific paper (on maturing sexual receptivity in the female rat), for example, was published about the time Neville Chamberlain had been duped by Hitler at Munich. My original story before consulting the *Times Index* was vaguely about a nineteen-year-old's first discovery, rather like a *Bildungsroman*. The post-Index story, with Munich now included, was an exercise in irony: young Nero fiddling with rats while Rome burned! And by the same compelling process, we invent the Dark Ages, making everything all of a piece until, finally, the diversity becomes too great and then we invent the Renaissance.

Once shared culturally—distributed in the sense discussed earlier—

narrative accruals achieve, like Emile Durkheim's collective representation, "exteriority" and the power of constraint.[48] The Dark Ages come to exist, and we come to cluck with wonder at the "exceptionality" of any nontraditional philosopher or deviant theologian who lived in its shadows. I am told that the ex-president and Nancy Reagan sent a letter of sympathy to a nationally known soap opera character who had just gone blind—not the actor, but the character. But that is not unusual: culture always reconstitutes itself by swallowing its own narrative tail—Dutch boys with fingers in the dike, Columbus Christianizing Indians, the Queen's honors list, the Europhilia that dates from Charlemagne.

What creates a culture, surely, must be a "local" capacity for accruing stories of happenings of the past into some sort of diachronic structure that permits a continuity into the present—in short, to construct a history, a tradition, a legal system, instruments assuring historical continuity if not legitimacy. I want to end my list of narrative properties on this rather "obvious" point for a particular reason. The perpetual construction and reconstruction of the past provide precisely the forms of canonicality that permit us to recognize when a breach has occurred and how it might be interpreted. The philosopher W. T. Stance proposed two philosophical generations ago that the only recourse we have against solipsism (the unassailable view that argues that we cannot prove the existence of a real world, since all we can know is our own experience) is that human minds are alike and, more important, that they "work in common."[49] One of the principal ways in which we work "mentally" in common, I would want to argue, is by the process of joint narrative accrual. Even our individual autobiographies, as I have argued elsewhere, depend upon being placed within a continuity provided by a constructed and shared social history in which we locate our Selves and our individual continuities.[50] It is a sense of belonging to this canonical past that permits us to form our own narratives of deviation while maintaining complicity with the canon. Perhaps Stace was too concerned with metaphysics when he invoked this process as a defense against solipsism. We would more likely say today that it must surely be a major prophylactic against alienation.

Let me return now to the original premise—that there are specific domains of human knowledge and skill and that they are supported and organized by cultural tool kits. If we accept this view, a first conclusion would be that in understanding the nature and growth of mind in any setting, we cannot take as our unit of analysis the isolated individual operating "inside her own skin" in a cultural vacuum. Rather, we must accept the view that the human mind cannot express its nascent powers without the enablement of the symbolic systems of culture. While many of these systems are relatively autonomous in a given culture—the skills of shaminism, of specialized trades, and the like—some relate to domains of skill that must be shared by virtually all members of a culture if the culture is to be effective. The division of labor within a society goes only so far. Everybody within a culture must in some measure, for example, be able to enter into the exchange of the linguistic community, even granted that this community may be divided by idiolects and registers. Another domain that must be widely (though roughly) shared for a culture to operate with requisite effectiveness is the domain of social beliefs and procedures—what we think people are like and how they must get on with each other, what elsewhere I have called "folk psychology" and what Harold Garfinkel has called ethnosociology.[51] These are domains that are, in the main, organized narratively.

What I have tried to do in this chapter is to describe some of the properties of a world of "reality" constructed according to narrative principles. In doing so, I have gone back and forth between describing narrative mental "powers" and the symbolic systems of narrative discourse that make the expression of these powers possible. It is only a beginning. My objective has been merely to lay out the ground plan of narrative realities. The daunting task that remains now is to show in detail how, in particular instances, narrative organizes the structure of human experience—how, in a word, "life" comes to imitate "art" and vice versa.

NOTES

1. See Judith Segal, Susan Chipman, and Robert Glaser, *Thinking and Learning Skills* (Hillsdale, N.J.: Erlbaum, 1985).
2. Howard Gardner, *Frames of Mind* (New York: Basic Books, 1983).
3. Michael Cole, *Culture in Mind* (in preparation); L. Vygotsky, *Mind in Society* (Cambridge: Harvard University Press, 1978); L. Vygotsky, *Thought and Language.* (Cambridge: MIT Press, 1962); J. W. Stigler, R. A. Shweder, and G. Herdt, eds., *Cultural Psychology* (Chicago: University of Chicago Press, 1990).

4. J. Seeley-Brown, A. Collins, and P. Duguid, "Situated Cognition and the Culture of Learning," *Educational Researcher* 18 (1988):32–42.

5. Harriet Zuckerman, personal communication.

6. T. Gladwin, *East Is a Big Bird* (Cambridge: Harvard University Press, 1970); R. Rosaldo, *Culture and Truth: The Remaking of Social Analysis* (Boston: Beacon Press, 1989); C. Geertz, *Local Knowledge* (New York: Basic Books, 1983); J. Bruner, *Acts of Meaning* (Cambridge: Harvard University Press, 1990).

7. E. E. Jones, *Interpersonal Perception* (San Francisco: Freeman, 1990).

8. For a fuller, more discursive account of the nature and products of narrative thought, see my *Actual Minds, Possible Worlds* (Cambridge: Harvard University Press, 1986), and my more recent *Acts of Meaning* (Cambridge: Harvard University Press, 1990). See also, T. Sarbin, *Narrative Psychology: The Storied Nature of Human Conduct* (New York: Praeger, 1986).

9. W. J. T. Mitchell, ed., *On Narrative* (Chicago: University of Chicago Press, 1981).

10. Paul Ricoeur, *Time and Narrative*, Vol. 1 (Chicago: University of Chicago Press, 1984).

11. W. Labov and J. Waletzky, "Narrative Analysis," in *Essays on the Verbal and Visual Arts* (Seattle: University of Washington Press, 1967); W. Labov, "Speech Actions and Reactions in Personal Narrative," *Georgetown University Roundtable on Languages and Linguistics* (1981):219–47.

12. Nelson Goodman, "Twisted Tales: Or Story, Study, or Symphony," in Mitchell, *On Narrative*.

13. Charles Taylor, "Interpretation and the Sciences of Man," in *Interpretive Social Science: A Reader,* ed. Paul Rabinow and William M. Sullivan (Berkeley: University of California Press, 1979), 28.

14. Ricoeur, *Time and Narrative*.

15. V. Propp, *Morphology of the Folktale* (Austin: University of Texas Press, 1968); see also V. Propp, *Theory and History of Folklore* (Minneapolis: University of Minnesota Press, 1984).

16. See, for example, Katherine Nelson, ed., *Narratives from the Crib* (Cambridge: Harvard University Press, 1989); and Jerome Bruner, *Acts of Meaning* (Cambridge: Harvard University Press, 1990).

17. Charles Taylor, "Interpretation and the Sciences of Man," in his *Philosophy and the Human Sciences* (Cambridge: Cambridge University Press, 1985), 15.

18. Hadley Cantril, *The Invasion from Mars* (Princeton: Princeton University Press, 1940).

19. Roland Barthes, *The Responsibility of Forms: Critical Essays on Music, Art, and Representation* (New York: Hill and Wang, 1985).

20. See, for example, Peter Elbow, *Embracing Contraries: Explorations in Learning and Teaching* (New York: Oxford University Press, 1986).

21. See Ellen Langer, *Mindfulness* (Reading, Mass.: Addison-Wesley, 1989).

22. Roy Harris, "How Does Writing Restructure Thought?" *Language and Communication* 9 (1989):99–106.

23. See Hilary Putnam, *Mind, Language, and Reality* (Cambridge: Cambridge University Press, 1975), 278.

24. Dan Sperber and Dierdre Wilson, *Relevance: Cognition and Communication* (Cambridge: Harvard University Press, 1986).

25. See Donald Spence, *Narrative Truth and Historical Truth* (New York: Norton, 1982). An unwillingness on the part of a patient to accept the psychoanalyst's version or interpretation of a narrative is likely to lead to an examination and reformulation by the latter of the former's story as having to do with the patient's "resistance." The patient's version is made to conform to the psychiatrist's version as a price for the therapy's continuation. While lawyers, typically, in translating the client's personal "story" into a legal narrative, offer the client options in how the "facts of case" shall be legally framed—whether things "add up" to a narrative about contracts, torts, or rights to due process, say—the final legal story is, nonetheless, forced into "canonical" narrative that conforms to prevailing biases in the society while also corresponding to some precedent in the law. So, for example, in recent American jurisprudence, the "facts of the case" in *Bowers v. Hardwick* are interpreted as a violation of the sodomy statutes of the State of Georgia rather than as an instance of the exercise of the individual's rights to privacy as guaranteed by the Fourth Amendment to the United States Constitution. The "fact" that a homosexual act is, in this case, between consenting adults is thereby ruled by the Court as "irrelevant" to the legal story. For a discussion of the effects of imposing "official" jurisprudential story forms on everyday narratives, see Kim Lane Scheppele's Foreword to a special issue on "Legal Storytelling" in the *Michigan Law Review* 87, no. 8 (1989): 2073–98.

26. Roger Schank and Robert Abelson, *Scripts, Plans, Goals, and Understanding* (Hillsdale, N.J.: Erlbaum, 1977).

27. Hayden White, "The Value of Narrativity in the Representation of Reality," in Mitchell, *On Narrative.*

28. Labov, "Speech Actions"; Barbara Herrnstein-Smith, *On the Margins of Discourse: The Relation of Literature to Language* (Chicago: University of Chicago Press, 1978).

29. Labov, "Speech Actions."

30. For a discussion of uses of this distinction by the Russian Formalists, see J. S. Bruner, *Actual Minds, Possible Worlds* (Cambridge: Harvard University Press, 1986).

31. Tzvetvan Todorov, *The Poetics of Prose* (Ithaca: Cornell University Press, 1977). For a good statement of Roman Jakobson's view, see his "Linguistics and Poetics," in *Style in Language,* ed. T. Sebeok (Cambridge: MIT Press, 1960).

32. Alastair Fowler, *Kinds of Literature* (Cambridge: Harvard UniversityPress, 1982), 37.

33. See Rueben Brower, ed., *On Translation* (Cambridge: Harvard University Press, 1959). It contains critical essays on the task of translating fiction and nonfiction into English by some of the great practitioners of the craft.

34. Shirley Brice Heath, *Ways with Words* (Cambridge: Cambridge University Press, 1983); Elinor Ochs and Bambi Schieffelin, *Acquiring Conversational Competence* (London: Routledge, 1983); Elinor Ochs, Carolyn Taylor, Dina Rudolph, and Ruth Smith, "Narrative Activity as a Medium for Theory-Building," 1989, Los Angeles, Department of Linguistics, University of Southern California; Carol Feldman, "Monologue as Problem-Solving Narrative," in *Narratives from the Crib,* ed. K. Nelson (Cambridge: Harvard University Press, 1989).

35. See especially Hayden White's *Topics of Discourse: Essays in Cultural Criticism* (Baltimore: Johns Hopkins University Press, 1978); Victor Turner, *From Ritual to Theater: The Human Seriousness of Play* (New York: Performing Arts Journal Publications, 1982).

36. *Michigan Law Review* 87 (1989): 8. Special issue on "Legal Storytelling."

37. See, for example, Susan Suleiman and Inge Crosman, eds., *The Reader in the Text: Essays on Audience and Interpretation* (Princeton: Princeton University Press), 190.

38. See Frank Kermode, "Secrets and Narrative Sequence," in Mitchell, *On Narrative.*

39. See Wolfgang Iser, *Prospecting: From Reader Response to Literary Anthropology* (Baltimore: Johns Hopkins University Press, 1989); see also Suleiman and Crosman, *The Reader in the Text.*

40. Wolfgang Iser, *The Implied Reader* (Baltimore: Johns Hopkins University Press, 1974).

41. Judy Dunn, *Beginnings of Social Understanding* (Cambridge: Harvard University Press, 1988).

42. Richard Rorty, *Philosophy and the Mirror of Nature* (Princeton: Princeton University Press, 1979); see also Charles Taylor, *Sources of the Self* (Cambridge: Harvard University Press, 1989).

43. See particularly Clifford Geertz's essay on "Thick Interpretation," in his *Local Knowledge* (New York: Basic Books, 1983); for a sampling of views on this approach to culture, see also Paul Rabinow and William Sullivan, *Interpretive Social Science: A Reader* (Berkeley: University of California Press, 1979); and Stigler, Shweder, and Herdt, *Cultural Psychology.*

44. See, for example, chapter 4 in my *Acts of Meaning* (Cambridge: Harvard University Press, 1990).

45. I am greatly indebted to Professor Ochs for letting a group of us in an informal seminar at UCLA during the winter term of 1990 view her tapes of these sessions and share her views on the processes involved.

46. See Eric Hobsbawm and Terrence Ranger, eds., *The Invention of Tradition* (Cambridge: Cambridge University Press, 1983).

47. But see Clifford Geertz, *Works and Lives: The Anthropologist as Author* (Stanford: Stanford University Press, 1988); James Clifford, *The Predicament of Culture* (Cambridge: Harvard University Press, 1988); and Michel Foucault, *Archaeology of Knowledge* (New York: Pantheon, 1972).

48. Emile Durkheim, *The Elementary Forms of the Religious Life* (New York: Free

Press, 1965). For a more psychological account of this process, referred to by the author as "ontic dumping," see, Carol Feldman, "Thought from Language: The Linguistic Construction of Cognitive Representations," *Making Sense: The Child's Construction of the World*, ed. Jerome Bruner and Helen Haste (New York: Methuen, 1987).

49. See entry for "W. T. Stace," *Encyclopedia of Philosophy* (New York: Macmillan, 1967).

50. J. S. Bruner, *Acts of Meaning*, chapter 4.

51. See Harold Garfinkel, *Studies in Ethnomethodology* (Englewood Cliffs, N.J.: Prentice-Hall, 1967).

2

Narrative Transformations

Francesco Corrao

The confines of the Psyche you will never be able to discover, not even if you go along all roads, so deep is the expression that belongs to it.
—Heraclitus of Ephesus

On 4 March 1908, at the twenty-third meeting of the Vienna Psychoanalytic Society (a name given that very year to what had been formerly called "The Wednesday Psychological Society"), Otto Rank read out a passage of a letter dated 1 December 1788 from Friedrich Schiller to Karl Korner, which defined in an extraordinarily precise manner the nature of the meaning of the "free association of ideas" in the Freudian sense, so much so that it induced Freud to quote the same passage in the second edition of *The Interpretation of Dreams,* published in 1909. Korner, a good friend of Schiller's, had lamented his scarce productivity and Schiller had retorted:

> The ground for your complaint seems to me to lie in the constraint imposed by your reason upon your imagination. . . . It seems a bad thing and detrimental to the creative work of the mind if Reason makes too close an examination of the ideas as they come pouring in—at the very gateway, as it were. Looked at in isolation, a thought may seem very trivial or very fantastic; but it may be made important by another thought that comes after it, and, in conjunction with other thoughts that may seem equally absurd, it may turn out to form a most effective link. Reason cannot form any opinion upon all this unless it retains the thought long enough to look at it in connection with the others. On the other hand, where there is a creative mind, Reason—so it seems to me—relaxes its watch upon the gates, and the ideas rush in pell-mell, and only then does it look them

through and examine them in a mass. You critics, or whatever else you may call yourselves, are ashamed or frightened of the momentary and transient extravagances which are to be found in all truly creative minds and whose longer or shorter duration distinguishes the thinking artist from the dreamer. You complain of your unfruitfulness because you reject too soon and discriminate too severely. (103)

In Freud's text, the quotation from Schiller is placed between two extremely interesting pages. The first one is about the effective method for analyzing dreams and pathological ideas. Freud writes:

What is in question, evidently, is to establish a psychical state which, in its distribution of psychical energy (that is, of mobile attention), bears some analogy to the state we are in before falling asleep—and no doubt also to hypnosis. As we fall asleep, "involuntary ideas" emerge, owing to the relaxation of a certain deliberate (and no doubt also critical) activity which we allow to influence the course of our ideas while we are fully awake. (We usually attribute this relaxation to "stress.") As the involuntary ideas emerge they change into visual and acoustic images. In the state used for the analysis of dreams and pathological ideas, the patient purposely and deliber-ately abandons this activity and employs the psychical energy thus saved (or a portion of it) in attentively following the involuntary thoughts which now emerge, and which—and here the situation differs from that of falling asleep—retain the character of ideas. In this way the 'involuntary' ideas are transformed into "voluntary" ones. (102)

The other page to which I wished to draw attention contains the following considerations:

Our first step in the employment of this procedure teaches us that what we must take as the object of our attention is not the dream as a whole but the separate portions of its content. If I say to a patient who is still a novice: "What occurs to you in connection with this dream?" as a rule his mental horizon becomes a blank. If, however, I put the dream before him cut up into pieces, he will give me a series of associations to each piece, which might be described as the "background thoughts" of that particular part of the dream. Thus the method of dream-interpretation which I practice al-ready differs in this first important respect from the popular, historic and legendary method of interpretation by means of symbolism and approxi-mates to the second or "decoding" method. Like the latter, it employs interpretation en détail and not en masse; like the latter, it regards dreams from the very first as being of a composite character, as being conglomerates of psychical formations. (103–4)

Immediately afterwards, in the continuation of the text, Freud shows himself at work, recounting his technical procedure in the analysis of

Irma's dream. The first movement is deconstruction aiming at segmenting the oneiric text and disarticulating the elements which compose it.

In the sixth chapter, on dream-work, he states again: "At bottom, dreams are nothing other than a particular form of thinking, made possible by the conditions of the state of sleep. It is the dream-work which creates that form, and it alone is the essence of dreaming—the explanation of its peculiar nature" (n. 506).

It is necessary to stress Freud's insistence on the principle of transformation, because this is the principle which later oriented the outstanding theoretical development that we owe to Wilfred Bion. In more recent times, the importance of this principle has been noted by M. Lavagetto (1985), who carried out a penetrating research on Freud and on literature. Bion specifically observes that dream-work is precisely what leads A to A1 and that the difference consists in a modification of an essentially formal nature.

Along parallel lines it is useful to remember, with an exemplification which is not arbitrary, that analogous results to those of dream-work are obtained by comic-work; by symptomatic work, in general, and by delirious work, in particular. Personally, I have repeatedly stressed the importance of logical transformations, that is, of those operations that lead a logical system A, for example a bivalent system, to another, nonbivalent system A1, and vice versa.

Coming back to dream-work, which constitutes the fundamental theoretical and practical paradigm of analysis, we may wonder what its rules of transformation are. They are well known to us, but they appear with a different type of enunciation in the sixth chapter of *The Interpretation of Dreams,* and in the essay *Über den Traum* (1901). The rules concern the forms of time, the forms of space, the forms of logic, and the modes of iconic or echoic representability, that is those of the translation of thought into representation, and lastly, the forms of discourse organization for the purposes of the dialogic-narrative communicability implied by secondary elaboration.

The following rules should be taken into consideration:

1. Temporal repetition represents the numerical multiplication of an object.
2. The present is the time in which desire is represented as fulfilled; the optative is substituted by the present.

3. The alternative "either . . . or" is represented by a conjunction "both . . . and," i. e. by an equivalence.
4. Simultaneity represents a logical connection, or, inversely, a logical connection is represented as simultaneity.
5. Causal relation is represented by means of the succession of two oneiric passages of differing length, so that the representation is inverted; that is to say, the beginning stands for the end and vice versa.
6. The direct transformation of one thing into another represents the cause-effect relationship.
7. As no representation is found for "no," two antithetical elements may be expressed through one of them alone or in a condensed manner.

These are the rules of transformation that Freud explicitly ascribes to the "primary process."

As is well known, the general framework of these rules of transformation is constituted by the processes of condensation *(Verdichtung)* and displacement *(Verschiebung)*. On the other hand, transformations and their rules are to be ascribed to the field of activity of representation, which constitutes the foundation of subjective experience of dreams; in this way transformations can all be seen as leading back to the semantic variations on the German terms centered on the root word *Stellung* (hence *Darstellung* [presentation, exposition, description], *Vorstellung* [representation, depiction], *Entstellung* [deformation, transposition], etc.) and are subordinated to their verbal translatability — if it is true, and we take it to be so, that the foundation of language is constituted by verbal representations.

In this light, it will not seem strange to consider these rules of transformation as rules pertaining to the dialogic-discursive production generated in the analytic situation (through mutual co-operation between analyst and patient), which can often take on a narrative form. Benveniste (1966) thus describes the analytic situation:

> Psychoanalysis seems to be principally distinguished from all other disciplines by the following: the analyst operates on what the subject says to him. The analyst is engaged in studying the patient's discourse, in examining his locutory, fabulatory, narrative behaviour, so that through this discourse there will gradually develop another discourse, supposed to be un-

conscious, which in turn will have to be uttered, recounted and understood. From the patient to the analyst and from the analyst to the patient, the whole process is enacted through language; but it is not in order to discover an empirical fact, recorded only in the patient's memory, that the analyst needs the patient to tell him everything, but because the empirical events only have reality because of their meaning and because of the discourse. The discourse confers on them the authenticity of experience regardless of their historical reality, or also, or more exactly, if the discourse eludes, transposes or invents the biography that the subject attributes to himself or herself. The constitutive dimension of this biography is its being verbalized, recounted, and hence assumed by the person who describes himself or herself in it; its expression is that of language, the relation between analyst and subject is that of dialogue *(dialogon)*. (93)

Analogously M. Lavagetto (1985) observes: "It is worth stressing that the specific object of psychoanalysis is the communicated, narrated discourse; is a text, perhaps a broken, fragmentary, pre-grammatical text, full of semantic lacerations, of illness" (135); "something," observes M. Bakhtin (1975), "which not even the most arid and flat positivism can treat in a neutral manner as a thing" (160).

And this is not all, because the analyst, like the historian, like the critic of literature or of ideologies, or like any other scholar of humanities, the anthropologist, the sociologist, etc., is not only forced to speak about words but has to speak about them using words in an interminable dialogic structure. For this reason the things the analyst is forced to go back to again and again are impregnated with time, meanings, history, stories, dialogue. Some critics, like those evoked by Schiller, might rush to a hurried dismissal of psychoanalysis, asserting that as we deal with discourse on discourse, with interpretations and not true facts, any type of scientific research becomes impossible. But the *fact,* in the case of analysis, is precisely interpretation, discourse, and interpretation of discourse, which can be assumed as such as soon as we can get rid of the positivistic model and of the arrogance of a one-way science, and as soon as we consider facts as a sort of circuit undergoing transformation which cannot be pinned down to a primarily unambiguous objective state. Bakhtin observes that:

> the exact sciences are a monological form of knowledge, the intellect contemplates a thing and speaks of it. Here there is only one subject, the subject that contemplates and enounces. Only a voiceless thing is present before him. But one cannot perceive, study the subject as such as if he or

she were a thing, because he or she cannot remain the subject without a voice: it inevitably follows that his or her knowledge cannot but be dialogic. (Ibid.)

From this point of view psychoanalysis is a very good representation of the rules which govern human sciences in general: no knowledge outside the dialogue (i.e., outside a linguistic-discursive field in which one text encounters another, and interweaves with it) can modify or be modified by it, broadening or shrinking it, or broadening or shrinking itself, over and above all possible or expected meanings. While the hermeneutic circle changes into an ellipsis, an ellipsis with two foci which incontestably constitutes the context outside which there is no intelligence of meaning or graspable understanding. "The context is always personal, an infinite dialogue, unendable, always open, without a first or a last word" (ibid.).

The latter considerations by various authors reflect the positive consequences of the present epistemological change of direction in psychoanalysis based on the concept of bipersonal field, whose function is described in terms of complementarity and cooperative poiesis of the analytic couple. The change was inaugurated by Freud (1937) himself with this formulation: "The delusions of patients seem to me to be the equivalents of the constructions which we build up in the course of an analytic treatment—attempts at explanation and cure." The formulation must be given a precise meaning; it does not postulate a delirious quality in the analytic construction, but attributes the dignity of a construction to the delirious formulation, just as it tends to comprehend delirium as an interpretative version of facts which are in themselves inaccessible but which nonetheless constitute intersubjective relations of reciprocity, like that which is set up in the analytic setting when the constructions of meaning are undertaken. It should be remembered that Freud maintains that at the center of every delirium there exists a nucleus of historical truth.

Usually he considers this truth as concerning an event which really occurred in a world of facts, and he thinks of a narrated story as a procedure suited to attaining the objective reality of the event. However, it may be much more effective to have a different perspective which assumes the characteristic of truth as intrinsic to narration, rather than attributing it to events, that is to say one which assumes truth as the structure of subjective experience, rather than as a characteristic of objective perceptions. I would like to be very clear on this subject. Schiller's texture of ideas, the text, the narrative plot, possesses a cognitive function inasmuch as it is not limited to evoking events, and what happened, but what may have happened or may yet happen, according to verisimilitude and necessity. But verisimilitude, the Aristotelian eikòs—observes F. Rella (1987) in a recent essay—does not propose a minor truth derived from a truth attainable with other discourses; eikòs, verisimilitude, is rather the plane of necessary truth, a plane which is specific to narration, and designates the imaginative truth that narration produces, setting up an intersection between the plane of its possibility and the plane of factual data. This truth is of a different nature from ontological truth, indeed it is not the essence of facts, but rather that truth which is produced when facts are organized along a meaningful line opening up in them the multisided dimension of what is possible. Possible and necessary appear to be antithetical terms, but actually we can state that truth is produced of necessity when facts are interwoven within a narrative logic illuminating some of them and obscuring others. This is a choice well known to any writer or storyteller. Once a narrative peripety is set in motion, the plane of events is transformed, more or less completely, in that the state of facts is not proposed reflexively, but through a dynamic process admitting some facts to the sense horizon and excluding others, in accordance with the logic or nonlogic of aspects of narration. A story may be either linear and resolve itself without peripeties, or complex, when it develops through peripeties and obeys them because it contains recognitions that arise from the very structure of the story. The narrative peripety, moreover, as a category, is the central dimension of all great narrations that have been handed down to us; it is the change that is produced in the opposite direction to the ongoing vicissitude, it is metabole, that is to say a temporal inversion. Not only history, not even philosophy and the exact sciences have this capacity for metabole, for temporal inversion, which instead is part of the structure of the story and is certainly inherited from myth. Hence mythical knowledge does not seem to have died out and disappeared (besides, *mythos* means story) but seems to have transmigrated into the narrative structure, into its truthlike fiction. Moreover, any historiographic reconstruction of real events cannot be anything but probablistic (historians tell us so) and involves a high degree of uncertainty. Analogously, any memory is nothing but retrospective signification *(Nachträglichkeit),* reconstructed by imagination, illusory and delusive at one and the same time. Moreover, according to the happy formulation by Roy Schafer (1983), "each account of the past is a reconstruction that is controlled by a narrative strategy. The narrative strategy dictates how one is to select, from a plenitude of possible details, those that may be reorganized into another narrative which is both followable, and expresses the desired point of view on the past" (193). Hence every reconstruction imperceptibly turns into an arbitrary narrative construction with respect to the silent and impassible event. At all events, any construction is always susceptible to change and transformation, within the analytic setting. As Schafer (1983) states:

> For whenever new explanatory aims are set up and new questions raised, new slants on the past will be developed and new evidence concerning the events of the past will become available; every construction constitutes a narrative text replacing the previous one, transforming it through interpretative variations that operate thematic revisions or reductions and generate new contexts, new meanings and new evaluations; while at the same time every construction is available for a possible new transformation. (Ibid.)

However, the production of successive narrative texts in analysis is not limitless, as every construction needs to be anchored in the here and now of the dialogue—the dialogic relationship, between analyst and patient and vice versa. The dialogue progressively takes on a regulatory function which facilitates the coherent self-organization of the multiple "life stories" produced by the analytic field, meaning an intersubjective, interpersonal context. It should be noted, as Schafer tells us, that analysts with different theoretical and technical viewpoints employ different narrative strategies, and consequently there develop analytic stories of a different type, with more or less divergent contents. The complications increase if we consider the narrative variations employed by the patient in relation to each possible different successive analyst encountered, as sometimes happens.

Despite the scope for complexity involved in this kind of constructionism (as it is indeed this), it should not to be feared that the transformational perspective and the narratological framework will lapse into an ungovernable chaos. First of all, it can be observed that the constructionist position is consistent with present-day general epistemologies, which propose a pluralistic and relativistic conception of events in the world, whether cosmological or anthropological, individual or collective, material, physical, or mental. Probably these epistemologies founded on the principle of uncertainty are the result of an ethical evolution of man, who intends to forego more and more his hubris, his cognitive arrogance.

The transformational model is the second point to dwell on. This is a cognitive model which, as I have already mentioned, was implicitly used by Freud and explicitly developed by Bion. This must be taken into account because it represents the analytic reality in which we live and affords new theoretical dimensions which are extremely productive. A correct use of the transformation theory obliges one to identify the rules of transformation as well as the invariants connected to them; for this purpose it is necessary to establish the limits of the field.

In *The Case History of Dora* (1905), Freud provides an exemplary testimony to narrative or narratological transformation, in the sense that, through the Freudian narration (which can also be defined as a written discursive representation) we can get an idea of the original analytic experience that Freud had with Dora. In the premise to his account of the case, Freud points out that it can be read as a roman à clef for the personal pleasure of anyone reading it. Understanding on the part of the latter will also depend on the invariants relating to his sexual curiosity; and this is not what Freud intends to concede to his reader. The invariants of pornographic literature are not the invariants of psychoanalysis (Bion 1965). The importance of *The Case History of Dora* in relation to problems of narrative transformation becomes very clear if one reads the minutes of the Vienna Psychoanalytic Society for the year 1908, during which the problem was dealt with several times in general terms and *The Case History of Dora* was specifically referred to by Stekel, who, after criticizing the boring and exasperating meticulousness of Sadger's case histories, which he describes as illegible, states: "Clinical histories, if they are not elaborated, prove wholly indigestible." There remains only one possibility, that is a scrupulous and artistic presentation as in *The Case History of Dora*. Freud himself in *Recommendations to Physicians Practicing Psycho-Analysis* (1912) writes:

> Exact reports of analytic case histories are of less value than might be expected. Strictly speaking, they only possess the ostensible exactness of which 'modern' psychiatry affords us some striking examples. They are, as a rule, fatiguing to the reader and yet do not succeed in being a substitute for his actual presence at an analysis. Experience invariably shows that if readers are willing to believe an analyst they will have confidence in any slight

revision to which he has submitted his material; if, on the other hand, they are unwilling to take analysis and the analyst seriously, they will pay no attention to accurate verbatim records of the treatment either. This is not the way, it seems, to remedy the lack of convincing evidence to be found in psycho-analytic reports. (114)

In conclusion, I would like to assume this general postulate: clinical accounts, interpretations during sessions, the explicative and hermeneutic theories of the analytic field, all together belong to the category of transformation groups of a narrative or narratological type. Though it is also true that operating narrative transformations of a literary, historical, or exegetic kind does not in the least mean effecting analytic transformations, yet one can also assume the opposite truth, namely that analytic transformations possess a narrative dimension to an extremely high degree. This dimension should be considered one of the fundamental parameters of the analytic field, that is to say a fundamental analytic category.

REFERENCES

Minutes of the Vienna Psychoanalytic Society. 1962. Vol. 1. New York: International Universities Press.
Bakhtin, M. 1975. *Voprosy Literatury I Estetiki*. Izdatel'stvo "Chudozestvennaja Literatura." Italian ed. 1979. *Estetica e Romanzo*. Milano: Einaudi.
Benveniste, E. 1966. *Problèmes de linguistique générale*. Paris: Gallimard. Italian ed. 1971. *Problemi di linguistica generale*. Milano.
Bion, W. R. 1965. *Transformations*. London: Heinemann.
Corrao, F. 1987. "Il narrativo come categoria analitica." In *Psicoanalisi e narrazione,* Egidi Morpurgo, ed. Ancona: Lavoro Editoriale.
Freud, S. 1900. *The interpretation of dreams. S. E.* Vols. 4 and 5.
———. 1912. *Recommendations to physicians practising psycho-analysis. S. E.* Vol. 12.
———. 1937. *Constructions in analysis. S. E.* Vol. 23.
Lavagetto, M. 1985. *Freud, la letteratura ed altro*. Turin: Einaudi.
Rella, F. 1987. *La battaglia della verità*. Milano: Feltrinelli.
Schafer, R. 1983. *The analytic attitude*. New York: Basic Books.

3

The Phenomenological Dimension of Representational Activity

Enzo Funari

In the following pages I will try to outline some reflections designed to illustrate aspects I consider fundamental to defining the concept of "representation" or, in other words, in determining the traits that make up representational activity and its nature.

I shall start from the premise that representation is not to be understood as one of the possible manifestations or phenomena of psychic and mental life but rather is the basic condition necessary for the realization of any psychic experience.

The theme of representation has undergone remarkable semantic and conceptual variations in modern thinking from Kant to the present day, according to the contexts and kind of theorization in which it has been employed. In this it has met the same fate as many other terms and concepts. In recent times especially, there has been a variety of usage which, though it may seem justified by the theoretical context to which it belongs, has not always proven to be founded in adequate explanation and argumentation. Nevertheless, within the scope of the theoretical construction proposed here, we can not only maintain that representation is the basic modality at the root of every possible psychic experience but also trace a historical thread that enables us to show how the theme of representation goes hand-in-hand with modern attempts to establish a psychological "point of view" unfettered by resort to explanations and anchorings taken from other disciplines such as biology and neurophysiology, for instance, not to mention the more recent examples from linguis-

49

tics and semiotics. Discerning this "point of view," which can be articulated in terms of a phenomenology of psychic life, in no way implies denial of the importance to research of observers from other disciplines. Rather, it is based on the conviction that a single object can be interpreted and investigated from different perspectives. In both psychological and psychoanalytic theorizations and theoretical constructs, we often note a tendency to resort to other fields to explain or understand certain phenomena, mixing, so to speak, different levels of observation and different kinds of practical and theoretical instruments. Let us take two examples which are in a sense opposite: on the one hand, the recourse to neurophysiological processes as the cause of psychic phenomena and, on the other, the appeal to myth as the explanation of the same psychic phenomena. As an attempt to explain the meaning of the psychic experience, both fail when placed on a different register. In the first case, what is observable on a transphenomenal plane, and thus on a natural level, is confused with what happens on the level of the phenomenal assumption. In fact, if the same phenomenal assumption could not occur in the absence, say, of the bioneurophysiological process and, more in general, as a function of a world of stimuli, that does not mean that it can be reduced to such a process or to such a world but rather that it requires another point of view that grasps its sense and its nature, albeit in relation to those other types of reality. Similarly, on the other hand and under different form, the use of the "mythical" explanation (in psychoanalysis, for example), which is the basis of the new tendency to follow a "narrative" dimension, runs the risk of using as an instrument of investigation cognitive dimensions which ought, in turn, to be subject to explication, in both the current and the etymological sense, that is, to be unfolded and grasped in their intimate articulation.

There can be no doubt that this is possible without dragging out the hoary question of ontic dualism between phenomenal assumption and material reality. If the phenomenal assumption—where, as I attempt to show, representation constitutes the cornerstone of the whole edifice—claims its own constitutive level, that does not keep it from maintaining a relation to another reality, which could be physical, biological, etc. without, however, deriving from that other reality. If you question the same things in a certain way—as Margolis (1984) claims—although material, they can support and express "nonmaterial" attributes. That is: it is not a sign of uncertainty and confusion when we identify one system and order of material things and another system and order of nonmaterial attributes. Differentiating the former from the latter doesn't imply falling into ontic dualism but rather supports the claim for more than one modality of apparition: thus, coming across an incongruity between lines of different attributes (material and nonmaterial) we recognize that "the real properties of things are not reducible to being all and only physical properties or properties of some other single kind." In other words, the consistence and function of an order relative to "material things" is not being denied here but a differentiation is being made between different orders of attributes, within a single type of experience in which nonmaterial attributes are not confused with or reduced to material attributes. Hence, mental activity or a certain kind of experience such as the dream cannot be reduced to merely physiological structures and processes and, in spite of that, such activities or experiences are embodied in those structures and those processes.

Dreams, for example (Margolis 1978; Moravia 1986) make clear a dimension that, though "embodied" in certain neurocerebral processes, is not those mechanisms. If an individual is terrified by a dream, what terrorizes him or her is not a physical event but occurrences and images that belong to another order of reality. Neural state N, notes Margolis, cannot be identified with the oneiric happening that frightens the subject.

It is here that we can take up the delicate question of what is meant in this field by phenomenological approach since the use of the term "phenomenology," even in a philosophical environment, projects lines of thought at variance among themselves. In psychology, moreover, it has been taken up at times in a simplified and casual way, as a pure description of the phenomenon investigated in all its directly observable elements, for instance. Bringing attention back to the phenomenological dimension in the field of psychic research requires, therefore, a network of arguments that makes it possible to determine the fabric of the experience we are dealing with, so that we escape, on the one hand, from a sort of psychologism (an accusation often aimed against psychological and psychoanalytical research in philosophical and epistemological quarters) and, on the other, from the more general risk of a naturalistic or spiritualistic outcome. At the outset a close dialectic relationship between a theoretical dimension and the technical tools is the indispensable grounding for defining any possible research aimed at psychic activity; in that sense, in the context of research on psychic life *stricto sensu* we necessarily stray from philosophical reflection proper, even though in the speculation that grows out of it we eventually outline themes based on that reflection. The rootedness of psychological research in its own operative environment of theoretical-practical order, while still not isolating it—as we have seen—from other scientific disciplines, doesn't likewise prevent it from a possible "importation" at the level of philosophical argumentation. Rather it merely prevents the use within its confines of this or that philosophical perspective, in a more or less direct or pertinent way, in the attempt once again to explain via an external route what emerges from the direct experience that springs from psychological research itself.

I see no consistency in a potential criticism determined to deny the legitimacy of a possible speculation through which we can produce a chain-link of concepts overlain with a set of methods/instruments in which it is expressed, within the specificity of the field of research under consideration.

Now it is in this theoretical-practical context that we can define a phenomenology of psychic activity as understood here: not a mere taking-up of what is directly observable but the tendency to discern the meaning, the structure, and the processes that determine psychic experience and thus both its cognitive and affective aspects in their articulations and in their expressive modalities. The very practice of empirical investigation, in this case linked to the field of the psyche, unlike mere theoretical speculations not only presents itself as an obvious instrument of research, but also proves to be a generative source of meaning. We might thus indicate this observational position as pragmatic phenomenology.

If this is the basic framework of the discussion, let us now see how it comes to life in the structures that lead on to progressively greater autonomy. The following treatment stems from what I outlined in the context of what I have termed "pragmatic phenomenology." No psychic experience is possible except through representational activity, which should be understood as the basic condition for psychic life to take place and as one of its functioning modalities which, per se, is distinct from any intuitive content or concreteness inherent in every kind and degree of experience. Such activity makes up the area of the phenomenal side, whose basic characteristic is the deliberateness as a function of which any psychic phenomenon necessarily refers to a more or less defined "reference mark (repère)" (hence "object" in the broader sense, not to be understood solely as empirical or external object, but nevertheless included in it). In the context of phenomenal assumption, this reference mark maintains its character of immanence. On the phenomenal representational level thus understood, a process of embodiment is effected in which phenomenal life in the very moment it manifests itself is embodied, so to speak, in the "encountered" which, though it may constitute the "external conditions" for it to arise, is not by virtue of that necessarily confined to the sense that is structured in psychic experience itself (viz. the example of the relation dream: neurocerebral processes or, on another plane, between a perception and the physical characteristics of the stimuli that can give rise to it). We'll have a chance to see how the aspect of embodiment finds proof, above and beyond the capacity indicated at a theoretical level, in the specification that can be drawn from psychological investigation in reference to corporeity as an original experience. Before proceeding in that direction, however, I think it fitting to take up again some considerations voiced elsewhere (Funari 1986), designed to further integrate the concept of representation proposed here, in order to confirm its primacy as a fundamental category in psychic life.

Etymological deconstruction of the term "representation" offers a significant contribution in this direction. "Represent" derives from the Latin *repraesentare* (re and *praesentare*); the prefix *re* indicates movement in an opposite direction, a return to a prior state and, more properly, a repetition or a nullification of a prior state (Devoto 1968). *Praesentare,* in turn, comes from *praesens,* a calque on *absens* in which *prae* (before, in front of) is substituted for the prefix *ab,* a signal of absence. One possible and credible reconstruction of meaning that the etymology suggests harks back to an event that reproposes and/or recovers a prior position (prae), preliminary condition for constituting any possible entity, furnishing that entity (ens) with the filling that *ab-sens* is without.

Representation can thus be understood as the presentation that tries again and reproposes itself in the different modes of repetition, of recovery, of return, of annulment or of the modification to the opposite of the prior state (viz. *re-velo,* "reveal," from "veil," where a return to the prior position indicates the form that denies it).

In the perspective proposed it should be understood that the language through which the etymon is expressed does not make up the reality which "explicates" the nature of representation but rather is the necessary vehicle through which representing manifests itself. In other words it is not language that determines the character of representing but vice versa.

What can be inferred from the etymological outline is that representation, understood as a basic expressive modality, takes shape as the prototype of every possible psychic experience, the working mode from which all possible meanings and their subsequent articulations stem.

At this point the proximity of the concept of representation to the concept *Vorstellung* becomes obvious. The prefix *vor* indicates, on the logical level, the precondition necessary for establishing any position whatsoever and for any phenomenal experience to come to life. This is indicated on the level of the experienced *(Erleben)* as a space, so to speak, that cannot be assigned either to the so-called "internal world" or to the "external world." This modality of functioning which, as stated above, by its very nature precludes this or that intuitive content or concreteness, shows up as an original readiness to experience that is filled, defined, and connoted on a case-by-case basis as a function of processes and contexts that bring about its categorical nature.

Consider for example expressions such as "my body," "my soul," "my mind," and so forth. Consider further the expressions that refer to their internal determiners, respectively: "physiological processes," "anatomical elements," for instance, on the one hand, and "thoughts," "emotions," on the other. All these expressions are indicative of the spontaneous manifestation—independent from the fact that they can be referred to the body or its "exterior"—of foreign objects or events, from which we differentiate ourselves. My body belongs to me, not I am my body. It is not I that am my soul or my mind; rather my soul and mind belong to me. It is as though I were forced to objectivize even that which I believe comes together to make up my essence, without wondering from what position I consider the issue or wondering to what "organ" my being belongs; position or organ through which I depict these object-events in a more or less generic or analytic way. But the spontaneous tendency guards and hides within itself a type of dawning or primitive experience that cannot, in its unreflected nature, be reduced to a process of substantialization, be it naturalistic, spiritualistic, and/or metaphysical. For it is reflected thought that always tries to "take away," that is, to remove and nullify this radical modality, depriving it of its generative spontaneity and, therefore, tries to go on to define it and force it schematically into an "outside" and an "inside." In carrying out this thought, however, through the multifarious and complex modalities in which it is expressed, the reflected thought tends to repeat what has already taken place in original experience, but with a predicative emphasis and articulation that further complicates the question by not recognizing the provenance.

The "outside" and the "inside," the mind and the body, are not to be identified as the matrices from time to time favored by this or that theoretic solution, but they constitute essential references that originate in representational activity itself. It is in representational intentionality that, through various types of experience, the first interior/exterior differentiations take shape. It is there that the subject's history acquires order and disorder in its encounter with the emerging effects of the activity of the organism, combined with effects stemming from contact with so-called "external objects." At this point the reader might object that I tend to explain by means of a dichotomy (moreover one already refuted) something that ought to be set up as a matrix avoiding that very dichotomy. The objection would be valid if we were to assume, as often happens in theoretical elaborations that tackle such problems, a point of view along a single axis. The point here, in fact, is to use a double point of view, a twofold modality of perspective and there is no reference to two counterposed or juxtaposed realities. The rivalry of two points of view gains consistency, as we will see in greater detail below, at a certain level of representational experience and it is encouraged by such activity but does not necessarily exhaust it since, as originally constituted, it exists without that distinction and only brings it into being during subsequent experiences. Hence the proposed description, if we operate from the point of view where the distinction is accepted, intends to "take back" the original dimension from which it comes and to which it belongs.

Returning to the categorical nature of representing, we see that it displays two distinguishable but closely linked characteristics: on the one hand, as a basic modality of experience, it retains an aspect unbound by any given content *(inexistentia)*, on the other it requires the indispensable concurrence of possible experiences in order to take place *(in existentia)*. As we shall see, however, Franz Brentano's point is taken up in a rather different conceptual context, which is understandable in light of the field of research in which it appears. The time is now ripe to delve into that area of psychological investigation which I will employ in an attempt to better justify the position I have termed pragmatic phenomenology. If by "phenomenology" we do not mean the mere description of phenomena but rather the search for a more direct point of contact with the meaning that is articulated inside those phenomena in the weft, so to speak, of their manifestation and their occurrence as intentional processes and hence as "the experienced" having tendencies and structures—then the "pragmatic" aspect is suggested by two planes of the argument: first by virtue of the fact that such investigation takes place within the "practice" of a discipline with its own instruments and methods but especially by the realization that, in the practice in question, the psychic phenomenon investigated holds within itself the forms and meanings, whether affective or cognitive, of the experience that unfolds in the "history" that involves it. But it is in the very research environment made up of psychic experience that the conditions are defined for further specification of what I have attempted to outline above. In this sense the history of attempts to make room for representational phenomenology seems to coincide with the intention to assign a place to psychology. From Kant's "obscure representations *(Vorstellungen)*" in *Anthropologie,* to Herbart's "ideas," through Helmholtz's "unconscious conclusions," up to Brentano's conception and hence to the Graz School, while on different theoretic groundings, there is an ever-present attempt to outline a plane discrete from other perspectives to be assigned to psychic events and to their respective instruments of research and reflection. This intention is often abortive since, as the case may be, it is subordinated, made hybrid, or practically nullified by theories and contrivances that refer to the most disparate disciplines (biology, neurophysiology, linguistics, etc.) to explain psychic experience. In outlining a train of thought that makes representational activity the linchpin of any discourse on psychic life and the fulcrum of the psychic experience, at some point we run headlong into the original thematization of Freudian research itself.

A careful reading of the *Studien* (1983–95) shows how the chance of encountering the psychic experience of the subject rests on the representational dimension. Both the concept of *Vorstellung* and the concept of *Kreisvorstellungen* make up the nexus to which the earliest Freudian investigation returns. The question is not a minor point in that writing. We witness the birth of an accepted semantic meaning of the term "representation" that, in the context, assimilates different positions and breaks new ground. In fact, it is in representation that we trace the modalities in which psychic life is expressed: in that sense Brentano's reading is adopted, but at the same time, unlike in the German philosopher's usage, representation not only keeps the character of a conscious event but can be referred to an unconscious and prereflective event; thus there is a reformulation of what was held by Kant in his *Anthropologie*, Herbart in his *Psychologie* of 1925–26, and Helmholtz in his *Optik* of 1866. The new ground consists of the fact that the argumentation concerning representational activity is not merely on a theoretical level but is part of a theoretical-practical framework set up with two aims: (1) to build a cognitive picture related to psychic life; (2) to furnish that picture with methodological and instrumental elements to carry out the required cognitive process.

A whole thus emerges made up of a representation meant as intentional activity, the basis for every possible psychic experience, whose expressive modalities and respective degrees of organization can manifest themselves on an unconscious and prereflective level, as well as on a conscious and reflective level, whose nature is related both to the cognitive aspects and to the emotional-affective aspects. It is from this perspective that the characteristics of an analytic relationship emerge, at least as it is understood here, i.e., as a possible laboratory in which to concretize theoretical aspects and thus as an empirical scenario or, following Kant in his *Critique of Pure Reason*, only experience can tell us what inclinations exist to be satisfied and what conditions can produce their satisfaction.

Within that perspective four observational guidelines, let us say, can be discerned. Their concurrence makes it possible to reconstruct and construct a progressive knowledge of psychic life: (1) the experience linked to the relationship of transference to countertransference; (2) the treatment of infantile neuroses and psychoses (for instance, the interpretation of symbolic play activity expressed in the transferential relationship); (3) the study of the expressive and behavioral activity of the newborn (action research); (4) the study of the conditions of fetal life in the intrauterine environment and of the relative variations that that situation undergoes at birth in the earliest external conditions.

While the first two points assume a more direct involvement on the part of the operator, the other two (4 in particular) maintain a level of observation more centered on a transphenomenal axis (objective registration of the data investigated, outside observation, etc.).

The combination of research experiences belonging to the here and now of the analytic relationship with aspects belonging to a reconstructive study undertaken to discover the processes of psychic life in a genetic-evolutional sense, supplies a very rich and complex picture which, starting from phantasmatic organization, can lead us to an adequate perception of reality. And it is precisely the concept of *phantasma* that lends itself to the grafting of the outcome of an empirical disciplinary study onto the more theoretical aspects of representational activity. In fetal life there is already a primitive psychic life in which "presentations" arising from the conditions in which the fetus itself is immersed follow one upon another. The presentational event manifests itself as a function of sensations coming from the organism of the fetus undergoing progressive and complex development, combined with the nature and functions of the environment made up of the maternal body. Such presentations are not attributable, however, to either one side or the other. Rather, they constitute primitive *Gestalten* that concur to form pleasurable or unpleasurable experiences as a function of states of tension or absence of tension. The general objective condition of containment, the regular rhythms of various processes (in the absence of specific genetic or viral disturbances, etc.) enable us to hypothesize the rise of a "basic presentation" visualizable as spherical, a first sheltering and nurturing "*den,*" the experienced, in other words, comparable to what could be called original *Ganzfeld* (whole field). In that sense, in their initial indifferentiation, linked, moreover, to the objective state of symbiosis, the various presentations come to constitute the earliest discretionary psychic elements, which nevertheless remain bound to a process of compensation by the general state of homogenization caused by "environmental" characteristics. Phantasmatic organization with its first presentations thus stands out as the first modality through which the urge to represent comes into function. In the *phantasma,* the nature of psychic experience cannot be divided along the lines of affect/cognition. It springs to life from the activity of the organisms involved and lays the foundation for subsequent articulations of psychic life from birth onwards, which will be present in the modes of hallucination, of memory, of daydreams, of perception, etc. The *phantasma,* understood as original psychic experience, keeps within itself the character of intentionality since it is connected to events and aspects which give rise to it and to its reaction. In it, at first, it is not so much the "object" or "objects" that are "presentified" but a space-event as an expression of immanence, that is, of a preservation of the indistinction between the earliest forms in which prereflective psychic activity is articulated and the earliest elements of the experienced, as products of sensory activity. A reality, therefore, to which not only what is expressed in the "closed" experience of the subject belongs, but to which the entire life that he or she encounters with things and the events of the environment in which he or she is placed belong; and this from the very beginning.

If the classic concept of immanence is meant to include activities like thinking and perceiving but not what belongs to the process connected to transitivity—which, upon inspection, definitively places an unclosable gap between intellectual activity and its "object"—here it is held that those aspects linked to transitivity also belong to the representational dimension, without implying a simple reduction of representation to the physical objects or the events implicated from time to time. If, for example, I chose to eat an apple or to deliver a kick to some object, all of this belongs to my representational being and to the respective organization of sense springing from single types of experience.

In this context, the traditional conception of the character of immanence is altered: that character does not concern only the sense of experience that remains within the subject but extends to include the meanings that spring from transitive activities. In other words, representing is not based on a purely mental dimension alone but also on what comes to life in the action-reaction dynamic. It gathers within itself the effects of corporeal activity combined with the effects of the "encounter" with what surrounds one's body. The multifarious and imponderable shapes that such "histories" assume represent the experienced woven by cognitive structures and by the emotional-affective dimension. Thus the *phantasma* is originally linked to corporeity and to the histories that spring from it. The representational path, that is, the progressive connection of representations that follow one upon another, ushers in its histories as the sole place in which psychic experience can come into being. This argumentation tends to eliminate all those conceptions in psychology and psychoanalysis that are based on a more or less explicit demarcation between mental and corporeal, between psychic and organic, etc. Furthermore in fact, these histories cannot be reduced simply to a mentalistic level. The aspects that make them up draw on the vicissitudes of nurturing and feeding, not only as facts but also as the effects of a welcoming or a holding in.

At this point, a very important question arises that cannot be dealt with here: it concerns the problem of the object and its coming into being, since the term "object," which recurs in psychological and psychoanalytic language, can at times have contradictory or flimsy meanings. This problem concerns subsequent branching out from the path that leads from phantasmatic organization (see for example phantasmatic objects) to the processes that make up what we can define empirically as "adequate perception of reality," processes that require an all-out labor of diffusion in the face of the primitive attitude on indifferentiation.

Even when the process that makes up the object has taken place, however, a situation arises in which we witness a dynamic combination between the "outsides" and the "inside" rooted in a sole type of possible concrete experience. Language itself betrays this aspect, revealing how we continually assign expressiveness and intentions derived from emotive-affective states to the "exterior" (an "easy home," a "threatening sky," a "happy country"), just as we can approach the "interior" only through forms, structures, and processes drawn from perceptual experience ("mental states," "impulses," "elements," etc.). In the words of Cesare Musatti (1958):

> We are continually forced to make abstract distinctions, to speak of a reality that is the object of our perception and of a perceptual activity aimed at that reality; and hence also to speak of a structure that belongs to that reality or of a structural function that belongs to our perceptual activity, although these are not in fact different things but the very same perceptual structuring: the one abstractly objectivized as a quality of the real and the other abstractly subjectivized as a factor of our subjective perceiving activity. We can even carry these abstract positions further if that seems momentarily useful in extending our analysis. We can do this, however, only as long as we maintain, in the course of the operation, our awareness of the construct that we've imposed and as long as we remain willing to review our positions on the basis of concrete reality: where an abstract subjective moment and an abstract objective moment (the structure of the world and the structuring activity) are no longer distinguishable and where only the unfolding of images, in the phenomenological sense, remains. (279)

There is another aspect which, like the preceding, merits further investigation. Our way of approaching emotions, things, and psychic events is centered mainly on visualization and spatialization. There can be discerned a widespread, spontaneous process of capture by means of vision of any type of experience whatsoever. The very modality of vision, however, albeit preponderant, does not resolve in itself the more general expressive modality of representation. Here too we can take advantage of knowledge that can be drawn from the evolution of psychic experience. When, during a certain phase, earlier moreover than was thought up to forty years ago, perceptive-visual activity begins to function effectively, it gives rise to a process of vicarious performance, dominating what reaches us from other areas of sensory experience. If vision promotes or helps accelerate development, it tends at the same time to cover up meanings coming from earlier experiences. Further study of early stages of psychic life can thus provide valuable suggestions for improving our knowledge of representing and our understanding of its roots.

We know, for example, that the reader of Proust's *Recherche* inevitably makes a visual representation of the characters, places, and situations described: the reader is spellbound by the text. But if, for an instant, the reader should activate a kind of suspended attention, the scent and flavor of the "madeleine" would come wafting in, as a potent aggregate of emotions and images and as a world covered by sight and word. The phantasma and the representing that bring this world into being, as its first expressive totality, reveal themselves to us, then, no longer as abstract concepts or as the effect of esoteric reminders but as aspects of the world we live in and are made of and thus as aspects susceptible to further investigation and enrichment precisely through a pragmatic phenomenology. This phenomenology is aimed at providing a general structure, and should not be thought of as a frame comprising whatever research developments on psychic life but rather as an open heuristic terrain on which different constructions can be built.

Keeping to the appointed track often seems to be an especially difficult operation, since the tendency to solve problems and place events either on the material or on the spiritual side seems to lure the thoughts of researchers irresistibly. In that way, however, we put into motion a diversion from the phenomenological dimension that offers itself both as a source of meaning and as the natural habitat for psychic life.

Translated by Philip Grew

REFERENCES

Breuer, J., and Freud, S. 1893–95. *Studies on hysteria. S. E.* Vol. 2. London: Hogarth Press.

Devoto, G. 1968. *Avviamento all'etimologia italiana.* Florence: Le Monnier.

Funari, E. 1986. La rappresentazione. In *Natura e destino della rappresentazione.* Milano: Raffaello Cortina Editore, 1–38.

Kant, I. 1781. *Critique of pure reason.*

Kant, I. 1798. *Anthropologie in pragmatischer Hinsicht abgefarbt.* Königsberg; English translation by M. J. Gregor, *Anthropology from a pragmatic point of view.* The Hague: M. Nijhoff. 1974.

Margolis, J. 1978. *Persons and minds.* Dordrecht, Boston, London: Reidel.

———. 1984. *Culture and cultural entities.* Dordrecht, Boston, London: Reidel.

Moravia, S. 1986. *L'enigma della mente.* Rome and Bari: Laterza.

Musatti, C. 1958. Struttura ed esperienza nella fenomenologia percettiva. *Rivista di Psicologia* 52, 4: 279.

4

The Unconscious and
the Representational World

Joseph Sandler

The interests of the psychoanalyst and the philosopher overlap because both are concerned, although for somewhat different purposes, with problems of the mind, with models of the mind. It is with some aspects of a particular psychoanalytic model of this sort that I will be concerned, that is, with aspects of what I shall refer to as the representational world.

I want first to address myself to a confusion that exists within psychoanalytic thinking in regard to the concept of "the unconscious." Although the idea of the unconscious mind and of unconscious mental functioning long antedated Freud, he was certainly influenced as a young man by the notion of the unconscious mind current at the time in the form propounded, for example by Eduard von Hartmann, Herbart, and Brentano. Nevertheless, Freud's was, as we all know, the first intensive and systematic attempt to investigate unconscious mental processes, especially in relation to pathology. Yet what Freud understood as "the unconscious" changed in the course of his writings, and one of his legacies has been a thoroughgoing contusion among psychoanalysts about the meaning of the term. So, before going on to the concept of the representational world and some of its implications, I should like to comment briefly on what we mean by the term "unconscious" and on some of the problems that have arisen about the meaning of the term.

You will recall that Freud attended Charcot's clinic at the Salpétrière in Paris for some months in 1885–86. Charcot was dealing with patients with gross hysterical symptoms—dramatic paralyses, fits, losses of sensation, and the like. He believed (as did many French psychiatrists) that hysteria indicated a mental dissociation of one, conscious, part of the mind from another, unconscious, part. This dissociation was thought to be due to an intrinsic mental weakness with a possible organic or constitutional basis. The evidence for such a dissociation—which could be artificially created or removed by hypnosis—impressed Freud deeply, and his visit to Charcot can be regarded as a turning point in the prehistory of psychoanalysis. On Freud's return to Vienna he began his well-known collaboration with Dr. Josef Breuer, and in their co-authored *Studies on Hysteria* (1893–95), emphasis was placed on the importance of inner emotional life and on the significance of the crucial distinction between conscious and unconscious mental activity.

For several reasons Freud parted from Breuer, and one of these was Freud's belief in the value of his theory of what he called the "defense neurosis." Contrary to the views of the leading French psychiatrists (e.g., Janet), Freud had come to believe that the dissociation from consciousness of an unconscious part of the mind was an *active* rather than a passive process. This view involved the concept of defense against wishes, memories, and feelings which were offensive and intolerable to consciousness, a view which in one way or another remained central to all his subsequent psychoanalytic thinking. He believed that the division into the conscious and unconscious parts of the mind occurred in everyone, not only in neurotic patients. At this time, of course, Freud had a theory of neurosis based on the idea of the repression of traumatically induced quantities of affect, together with unacceptable memories associated with that affect. Treatment was based on the view that such emotions could be released through bringing them and the associated memories into consciousness, with consequent release of affect through abreaction or catharsis.

With the publication of *The Interpretation of Dreams* in 1900 the simple distinction between what was conscious and what was unconscious was not longer maintained by Freud. In the model of the mind put forward there—the topographical theory—Freud described two sorts of unconsciousness. He contrasted this view with that of the philosophers, and remarked

> The new discovery that we have been taught by the analysis of psycho-pathological structures . . . lies in the fact that the unconscious (that is, the psychical) is found as a function of two separate systems and that this is the

case in normal as well as in pathological life. Thus there are two kinds of unconscious, which have not yet been distinguished by psychologists. Both of them are unconscious in the sense used by psychology; but in our sense one of them, which we term *Ucs.* is also *inadmissible to consciousness,* while we term the other the *Pcs.* because its excitations—after observing certain rules, it is true, and perhaps only after passing a fresh censorship . . . are able to reach consciousness. (1900, 614–15)

The deeper sort of unconscious was the *system* Unconscious, or the so-called *dynamic* Unconscious, which was regarded as containing instinctual drives and wishes which, if they were allowed to emerge into consciousness, would constitute a danger, a threat, and would give rise to the most unpleasant feelings. The wishes arising in the Unconscious were thought of as constantly being propelled toward gratification through discharge, but if they were expressed in consciousness (i.e., if they reached the system *Conscious*) or were expressed in behavior, this could only be achieved in a distorted or censored form. The other sort of unconsciousness, that attributed to the system Preconscious, was conceived of as containing knowledge, thoughts, and memories of all sorts which were not defended against, which were not objectionable, but which could enter consciousness freely at the appropriate time and be utilized by the individual not only for rational tasks. They could also be seized upon by wishes from the system Unconscious as these repressed wishes pushed upwards from the depths to the surface. It should be noted that in all this, what is *descriptively* unconscious is not simply the system Unconscious but also the system Preconscious.

The system Unconscious of the topographical model can be regarded as being characterized by a very primitive mode of functioning which Freud designated as the *primary* process. Logical and formal relations between the elements in the Unconscious are absent, and simple rules of primitive association apply. Drives and wishes in the Unconscious system function only according to what Freud termed the *pleasure principle,* that is, they seek discharge, gratification, and relief of painful tension at all cost. The systems Preconscious and Conscious could be considered as being in direct opposition to this. Here the *secondary process,* that is logic, reason, and the knowledge of external reality and of our conscious ideals and standards of conduct, predominate. In opposition to the system Unconscious, the Preconscious and Conscious systems follow, or attempt to follow, what Freud in 1911 called the *reality principle.* It seems obvious

that situations of conflict—for example, between sexual wishes of a primitive sort and the persons's moral and ethical standards must inevitably
and constantly arise, and that some sort of solution—which might or
might not be pathological—would be sought which would take all the
opposing forces into account.

Toward the end of this phase of psychoanalysis a number of inconsis-
tencies began to be apparent in Freud's view of the mental apparatus and
its functioning. Problems arose in connection with the "descriptive" and
"systemic" use of the word unconscious. The term "preconscious," which
at one time referred to mental content which could be freely accessible to
consciousness, also designated a system and, moreover, Freud found it
necessary again to postulate a repression barrier between the Preconscious
and the Conscious, an idea mentioned years before in the *Interpretation of
Dreams*. I do not want to go into the difficulties which led, in 1923, to
Freud moving from the topographical model to his second topography,
known in the Anglo-Saxon world as the structural theory of the mind, a
theory which made use of a model involving a tripartite division of the
mental apparatus into the major structures or agencies of id, ego, and
superego (Freud 1923).

In this theory the id corresponded roughly to much of what had been
encompassed by the concept of the system Unconscious in the past.
However, a large part of the ego and of the superego were also, descriptively speaking, unconscious, and consciousness was now seen as a sense
organ of the ego. From this point on a major confusion arose in regard
to the term "unconscious," for at times it was used to refer to the system
Unconscious of the first topography, of the model put forward initially in
The Interpretation of Dreams. At other times it referred to everything that
was, descriptively speaking, unconscious. In the latter sense, it covered
the workings of much of the ego and the superego. It was very natural
that the *adjective* unconscious brought about the creation of the *noun* the
"unconscious," but now the unconscious referred to much more than the
system Unconscious of the first topography. The resulting confusion,
which was evident even in some of Freud's later writings, has certainly
permeated the writings of psychoanalysts ever since, and there is not
doubt that in our current and general use of the term the "unconscious"
we include organized secondary process functioning and the functioning
of the unconscious ego in general, as the term to refer simply to all that

is, descriptively speaking, unconscious, and it is time that psychoanalytic theoreticians fully recognized this.

Relevant to the concept of the unconscious is a fundamental distinction between two very different areas of the mind—what I shall refer to as the "experimental" and the "nonexperimental realms." In a paper written together with W. Joffe we said:

> The realm of subjective experience (in German *Erlebnis* but not *Erfahrung*) refers to the experience of the phenomenal content of wishes, impulses, memories, fantasies, sensations, percepts, feelings and the like. All we "know" we know only through such subjective phenomenal representations, which may vary widely in content, quality and intensity.
>
> Having said this, we would add immediately that experiential content of any sort, including feelings, can be either conscious or unconscious. Implicit in this is the view that an individual may "know" his own experiential content outside consciousness, that ideas can be experienced and feelings felt outside conscious awareness; and that he does not know that he unconsciously "knows." All this makes necessary the conceptualization of the existence of what we can call a representational "field" or "screen" upon which content can appear and be assessed. And, we would stress again, this content may or may not possess the quality of consciousness. In sharp contrast is the "non-experiential realm." This is the realm of forces and energies; of mechanisms and apparatuses; of organized structures, both biological and psychological; of sense organs and means of discharge. The non-experiential realm is intrinsically unknowable, except insofar as it can become known through the creation or occurrence of a phenomenal event in the realm of subjective experience. From this point of view *the whole of the mental apparatus is in the non-experiential realm,* capable of becoming known to us (only to a limited extent) via subjective experiences of one sort or another. (Sandler and Joffe 1969, 82)

Thus the concept of "the unconscious," as we use it today, includes the systems Unconscious and Preconscious of Freud's topographical model, the whole of the nonexperiential realm as I have described and the unconscious aspects of what has been referred to as the world of subjective experience—the experiential realm. Of course it is true that the idea of unconscious phenomena, unconscious awareness of, for instance, fantasy content, is a controversial one—a controversy I gladly leave to the philosophers. Yet as a working concept it is a useful one, particularly so when we work with a psychoanalytic model of the mind.

One of the reasons for the persistence in our thinking of a more general concept of the unconscious than that put forward by Freud in 1900 has been the increasing awareness of the inability of Freud's structural theory of 1923 to account fully and satisfactorily for psychic conflict as it is shown in the clinical psychoanalytic situation; as a consequence the concepts of the first topography remain—the Unconscious, the Preconscious, and the Perceptual-Conscious systems. But it is essential to keep in mind the double meaning of the term "the unconscious," in particular its extended meaning in which it refers to everything that is, descriptively speaking, unconscious. This is a topic I have considered at some length elsewhere (Sandler 1974), and I do not propose to go into it again now, except to say that it is becoming increasingly clear that psychic conflict cannot satisfactorily be considered in terms of conflict between the id, ego, superego, and external world. There is confusion about the concept of "the unconscious"; its double meaning, which I have commented on, has led many people to adhere to the view that all unconscious wishes are instinctual wishes, that is sexual or aggressive, whereas it is clear in the clinical situation that there is a whole spectrum of unconscious strivings with very different motivations. Some of the motivating forces may indeed be instinctual, but others relate to the need to gain feelings of safety (Sandler 1960). The need to avoid anxiety or any other painful affect is a particularly strong motivating force. Anxiety can be as strong a propelling factor in unconscious wishes as sexuality and aggression in their various forms.

Following on an attempt to fit clinical observations more closely to theory, and theory more closely to clinical observation, it was felt appropriate to construct a frame of reference which would coexist with the structural theory. This frame of reference was referred to as the representational world (Sandler and Rosenblatt 1962) and I shall try to describe the ideas involved very briefly.

In the context of what follows, the term "representation" has at least two meanings. On the one hand it can be considered to have a more or less enduring existence as an organization, schema, or set of rules that is constructed out of a multitude of impressions, an organization or structure in the nonexperiential realm. The classical "body schema" or "body image" is a representation in the sense described. However, "representation" also refers to contents of the experiential realm, to images and other subjective phenomena, including feelings. The child who undergoes many subjective experiences in his interaction with his mother—mother feeding, mother talking, mother scolding, and so on—gradually creates a mother representation which is outside subjective experience—as I have said, an organization, a schema, or set of rules for organizing the data of subjective experience. So we can have an experiential representation and a nonexperiential representation, and although the two are intimately connected, in that the mother schema, for example, can give rise to thoughts and fantasies about mother, such a representation is qualitatively different from the subjective image or experience involved in these thoughts or experiences. However, in spite of this important difference, it is useful at times to speak of, for example, object representations or self-representation or representations of self and object in interaction, without distinguishing—except where necessary—which of the two meanings of "representation" is being used. I quote from our original paper on the representational world:

> In all our considerations, we have made use of a notion that seems to us to be a central one in psychoanalysis, that of the child's subjective *world*, a world that is only gradually differentiated in the course of development as a consequence of processes of biological and psychological adaptation. (Sandler and Rosenblatt 1962, 130–31)

Freud had differentiated between the external and internal worlds of the child, but his use of the terms "internal" and "external" was meant to be purely descriptive. If we take into account our current knowledge that perception of objects in the external world cannot take place without the development, within the mind of the child, of an increasingly organized and complex set of representations of external reality, and of the child's interaction with that reality, then we have to go further than a purely descriptive differentiation between "internal" and "external," and will have to approach the problem of the child's "world" from a different point of view.

> The representations that the child constructs enables him to perceive sensations arising from various sources, to organize and structure them in a meaningful way. We know that perception is an *active process* by means of which the ego transforms raw sensory data into meaningful precepts. From this it follows that the child creates, within its perceptual or *representational* world, images and organizations of his internal as well as his external environment. It is well-known that the infant constantly confuses aspects of what we as *observers* would describe as "internal" and "external" reality within its representational world. All this means that in order to know what

is "outside," the child has to create a representation of that "outside" as part of his representational world. . . . The notion of body representation can be extended to that of self-representation. . . . The self-representation is, however, much more than a body representation. It includes all those aspects of the child's experience and activities that he later feels (consciously or unconsciously) to be his own. It has a status that parallels that of object representations, except that it refers to the child himself. By the "self-representation" we mean that organization that represents the person as he has consciously and unconsciously perceived himself, and that forms an integral part of the representational world. (Sandler and Rosenblatt 1962, 131–34).

The representational world has been compared to a stage set within a theater, with the characters of the stage representing the child's various objects, as well as the child himself. Moreover, there are representations of the child and object in interaction. The theater which exists in the nonexperiential realm contains the stage, and involves various functions such as scene shifting, raising or lowering the curtain, and all the machinery auxiliary to the actual stage production, a production which makes its appearance in the experiential realm.

Freud always saw the unconscious wish as consisting of a motivating energy or force which had become connected with a mental representation of some sort. For Freud unconscious wishes always had an instinctual force behind them, but we can now take the view that only *some* unconscious wishes are instinctual, and—as I indicated earlier in this chapter—others are driven by the need to do away with painful feelings and to gain or regain states of safety and well-being. In what follows I want to discuss the way in which unconscious wishes or wishful fantasies find expression—I could say find representation—in conscious experience and behavior. You will recall that in the topographical theory of 1900 Freud postulated a censorship between the system Unconscious and the system Preconscious and referred to a further censorship between the systems Preconscious and Conscious. These censorships, which have the function of protecting consciousness, remained in the second topography, that is, in Freud's structural theory of 1923, but were conceived of as the ego's *defensive* organization, a way of protecting consciousness from being overwhelmed by uncontrollable and painful subjective experiences—or, as Freud put it in 1926, a way of avoiding the experience of trauma. Nevertheless, the concept of censorship is still a useful one, particularly when we come to consider the transformation of representations in the formation of the dream—the "dream-work" as Freud called it (Freud 1900).

If an unconscious wish is to be defended against, it needs to be modified in some way so that it is acceptable to consciousness. But in order for this modification to take place it has to be evaluated first, which means that it has to be represented in the unconscious part of the experiential realm in order to be assessed. This implies that we have to conceive of sophisticated unconscious processes producing and constructing experiential content which is "scanned" by a sort of internal eye operating outside consciousness. The content is assessed from the point of view of its acceptability to consciousness, then modified and disguised, given a degree of "plausibility" and rational organization, in order to make it acceptable. In other words, representational transformations have to occur, and in these transformations the various mechanisms of defense are employed to bring about representational change. So, to take a simple example, the unconscious representation of an aggressive wish to attach to an ambivalently loved object may arouse anxiety, may therefore be regarded as unacceptable to conscious awareness, and be transformed, through the use of the mechanism of projection, into a representation in which the object is attacking the person. Indeed, it is perhaps of interest that all the mechanisms of defense can be schematized in terms of the representational changes which they bring about in order to make the content acceptable to the individual's consciousness, to make the content "ego-syntonic."

Unconscious wishes and wishful fantasies, whatever their origin, have as an essential component the mental representation of self and object in transition. There is always a role for the object in the wish-fulfillment that is desired, just as much as there is a role for the self. So the child's wish to cling to the mother does not only involve a representation of the child clinging, but also of the mother responding to the clinging, perhaps by bending down and holding the child.

As psychoanalysts we accept the theory that such unconscious wishes, unless they are completely repressed, can gain fulfillment in a disguised and distorted way. We can no longer accept the view that wish-fulfillment comes about through the discharge of quantities of energy, and in this connection I would like to put forward a proposition for your consideration, that is, that there is a close connection between conscious representation and unconscious wish-fulfillment. In order to do this, I want to turn briefly to the psychoanalytic theory of the dream. The dream can be regarded as a particular perceptual experience, a hallucination occurring at night, moreover a hallucination that can in many instances be remembered later, in that we are all licensed to have bizarre experiences provided that these experiences can be identified as dreams, though we are, of course, not normally licensed to hallucinate while awake. The dream is, we could say, a permissible and socially acceptable psychotic experience.

In his well-known seventh chapter of *The Interpretation of Dreams,* Freud pointed out that wishes could be fulfilled by means of achieving what he called an *identity of perception.* To put it in its simplest form, the wish has as its aim the reexperiencing, through perception, of a past situation which brought about gratification. So, for example, if memory traces of the experience of being satisfactorily fed are laid down in the infant, the oral wish recurring when the baby is hungry again would be essentially a wish to reexperience, through the perceptual apparatus, a situation which is perceptually identical with the earlier gratifying experience, that is the satisfying situation of being fed. Freud, in speaking of the hungry baby, said:

> A change can only come about if in some way or other (in the case of the baby, through outside help) an "experience of satisfaction" can be achieved which puts an end to the internal stimulus of the unfulfilled wish. An essential component of this experience of satisfaction is a particular perception (that of nourishment, for example)—the mnemic image remains associated thence forward with the memory trace of the excitation produced by the need. As a result of the link that has thus been established, next time this need arises the psychical impulse will at once emerge which will seek to . . . re-evoke the conception itself, that is to say, to re-establish the situation of this original satisfaction. An impulse of this kind is what we call a wish, the reappearance of the perception is the fulfillment of the wish. . . . Thus the aim of this . . . psychical activity is to produce a "perceptual identity"— a repetition of the perception which was linked with the satisfaction of the need. (Freud 1900, 565–66)

From the idea that the wish seeks fulfillment through the achievement of an experience which is perceptually identical with the earlier experience of satisfaction, Freud proceeded to show how the process of wish-fulfillment through a simple hallucination of the previously gratifying experience has to be modified. He discusses what he called the "round-about path to wish-fulfillment which has been necessary by experience," and describes the development of *thought* as a substitute for the hallucinatory wish. Above all, however, it is the dream which shows us the path taken by the process of wish-fulfillment.

In regard to the dream we can say that what we find is a perceptual identity—an identity of perception with the unconscious wish—thoroughly and usually successfully disguised by the operation of a whole series of mechanisms which range from the primitive to the more sophisticated. In a paper on this topic published in 1976, I commented:

> What I mean is simply this; a dream would be useless to the dreamer unless, at the time, he could also function as the observer of the dream. Similarly, a daydream would be valueless as a wish-fulfillment unless it were in some way perceived . . . a work of art would have no function in satisfying an unconscious wish unless the artist was aware of the act of creating and of the qualities of the creation itself. . . . If wish-fulfillment comes about through the attainment of an identity of perception we are faced with the problem of how it is that the attainment of this identity in a highly disguised and symbolic form can bring about a wish-fulfillment. How is it that to dream that some strange person presents another with a posy of flowers, while the dreamer stands aside as an observer, can provide the gratification of a sexual wish during the dream? Or that the construction of a work of art, full of symbolic and disguised wish-fulfillments, can affect the gratification of crude unconscious wishes by means of the expression *and the perception* of the symbolic representations.
>
> I suspect that the answer may lie in an ability of the individual to understand the symbolic meaning of his dream (or of any other "derivative," for that matter) *unconsciously*. What is crucial here is the absolute necessity for the person to protect his own consciousness from his unconscious knowledge. The point I want to stress is that perception can provide gratification and that it can do so not only by representing the wished-for situation, but also by doing so in a *disguised* form. While perception can provide gratification only momentarily in the case of pressing biological needs, in the case of psychological needs and wishes (including wishful fantasies) direct or indirect gratification via perception can be much more substantially obtained; moreover, it can be reached symbolically, and we have only to consider the phenomenon of sublimation . . . to be aware of this process of unconscious wish-fulfillment occurring without direct bodily stimulation. (Sandler 1976, 38–39)

I should like to propose that we can regard all wish-fulfillment as being brought about through what we can call some form of actualization. Let me quote again:

> The commonest way of making something "real" or "actual" is to act on the real world in such a way that our perception comes to correspond to

the wished-for reality; also we may act upon ourselves in order to attain this correspondence. Commonly we do both but there are other forms of actualization. We may include *illusional* actualization, in which the perceptual process distorts the sensory data arising from the external world in the direction of wish-fulfillment, although normally such an illusion can be corrected by later experience. If it cannot, we have *delusional* actualization, a process which is by no means restricted to psychotics. Wish-fulfillment through *hallucinatory* actualization is, of course, common in psychosis. Actualization through *daydreams* is normally less satisfying than actualization by way of direct perceptual experience, although much will depend on the sensory intensity of the daydream images and the capacity of the individual to suspend "disbelief" temporarily during daydreaming. . . . Freud's masterly description of the "dream-work" needs, I believe, to be supplemented by an equal emphasis on the opposite *centripetal* process of perceiving the dream content and unconsciously translating it back into its latent meaning, so that wish-fulfillment is obtained by means of an identity of perception. In a sense there is an unconscious "understanding-work" which goes in a parallel but opposite direction to the dream-work as described by Freud. What is true of the dream can also be regarded as true for other "derivatives," for other surface expressions [representations] of unconscious wishes and fantasies. This allows us to add something further to the idea put forward previously that all wish-fulfillment is brought about by some form of actualization. The additional element is that *the perceived manifest actualization is unconsciously understood and unconsciously translated back into its latent meaning.* In terms of the topographical model this "decoding" and understanding would take place in the Preconscious system, while in the structural model it can be attributed to the unconscious ego. Essential to the whole process is the need for consciousness to be protected from the knowledge of what is going on. (Sandler 1976, 39–40)

From the point of view of the thesis put forward here, such activities as sublimations can be regarded as symbolic actualizations which are *unconsciously understood* by the individual concerned in terms of the significance of the activity being pursued, even though he is not *consciously* aware of the meaning of what he has produced in the form of a disguised or symbolic representation. The person's consciousness is in this way protected from awareness of the unconscious wishful fantasy being gratified or fulfilled.

Finally, I want to conclude by commenting that what goes on in the unconscious is not at all directly accessible to us — so we need to construct models of the mind that are useful for our work. In this chapter I have tried to present, in a very sketchy form, a frame of reference which can be used alongside other psychoanalytic methods, a way of thinking which allows a number of processes to be viewed from a representational perspective. I hope that you have found it of some interest, and may find it of some use.

REFERENCES

Breuer, J. and Freud, S. 1893–95. *Studies on hysteria. S. E.* Vol. 2. London: Hogarth Press.
Freud, S. 1900. *The interpretation of dreams. S. E.* Vols. 4 and 5.
———. 1923. *The ego and the id. S. E.* Vol. 19.
———. 1926. *Inhibitions, symptoms and anxiety. S. E.* Vol. 20.
Sandler, J. 1960. The background of safety. *Int. Psycho-Anal.* 41:352–65.
———. 1974. Psychological conflict and the structural model: Some clinical and theoretical implications. *Int. Psycho-Anal.* 55:53–62.
———. 1976. Dreams, unconscious fantasies and identity of perception. *International Review of Psycho-Analysis* 3:33–42.
Sandler, J., and Joffe, W. G. 1969. Towards a basic psychoanalytic model. *Int. Psycho-Anal.* 50:79–90.
Sandler, J., and Rosenblatt, B. 1962. The concept of the representational world. *Psychoanal. Study of the Child* 17:128–45.

II

REPRESENTATIONS AND NARRATIVES IN DEVELOPMENT

5

Maternal Representations during Pregnancy and Early Infant-Mother Interactions

Massimo Ammaniti

In this chapter I should like to discuss the effect of representations on intergenerational relationships and in particular the influence of the maternal psychic world and its internal relations on the attachment style and quality of the interpersonal relationship of a mother to her baby.

In Freud's thought one of the leading ideas throughout his theoretical construction was undoubtedly represented by the hypothesis that any relation experienced both on the conscious and unconscious level with one's own parents during infancy will have a decisive influence on the development of the baby's personality. In his paper *On Narcissism: An Introduction* (1914), Freud deals with parental roles during this intergenerational process, focusing on the function of parental "compulsion to ascribe every perfection to the child" (91), and in the subsequent lines he adds "the child shall fulfil those wishful dreams of the parents which they never carried out" (91). In a later essay, *Group Psychology and the Analysis of the Ego* (1921), Freud faces the other aspect of this process, in fact he considers the identification mechanism of the child which represents "the earliest expression of an emotional tie with another person" (105). Although Freud refers to the identification with the father of one's "personal pre-history" through which one "should like to grow like him and be like him" (105), he describes this kind of link in a baby as the first relationship it has with its mother.

It is interesting to notice that within the concept of compulsion to ascribe one may already foresee Klein's later discovery of projective identification. This mechanism is not only intrapsychic but also intersubjective and may entail in itself the modification of the object, on which the projection takes place, not only in fantasy but also in reality. With Bion the concept of projective identification is further developed particularly in the context of mother-child relationships according to the "container" model. Following this model the mother, who is caring for the baby, is capable of attending and being tolerant toward the baby's needs, his distress, his anger, and also toward the love which the baby expresses, and in this way she will communicate and reassure the baby that she is capable of containing and responding to these feelings.

Another contribution toward the comprehension of the intersubjective mechanisms has been given by Sandler (1976), who speaks about the concept of actualization or rather of "a wished-for role interaction, with the wished-for or imagined response of the object being as much a part of the wishful fantasy as the activity of the subject in that wish or fantasy" (64). As Selma Fraiberg (1980) writes, "in every nursery there are ghosts . . . visitors of the unremembered past of the parents. . . . These unfriendly and unbidden spirits are banished from the nursery . . . the bonds of love protect the child and his parents against the intruders" (164). It can happen that in some cases the family appears to be possessed by its ghosts and the parents and their child may find themselves reenacting a moment or a scene from another time with another set of characters. In this situation the baby is already in peril, showing the early signs of emotional starvation, because he is burdened by the oppressive past of his parents.

If these contributions we referred to are set within a clinical context, very interesting evidence has recently emerged on intergenerational transmission during research projects whose background is the theory of attachment by Bowlby (the Minnesota Project conducted by Morris [1980]; the Amherst Project conducted by Ricks and Noyes [1984]; and the Berkeley Project conducted by Main, Kaplan, and Cassidy [1985]). These studies on intergenerational transmissions are certainly interesting for our understanding of the affective world and individual relational styles, and permit the investigation of the dynamics through which internal working models and parental mental representations influence the child's attachment development (Main, Kaplan, and Cassidy 1985).

In the case of those mothers who have a sufficiently balanced representational world, corresponding to the internalization of infantile experience
with sensitive attachment figures which are ready to respond to the baby's
own affective signals, it is very probable that the baby will show a secure
attachment. Babies with secure attachment show good ability to explore,
good affective configuration, and a considerable personal ego-resilience.
Even affective regulation and modulation are correctly influenced. These
children reveal good and positive feelings which influence and enrich
relationships, but are at the same time capable of tolerating negative
affects (Ainsworth 1978). If we consider the representational world of
the mothers of the secure babies, it will enable us to have a better
understanding of intergenerational transmission's processes of personal
affective configuration. In this case we will be dealing with women who
have coherently worked out their own childhood relationships with their
parents, recognizing in them a relevant value for their own personal
history and their present mental state. A decisive point is not so much the
fact that childhood history be positive or negative, as the way in which it
has been lived through and has been mentally elaborated during adult
age; we may add that what counts is coming to terms with one's own
parents. These mothers not only give value to relations but maintain a
balanced view of themselves within their relationships with others, are
capable of forgiving any injury, are coherent in describing early experiences, and do not idealize their own parents. This personal orientation
enables the mother to respond affectionately to her baby's demands for
safety and his need for independence. Thus the baby will interiorize a
feeling of relational trust; in fact the baby expects his mother to pay
attention to his demands and communications and to be able to understand them.

Very different is the case of the mothers we may call enmeshed, who
maintain a very strong dependence on their own original family. In fact
they seem to be incapable of deidentifying themselves from their own
childish relations—they still show hostility and resentment toward what
happened to them during infancy, and still try to ingratiate themselves
with their parents although they are already adults. These mothers are
generally incoherent in describing their own attachment relations and
their own childhood experiences. When we observe children brought up
in this affective climate we will notice a very marked ambivalence toward
the mother, with an anxious seeking of a relationship with her and with

reactions of anxiety, fear, and anger always directed toward the mother. These children show a low affective activation threshold, even small episodes of stress or conflict are sufficient to give way to apprehension and fear, which inevitably interfere with self-confidence and seeking behaviors. If, instead, the mother is not responsive to her baby's expectations, or doesn't support his attachment, or doesn't encourage his seeking needs, or doesn't comfort him during his moments of stress and suffering, the baby will be directly influenced in his attachment to his mother and in his representation of himself and others. This may be noticed in the mothers of avoidant babies of whom I will give a clinical and observational example. We are dealing here with affectively detached mothers who seem incapable of valuing their attachment relations, who find it difficult to remember early experiences, and who don't show affective responses to their memory of early and painful situations. If we consider the level of mental functioning in these women, what will be noticeable is a certain incoherence between their semantic memory regarding rather generalized and abstract memories (such as "my mother used to be generous") and episodic memory referred to specific events (such as "that time my mother got very angry with me") which don't give support to their generalizations. We may explain this by saying that defensive mechanisms of splitting and denial which are being used effectively cancel painful memories and experiences and maintain an idealized vision of the self and of others. The same defensive style will be noticeable in their children, who will tend to escape from self-involving affective interactions, and who will adopt defensive strategies to eliminate any negative effect, such as anxiety and anger. The picture I have been tracing out focuses on the continuity and intergenerational transmission of affective configuration and representational working models of the Self and of significant others. Researches which have been carried out in different countries seem to agree in pointing out this fact.

To better understand the meaning of the intergenerational influences and transmission, I would like to introduce the case of particular little baby boy, Andrea, belonging to the anxious-avoidant category (subcategory A1) and consider him in relation to his own mother. At one year of age we had a Strange Situation with Andrea according to Ainsworth's procedure. The child appears extremely avoidant, detached, and distant, unable to communicate his affects and moods. He shows neither distress in the new environment nor attachment to the mother, and doesn't seek attention or comfort. Also, a stranger's presence doesn't worry him; he continues to play even when his mother goes out and then comes back. When an adult is present (be it his own mother or a stranger) Andrea seems to concentrate only on his own toys, but then when he remains alone in the room after his mother has left him, he stands up and starts moving about the room in a free and easy way. It might be interesting at this point to quote from what Balint and Balint (1959) wrote about the world of the philobate, which consists in a well-known space filled by dangerous and unforeseeable objects.

As Balint and Balint write, "We may therefore say that the philobatic world consists of friendly expanses dotted more or less densely with dangerous and unpredictable objects" (34) and in his relationship with any object what is very important is to look at it from a distance. His 28-year-old mother, Angela, was interviewed by us during her eighth month of pregnancy using an interview (IRMAG)* which we have devised and which explores the mother's mental representations of herself as a mother and of her future baby.

During the course of the interview it appears that Angela has faced this, her first pregnancy, alone, because her original family is not resident in Rome. Regarding the choice of having a child, she says "Well, I really wanted it. I have always adored children, we've been married for about two years and it seems like the right moment for me—it really was, I wanted it. I don't know how much my husband did really." She has also decided to give up working to dedicate herself completely to the child, even though this choice was criticized by her in-laws. She was "terrified" at the idea of letting her in-laws know about her pregnancy, while with her mother it has been different, their relationship has always been very open. Her husband "was pleased—she says—but I think I probably forced the thing." Every now and then she has nightmares, and feels

---

*Interview of Maternal Representations during Pregnancy (IRMAG): the interview data for the investigation are maternal responses to a semistructured interview. In the IRMAG, questions are asked about the following areas of personal experience: 1) the woman's and the couple's desire for a baby; 2) the emotional reactions of the woman, of the couple, and of the other family members to the pregnancy; 3) the emotions and changes in the woman's life, in the life of the couple, and in relation to the original families during pregnancy; 4) the perceptions, positive and negative emotions, maternal and paternal fantasies, the internal child's psychological space; 5) future expectations and possible life modifications; and 6) the personal historical perspective.

afraid of the birth, of giving birth to a baby who's malformed, but she can't talk about this with anybody, not even with her husband who is a very closed type of person. She began to feel the fetal movements at about the fourth month; she didn't want to know the sex of the baby, sometimes imagining it as a boy and sometimes a girl. They have not been able to find a name for it. She can't either imagine or dream what the baby is going to be like. When she imagines it after the birth she asks herself a lot of questions, she thinks about its school, about when it'll be grown-up, but then she feels that she's day-dreaming too much. She'd like a calm and contented baby, "a little being who is also passive"; she feels a bit worried since she doesn't have any experience with newborn babies, having seen a newborn baby for the first time the week before. She has known children about five or six months old who were quite lively and she's frightened of it. About her infancy she reports that her parents are divorced and that there was no relationship with her father, but with her mother it was different. She always ran around, busy in the house, and her brothers and herself always had to be good, silent, and quiet. With her child she thinks it will be different, that she'll have much more time; she gave up working for this reason: "I definitely want to be available to my child, perhaps because that's what I missed as a child." It appears during this interview that Angela faced this pregnancy as her own choice, maybe as a mission that she has undertaken by herself against her husband's and her in-laws' ideas. Care of her baby will play the role of compensating her for the deprivations and pains of her childhood; it is a secret baby, ideal, who lives inside her but who has neither a face, nor sex, nor name.

This "phantasmatic baby" (Lebovici 1983) is inevitably a "passive little being." He is the object of his mother's narcissistic desires, capable of giving the mother a personal completeness and enabling her to defeat her feeling of inadequacy and failure. However, Angela seems scared by the baby who is going to be born, she fears he might be too lively and aggressive, representing an aspect of her own infantile Self, not recognized and full of anger and resentment at not having been sufficiently looked after and loved.

When the child is one year old we again interviewed the mother according to the Adult Attachment Interview (AAI) procedure elaborated by Main and Goldwyn.

She talks about her life during childhood in a small provincial town, with her very stern father who worked at home. She and her brothers had very little room for themselves and couldn't move about. With her parents "there was no relationship" and she adds "perhaps that's exactly why I made my decision to devote myself to the child, because my father was practically never there . . . he was on a pedestal and you couldn't go near him." Her mother was very much more available, but she had a lot of work too. As a child she knew she wasn't allowed to ask for anything, not expect anything from anyone, "so the mere fact of just telling her about something I wanted was already a sign of a good relationship to me."

During the interview she seems more and more upset talking about her father: "it's still difficult for me to talk about it, my father left home . . . goodness, it makes me so cross that I still find it difficult to talk about it." She cries and says that when she was thirteen her father left home to go and live with a young woman who lived in the same building and he started a new family with her. She has stopped seeing her father now; she's never forgiven him for leaving her, but then immediately she corrects herself and says: for leaving my mother.

During pregnancy she spoke to him to tell him about the baby; when the child was born she telephoned him from the clinic, but he didn't come to see her. Regarding the child she says that she's quite jealous and when he sometimes stays with her sister-in-law she feels worried about it. During this interview her adolescent disappointment at having her womanhood refused by her father comes to light; her father in fact chose another young woman who was almost the same age as herself. Keeping this fact in mind we may suppose that Angela tried through her own pregnancy to give her own father a baby in the unconscious intent of bringing him back to his family, and thus of succeeding where her own mother had failed.

If we now consider the interview from the point of view of the attachment motivational system, the interview of this woman can be classified in the "Dismissing of Attachment" category (DS2), characterized—as Main and Goldwyn say—by "an implicit devaluing of attachment; one or both parents may be described with a cool, active devaluation and derogation. Surprisingly, despite or perhaps because of an overriding active coolness towards relationships, the adult may occasionally make strikingly personal, perceptive or even passionate remarks about individuals or about aspects of childhood, suggesting an underlying vivacity" (107–8).

I should now like to speak about another case, Marco's, a little boy who was tested with the Strange Situation Test when he was one year old. From the very start it was evident that Marco, although he appeared to be reasonably independent and interested in his toys, had actually a greater interaction with his mother. When confronted with a person he didn't know he hesitated and showed initial confusion, but then accepted to play; anyway, when his mother left him he showed distress and called her back, sounding alarmed. When his mother did come back to the room where he was, his first reaction was happiness at having her back, though he very soon started playing again, turning away from her. What we noticed was that after Marco was left alone after his mother had gone, he tried to control himself, later when his tension grew he started whimpering and tried to reach the door and his mother. During the last test when his mother came back Marco acted offended, he tried to wriggle out of her arms, he was probably angry at having been left.

It's quite evident that his behavior is at times avoidant, but he still shows secure attachment (subcategory B1) for the simple reason that he is capable of expressing his own emotions and of expecting an active response from his mother.

At this point we can begin examining Marco's mother's world, starting off from the interview we had with her when she was seven months' pregnant. Marco's mother is a tall, good-looking woman, 31 years old, with a pleasant and active appearance. Her way of answering questions is bright and humorous and shows good insight. Her pregnancy hadn't been expected or planned. She had been used to independent work, and felt very much involved in her job as an advertiser. "My pregnancy" she says "totally changed the rhythm of my daily routine." Since she was physically unwell from the very start, she "also had the feeling of being hindered." After learning she was pregnant, she and her partner decided to marry, as till then they had simply been living together. After a while she had settled down and started getting organized and used to what a pregnancy really means and implies. All of this she says showing emotional participation, and when her feelings are particularly roused she laughs. She says she's kept traveling on business, in the country and abroad, because her work must always be of the same standard. So, despite initial perplexities because this particular moment was not ideal for having a baby, her decision to keep it came immediately. This radical change in life disorientated and fascinated her at the same time. Her husband and both their families backed her in her decision; her pregnancy was altogether welcomed as a joyful event, just because her own parents considered that not having children at the age of 31 was a real lack, although there had never been recriminations on their part.

What is constantly and strikingly evident during the interview is her difficulty in accepting the novelty of her new state; it's such a change and it makes her have to face new experiences. "When one is 31 this means stepping into something new and ponderous, making up one's mind is no trifling matter." Her relationship with her husband has become closer; with her mother as well bonds have become stronger. Her mother is described as "brimming with her liveliness and joy and very young." During these last months of her pregnancy she keeps thinking about her baby, before falling asleep in the evenings she tried to imagine what her baby is going to be like. She also goes through moments of anxiety, fearing the baby might not be well; she thinks about childbirth but can't figure out what it's going to be like. When she feels her baby moving within her she says "it's anomalous, feeling the baby moving inside me makes me realize I'm growing fond of it, and it can be amusing at times, but it's not an everyday normal experience." The baby seems to move more when she feels tense, so she is sure her feelings pass through to her baby.

Through ultrasound screening she knows it's going to be a baby boy, but she doesn't really care, saying "a baby boy or a baby girl makes no difference, it annoys me when people seem to prefer one to the other." About the ultrasound screening she commented on having had the feeling that her baby was suffocated by her own tummy because he lived in a situation which was totally different from her own: "he wasn't living in open air and seeing light, he couldn't move about as I could."

Thinking forward to the near future she says, "I shouldn't like the baby to sleep in my own bedroom, I should like him to be independent from the very start." As a mother she knows she will have to follow the baby's rhythms. "Every baby has its own ways, I don't feel I could force him to sleep at nights and keep awake during the day-time." After her baby is born she thinks she'll need some help. Certainly also her mother will help, but then she adds, "I shouldn't like to hand him over to her alone, she might end up by having the upper hand."

When she thinks back to her childhood she remembers her mother played an important role, having had to act both as a mother and a father.

She had been a very important everyday presence: "I needed her love and her love flowed toward me incessantly." Growing up, when she was about 20 she started to feel that her mother was somewhat oppressive, whereas in her earlier years she had been the only important person. Because her father had always worked very much out of home, when he came back he was tired and needed to rest and was never inclined to play or develop common interests and have fun with his children.

Thinking of herself as a mother she fears she might follow in the footsteps of her mother and become an anxious mother. "I do hope I won't become like her . . . I shouldn't like to expect my own child to come back to me so completely, that's what our mother expected of us children." Again, speaking of her own mother she adds, "I shouldn't like my mother to need my baby too much and I don't want my child to be left with her 24 hours out of 24."

We met Marco's mother again when the baby was four months old. Altogether her experience of motherhood and nurturing had been a very positive one; she had feared it might all have been more of a burden. She had discovered her anxiety with her baby: "anything seems to scare me to death, like if it happens for example that he doesn't manage to swallow something." The baby is growing well: "he is a strong baby, capable of making himself understood, he knows what he wants . . . he is not like those babies who will just stay put." He sleeps in his parents' bedroom, because she wants to be able to watch over him and is afraid he might choke while sleeping. Breast-feeding was a good feeling, she did enjoy the idea of being of physical support as well. Speaking about these months she says she felt completely different from what she was before: "it's been not only a great change in my physical habits but also my mental habits, . . it's a totally different style of life." After her pregnancy she's felt greater closeness with her own mother, the only risk being that as her mother is very young, she may take her grandchild for her own child and interfere between herself and her baby. "This is why we would rather the baby was cared for by his father than by his grandmother." When talking about the baby's future she hopes it will grow into an independent confident little being and that she herself won't make the mistake of becoming an anxious mother.

When the child is one year old we again interview the mother according the Adult Attachment Interview (AAI). Talking about her relationship with her own mother during childhood she says "it was very close, it had to make up for the father not being there." When speaking about her mother she says she was a very tender woman, very close, intelligent, lively, and amusing. When she is asked to give examples she remembers that when she and her brother were young their mother used to wake them up in the morning and cuddle them: "it is quite typical that children don't want to get up, because it's cold, because they are sleepy; my mother never used to just call us, she would slip into bed with us, she would cuddle us . . . she would help us in our waking up."

So we start recognizing a very protective mother, whose feelings of security depend upon her child. Anyway, although this attitude does provide a certain feeling of stability and reassurance, at the same time it also creates a certain ambivalence. This is clearly evident from an episode about when Marco's mother got hurt when she was a little girl: "I remember when . . . I fell and skinned my knees and my mother dressed my wound with peroxide; unfortunately during the night the dressing slipped out of place and took off the skin on my knee and I cried. I do remember this, but my mother kept telling me to be quiet." Apart from the relationship with her mother her grandfather was an important figure, "a man who taught . . . to love certain studies . . . to want to know the world . . . to travel."

It is possible that the identification with this grandfather helped her to detach herself from her very protective family, who, when she was young girl, went to the extent of threatening to call in the police to make her come back early from her evening outings. Becoming independent of her family was rather traumatic: "up to the age of 20 I stayed at home and followed their rules . . . after that I couldn't stand it any longer and left, I suddenly had a fight with them and went off and lived on my own. I had great difficulties, that was my reaction, because I felt oppressed by their way of bringing children up, because it wasn't really anyway at all, actually it was their own fears and their own anxieties."

Speaking about her present relationship with her parents, she notices that while once she just passively accepted whatever they wanted, now "there is an equally and contrary reaction in the sense that I hardly accept anything they might suggest." Speaking about her own child she understands she doesn't want to repeat her parent's mistakes, but when she is away from her son it is "as if the umbilical cord were been torn . . . I feel . . . actually I don't feel well."

The general picture is quite coherent, showing a certain balance and a certain personal autonomy. Having in mind the classification system proposed by Main and Goldwyn, the interview orientates us toward the F5 Classification, that is Free-Autonomous regarding attachment, but somewhat resentful and conflicted. As Main has come to write: "these are individuals who are moderately angrily preoccupied with their relationships to their attachment figures, but are nonetheless strikingly coherent, or even humorous" (121).

Let's now try to draw some conclusions, though of necessity brief: from what we've been able to see the two mothers faced pregnancy and childbirth in two different ways.

In the case of Angela we might propose the hypothesis that she may have tried to work out her messianic fantasies through her baby, considering her personal mental organization which is dominated by schizoid defenses. It is possible that this pregnancy was started with the secret desire to reconquer her father, giving him a baby like the young woman he had gone away with had done.

Anyway, Angela got her expectations severely frustrated because her real baby did not personify and realize her own fantasies and probably Angela had simply gone on living in a secret expectancy of a baby Messiah. During her relationship with her real baby Angela feared that he might expect a tension and fondness and might express resentment and anger for not being adequately looked after, that is, she feared he might embody her own childhood tendencies which she herself had not been able to express during the general atmosphere of her childhood.

As Mary Ainsworth has clearly evidenced, when a mother is not sensitive and ready to respond to any affective signs of pain and distress from her baby she will discourage further requests and behaviors; the baby will very soon learn to control these expressions of affection so as to avoid receiving a refusal.

Let's assume that Angela went on living and expecting a messianic baby who would enable her to draw her own father back to her, whereas toward Andrea she kept feeling a kind of psychological distance for the reason that the baby didn't embody her fantasies. One may question what exactly took place from his very first days of life. Did Angela manage to interact with her own baby, did she hold him correctly, did she manage to encourage fondness, did she recognize his needs and aliments? Our hypothesis, which was confirmed by interactions observed during the Strange Situation Test, is that Angela couldn't become attuned with her baby, was incapable of giving him comfort, and didn't initiate an affectionate dialogue, which is possible only when the mother accepts the baby as an individual. In this particular situation, what may take place is a kind of transmission of the defensive system between mother and baby, based on a splitting and isolation of affect mechanisms which will do away with the subjective experience of suffering, will not be understood and worked out by the mother, and therefore won't be internalized by the baby.

It is reasonable to suppose that in the case of avoidant children the splitting mechanism may not only have a defensive function but also a facilitating function, or better an enabling function (Shapiro and Perry 1976; Alvarez 1989) which will actually help the child's development. The child can concentrate on one task or thought (as was the case with Andrea during the Strange Situation when he was totally absorbed in his playing) and this will happen only when the child can ignore other thoughts, tasks, and subjects with the capacity to put aside those others and be able to forget. Mary Main suggests that the avoidant child or detached child, according to Bowlby's earlier definition, may be the victim of an irresolvable and self-perpetuating conflict caused by his mother's aversion to physical contact: the infant cannot approach because of the parent's rejection and cannot withdraw because of his own attachment. The only way for the child to solve this conflict is to learn to control and limit real interactions and live all his desires in an idealized separate world in which he can act out a perfect union with the mother. The idealization entails the refusal to perceive or report normal human and expectable limitations preventing information and experiences that would distress him. In this way negative affects such as anger, resentment, or envy are screened away and eliminated so as to reduce conflicts with the attachment figures and consequently save the relationship with them.

As Lebovici (1983) very clearly pointed out, all forms of development and organization of mother-to-baby interactions, particularly those involving affects, are strongly conditioned by maternal phantasms, and we may also add by their being permeable to new experiences the mothers may be living through. While in the case of Angela her personal phantasmatic configuration is somewhat fixed, in the case of Marco's mother there is a whole wealth of changes being experienced during pregnancy; she is therefore capable of modifying and taking new decisions regarding her job and her own private life. She can assert her own independence which during adolescence she had made use of to overcome her own regressive tendencies toward her mother. In this she may have been helped through a counteridentification (Palacio-Espasa 1991) with the complementary image of the grandfather, who helped her to detach herself from her family world and open herself up to the outside world. Pregnancy appears to have triggered off the separation-individuation process toward her own mother. On the one hand, in fact, she too wants to face motherhood like her own mother did, identifying herself with a good internal mother which helps her to fulfill this more mature function, on the other hand regressive tendencies reemerge when she identifies herself with the fetus and feels she is suffocating, trapped in a strongly asymmetrically biased relationship which restricts her ability to see and foresee. This is the way in which the mother is preparing to welcome her baby-to-be, who represents all aspects of her own infantile Self. This second example is typical of the changes which may take place during pregnancy in the woman's life; this, as Bibring et al. (1961) suggest, is "a turning point that brings with it unsettling and dislodging of habitual solutions," reaching completion after the baby is born.

The integration taking place between deeper fantasies, daydreaming, and the tangible reality of her relations toward herself, her husband, and her child allows her to be a sensitive mother, watchful to any sign of distress in her child, although, with a good degree of insight, she at times senses the danger of becoming too anxious and worrying following her own mother's example.

Another difference between the two women is the different attitude about the knowledge of the sex of the fetus. As Chaves Winestine (1989) points out, there are basically two groups of women: the ones who seem to want to know about the sex of the fetus and who show a practical and rational attitude and therefore accept at the early stage the baby's presence and individuality, while the others refuse any form of information and seem to prefer to live by amorphous fantasies.

In this last group "women enjoy pregnancy for its own sake more than for the sake of the child" (Chaves Winestine 1989, 1027); this seems to be the case with Angela.

Still there is one aspect which clearly differentiates the two women and which mainly regards the way in which each personal experience and each infantile history has been worked out. In fact, in our first example Angela built up her own autobiography, to refer to Bruner's point of view, in which she chooses to represent herself as a deprived little girl who has been obliged to cope independently with everything by her mother who was too busy working and her father who betrayed her. In our second example, by contrast, the woman appears to have lived through a very close relationship with her mother, thus hindering the possibility of her reaching autonomy.

Angela started her pregnancy in an idealized world of messianic fantasies which undoubtedly are a hindrance to her own perception and experience of pregnancy, so as to be able to escape her resentments and mortifications. This is very different from our second example in which Marco's mother is in touch with a good internal mother, without in any way falling back into a regressive position.

What is interesting is that what we have been noticing has many points in common with the research of Dana Breen (1975), who like us reveals the danger of an idealized maternal image, which she defines as "perfect-all-sacrificing-contented-never-angry" (117)and which will interfere with the possible acquisition of maternal identity if it remains unmodified even after the baby is born.

Let's now draw some conclusions about the two cases presented. It appears that there exists in Angela a phantasmatic fixity, modestly modifiable by the conscious fantasies and the experiences she lives through in pregnancy, initially, and in the relationship with her child, later. Very different is the second case in which the pregnancy reactivates infantile fantasies connected to the mother which can be modified and modulated by the experience she is living. So the modifiability of the phantasmatic world assumes great importance also in relation to the child: in the first case it entails a focus of the mother on the personal fantasies and in the second case the competence to interact with the child and understand his affective signals, decisive experience toward the development of the infantile attachment.

At this point we may want to question what it is that determines the child's destiny, keeping in mind that, as Fraiberg writes, "history is not destiny." Certainly, if the parent is in contact with his own sufferings this constitutes a powerful deterrent against repetition in parenting, while repression and isolation, very active mechanisms in Angela's world, provide the psychological requirements for identification with the betrayers and the aggressors.

Another important aspect is the parent's capacity to distinguish between what is called reality and what is called phantasy. We can consider this as the ability and wisdom to tolerate ideas and emotions without making recourse to narcissistic projections on one's child which have the double aim of protecting the child from the experience of the loss of his objects and protecting the parent himself from the possibility of reexperiencing through his child his own infantile losses. And while these projections erase the limits between phantasy and reality, more mature projections point to further procedures aimed at working through mourning still unsettled after childhood and adolescence.

REFERENCES

Ainsworth, M. 1978. *Patterns of attachment.* Hillsdale, N.J.: Erlbaum.

Alvarez, A. 1989. Development toward the latency period: Splitting and the need to forget in borderline children. *Journal of Child Psychotherapy* 15: 71–83.

Ammaniti, M.; Baumgartner, E.; Candelori, C.; Pola, M.; Tambelli, R.; and Zampino, F. 1990. Rappresentazioni materne in gravidanza: Contributi pre-liminari. *Rivista di Psicologia Clinica* 1: 36–50.

Ammaniti, M., ed. 1989. *La nascita del S___.* Roma: Laterza.

Ammaniti, M., and Dazzi, N., eds. 1990. *Affetti.* Roma: Laterza.

Balint, M., and Balint, E. 1959. *Thrills and regressions.* New York: International Universities Press.

Benedek, T. 1966. Psychobiological aspects of mothering. *American Journal of Orthopsychiatry* 26: 272–78.

Bibring, G. L. 1959. Some considerations of the psychological process in preg-nancy. *Psychoanal. Study of the Child* 14: 113–21.

Bibring, G. L., et al. 1961. A study of the psychological processes in pregnancy and the earliest mother-child relationship. *Psychoanal. Study of the Child* 16: 9–23.

Bowlby, J. 1969. *Attachment and loss.* Vol. 1, *Attachment.* New York: Basic Books.

———. 1973. *Attachment and loss.* Vol. 2, *Separation.* New York: Basic Books.

———. 1979. *The making and breaking of affectional bonds.* London: Tavistock.

———. 1980. *Attachment and loss.* Vol. 3, *Loss.* New York: Basic Books.

Brazelton, T. B., et al. 1982. *La dynamique de nourrisson.* Paris: E.S.F.

Breen, D. 1975. *The birth of a first child: Towards an understanding of femininity.* London: Tavistock.

Bretherton, I. 1987. New perspectives on attachment relations: Security, commu-nication and internal working models. In *Handbook of infant development,* 2nd ed., edited by J. Osofsky, 1061–1100. New York: Wiley.

Bruner, J. 1990. *Acts of meaning.* Cambridge: Harvard University Press.

Chaves Winestine, M. 1989. To know or not to know: some observations on women's reactions to the availability of the prenatal knowledge of their babies' sex. *Am. Psychoanal. Assn.* 37: 1015–30.

Chertok, L. 1969. *Motherhood and personality.* London: Tavistock.

Courvoisier, A. 1985. Ecographie obstétricale et fantasmes. *Neuropsychiatrie de l'enfance et de l'adolescence* 33: 103–6.

Deutsch, H. 1945. *The psychology of women: A psychoanalytic interpretation.* Vol. 2, *Motherhood.* New York: Grune and Stratton.

Erikson, H. 1959. *Identity and the life cycle.* New York: International Universities Press.

Erikson, H. E. 1964. Inner and outer space: Reflection on womanhood. *Daedalus* 93: 582–608.

Fraiberg, S., ed. 1980. *Clinical studies in infant mental health.* London: Tavistock.

Freud, S. 1914. *On narcissism: An introduction. S. E.* Vol. 14. London: Hogarth Press.

———. 1917. *On transformations of instincts as exemplified in anal erotism. S. E.* Vol. 17. London: Hogarth Press.

———. 1921. *Group psychology and the analysis of the ego. S. E.* Vol. 17. London: Hogarth Press.

Klein, M. 1946. Notes on some schizoid mechanisms. In *The writings of Melanie Klein,* Vol. 3. London: Hogarth Press.

Lebovici, S. 1983. *Le Nourrisson, la mère et le psychanalyste.* Les interactions précoces. Paris: Le Centurion.

Leff, J. R. 1983. Facilitators and regulators: Two approaches to mothering. *British Journal of Medical Psychology* 56: 379–90.

———. 1986. Facilitators and regulators: Conscious and unconscious processes in pregnancy and early motherhood. *British Journal of Medical Psychology* 59: 43–55.

Lester, E. P., and Notman, M. T. 1988. Pregnancy and object relations: Clinical considerations. *Psychoanalytic Inquiry* 8: 196–221.

Lumley, J. M. 1980. The image of the foetus in the first trimester. *Birth and Family Journal* 7: 5–14.

———. 1982. Attitudes to the foetus among the primigravidae. *Australian Pediatric Journal* 18: 106–9.

Main, M. 1981. Avoidance in the service of attachment: A working paper. In *Behavioral Development: The Bielefeld interdisciplinary project,* edited by K. Immelman, G. Barlow, M. Main, and L. Petrinovitch. New York: Cambridge University Press.

Main, M., and Goldwyn, R. 1989. Adult attachment interview. Unpublished manuscript, University of California, Berkeley.

Main, M.; Kaplan, N.; and Cassidy, J. 1985. Security in infancy, childhood and adulthood: A move to the level of representation. In *Growing points of attachment theory and research,* edited by I. Bretherton and E. Waters. *Monograph of the Society for Research in Child Development* 50 (1–2 Serial n. 209): 66–104.

Mandler, J. M. 1983. Representation. In *Handbook of Child Psychology,* edited by P. Mussen, Vol. 3. New York: Wiley.

Mebert, C. J., and Kalinowsky, M. F. 1986. Parents' expectations and perceptions of infant temperament: "Pregnancy status" differences. *Infant Behavior and Development* 9: 321–34.

Morris, D. 1980. Infant attachment and problem solving in the toddler: Relations to mother's family history. Unpublished doctoral dissertation. University of Minnesota.

Palacio-Espasa, F. 1991. Fantasie dei genitori e psicopatologia del bambino. In *Fantasie dei genitori e psicopatologia dei figli,* edited by Società di Neuropsichiatria Infantile. Rome: Borla.

Pines, D. 1972. Pregnancy and motherhood: Interaction between fantasy and reality. *British Journal of Medical Psychology* 45: 333–43.

———. 1982. The relevance of early psychic development to pregnancy and abortion. *Int. J. Psycho-Anal.* 63: 311–19.

———. 1988. Adolescent pregnancy and motherhood: Psychoanalytic perspective. *Psychoanalytic Inquiry* 8: 234–51.

Ricks, M. H., and Novey, D. 1984. Secure babies have secure mothers. Unpublished manuscript, University of Massachusetts, Amherst.

Sandler, J. 1976. Actualization and object relationships. *J. Philadelphia Assn. Psychoanal.* 3: 59–70.

Shapiro, T., and Perry, R. 1976. Latency revisited: The age of seven plus or minus one. *Psychoanalytic Study of the Child* 30: 156.

Soifer, R. 1971. *Psicologia del embarazo, parto y puerperio.* Buenos Aires: Ediciones Kargicman.

Soulé, M. 1982. L'enfant dans la tête, l'enfant imaginaire. In *La dynamique du nourrisson,* edited by T. B. Brazelton, et al. Paris: E. S. F.

Stern, D. N. 1985. *The interpersonal world of the infant: Views from psychoanalysis and developmental psychology.* New York: Basic Books.

———. 1989. Representation of relationship experience. In *Relationship disturbance in early childhood: A developmental approach,* edited by A. J. Sameroff and R. N. Emde. New York: Basic Books.

Winnicott, D. W. 1958. *Through paediatrics to psycho-analysis.* London: Tavistock.

Zeanah, C. H.; Keener, M. A.; Stewart, L.; and Anders, T. F. 1985. Prenatal perception of infant personality: A preliminary investigation. *Journal of the American Academy of Child Psychiatry* 24: 204–10.

Zeanah, C. H.; Keener, M. A.; and Anders, T. F. 1986. Adolescent mothers' prenatal fantasies and working models of their infants. *Psychiatry* 49: 193–203.

Zeanah, C. H., and Barton, M. L. 1989. Introduction: Internal representations and parent-infant relationships. *Infant Mental Health Journal* 10: 135–41.

6

Three Roads Intersecting: Changing Viewpoints in the Psychoanalytic Story of Oedipus

Robert N. Emde

This essay will present three retellings of the psychoanalytic Oedipus story, each of which gives us a different pathway for viewing the classic drama and its conflicts. We will also portray three roles of the psychoanalytic hero Oedipus, and conclude by indicating some new directions in our research-based thinking about the oedipal drama in childhood.

The psychoanalytic story of Oedipus is centered around the fifth-century B.C. Greek drama provided by Sophocles. Freud considered this story a core narrative for psychoanalysis and, in fact, stated that the Oedipus complex, based on his version of the Sophoclean story, was not only a precious discovering of psychoanalysis but one that distinguished psychoanalysts from others, based on whether they recognized it or not (Freud 1900).

Freud, however, was highly selective in his retelling of the Oedipus story. It was as if he traveled one road to his understanding of the drama some ninety years ago. I believe two other retellings of the Oedipus story can now be added and that all three versions are relevant today.

Three Views of Oedipus Rex

It is well known that the ancient Greeks were fond of the number three and the significance of triangles. Our story is no exception. Three angles of perspective occur throughout Sophocles' *Oedipus Rex*. The oracle is consulted three times; the riddle of the Sphinx has three parts; the Sphinx herself if tripartite (lion, woman, and bird); and, as the title of my chapter indicates, the fatal incident of parricide takes place where three roads meet. There are, of course, threesomes of people who are prominent; such people become intimately involved, you might even say "triangulated." But without exhausting the point, let me acknowledge the Greek fondness for three in the retellings of the story. Each offers a different version of the drama, along with a different approach to the analysis of conflict.

To set the stage in a traditional way, let me forecast the retellings. One has Oedipus as a provocateur, another as victim, and still another as a seeker of secret knowledge. The first retelling calls for an individual/intrapsychic level of action, the second an interpersonal level, and the third an intersystemic one. Oedipus is tragic hero in each of these retellings, but the meaning of each story is different. I will begin with Freud's retelling of the Sophocles drama, since the two others add increasing levels of complexity and are more revealing when superimposed on Freud's original template.

Oedipus as Provocateur

In Freud's original retelling for psychoanalysis, there is an emphasis on Oedipus as provocateur. The level of interest is *intrapsychic*. Freud tells a story involving a conflict of wishes and of intentions, as well as a history of conflicted events and entanglements. Throughout, circumstances are set in motion *by the individual*. Correspondingly, repression and denial happen within the individual. Let us hear about it in the voice of Freud, writing in 1900:

> Oedipus, son of Laius, King of Thebes, and of Jocasta, was exposed as an infant because an oracle had warned Laius that the still unborn child would be his father's murderer. The child was rescued, and grew up as a prince in an alien court, until, in doubt as to his origin, he too questioned the oracle and was warned to avoid his home since he was destined to murder his father and take his mother in marriage. On the road leading away from what he believed was his home, he met King Laius and slew him in a sudden quarrel. He came next to Thebes and solved the riddle set him

by the Sphinx who barred his way. Out of gratitude the Thebans made him their king and gave him Jocasta's hand in marriage. He reigned long in peace and honor, and she who, unknown to him, was his mother bore him two sons and two daughters. Then at last a plague broke out and the Thebans made enquiry once more of the oracle. It is at this point that Sophocles' tragedy opens. The messengers bring back the reply that the plague will cease when the murdered of Laius has been driven from the land. . . .

The action of the play consists in nothing other than the process of revealing, with cunning delays and ever-mounting excitement—a process that can be likened to the work of a psycho-analysis—that Oedipus himself is the murderer of Laius, but further than he is the son of the murdered man and of Jocasta. Appalled at the abomination which he has unwittingly perpetrated, Oedipus blinds himself and forsakes his home. . . . His destiny moves us only because it might have been ours—because the oracle laid the same curse upon us before our birth as upon him. It is the fate of all of us, perhaps, to direct our first sexual impulses towards our mother and our first hatred and our first murderous wish against our father. Our dreams convince us that that is so. King Oedipus, who slew his father Laius and married his mother Jocasta, merely shows us the fulfillment of our own childhood wishes. . . . Like Oedipus, we live in ignorance of these wishes, repugnant to morality, which have been forced upon us by Nature, and after their revelation may all of us well seek to close our eyes to the scenes of our childhood. (261–64)

It is hardly necessary to review the coherence of this retelling of the story for a Victorian Age of repression and guilt about sexual impulses. This retelling also had special coherence for a psychoanalytic theory of neurosis and its origins in conflicted childhood wishes, one that dominated clinical thinking for the next fifty years.

Oedipus as Victim

The next retelling brings in more elements of the whole story, and of other motivating events in the family. Again, Oedipus is the hero, struggling, but he comes across in many respects as more virtuous. This retelling emphasizes the interpersonal and intergenerational aspects of the struggle. Conflicts are activated between the individual and others. Repression is overt rather than covert, although there may be deceit.

The story goes as follows. Long before Oedipus's birth, his father, Laius, consulted an oracle and was told that he should beware of bearing a son for, according to a curse, such a son would kill him and marry his mother. (In a version of the legend that surrounds the play but is not in it, the audience knew that his curse was issued by King Pelops because Laius had raped and sodomized his illegitimate son, Chrysippus. The legend also has it that Laius avoided intercourse with Jocasta and that she may have seduced him in order to have a son.) When Oedipus was born, Laius and Jocasta abandoned the young infant in order to thwart the prophecy. To make sure of his demise, Laius pierced the heels of the baby Oedipus and tied his feet together, leaving him on a hill. Oedipus, who got his name—that is, swollen feet—from this form of maltreatment, was saved by a shepherd and later adopted by the king of Corinth. Later, when the grown Oedipus left the home where he was reared, he encountered another traveling party at a crossroads where three roads met. Those meeting him provocatively gave an order for Oedipus to give way and although they did not identify themselves they pushed him off the road. A fight ensued. Oedipus killed all except one.

In this retelling, Laius is provocative in the extreme. Intergenerational conflicts go back before Oedipus was born and Jocasta is complicitous. She wants a son but then participates in the newborn's abandonment. Later, she becomes a willing wife for a triumphant Oedipus who has saved the City of Thebes. When the Oedipus of the drama then begins to unravel the mystery of the past—of parricide and of incest—Jocasta makes a plea not to pursue matters further. Many men, she says, before this time have encountered ideas from dreams and from oracles about sleeping with their mothers; these ideas are best ignored.

Oedipus in this version of the drama is the victim of child abuse, neglect, and seduction. Conflicts are interpersonal with shame, public and private; moreover, there is little guilt. For today, therefore, this version of the Oedipal drama is about struggling with intergenerational conflict and trying to develop in the midst of child maltreatment. Freud began with a childhood seduction and abuse theory of neurosogenesis; he then abandoned it for his theory of universal, biologically based oedipal wishes in the child, causing intrapsychic conflict although repressed in the adult. We can see now that this retelling supplements the Oedipus complex with intergenerational conflict that is all too real. Clinical experience has shown that there *are* naturally-occurring urges of love and hate that arise toward parental figures at particular phases of development. But clinical experience has also shown that child maltreatment and seduction are widespread. In the idiom of the metaphor, their effects can be devastating by deflecting an individual from a developmental path.* [Note: In the above account I have made use of a number of literary and psychoanalytic criticisms. In particular, I am grateful for discussion in Devereux 1953; Kanzer 1950; Rascovsky and Rascovsky 1968; Ross 1982; Pollock and Ross 1988.]

Oedipus as Seeker

This retelling adds more to the "whole story." All through the drama there is a search for secret knowledge. Oedipal conflicts involve exclusion in relation to others. We are reminded that the drama of Sophocles takes place in the course of one day. It is similar to a detective story, with Oedipus trying to find out the facts that have been withheld from him. The level of action for this retelling is beyond the intrapsychic and interpersonal. It is now *intersystemic.*

I will summarize this retelling of past events so the secrets can be more completely understood. Things go along in quite an ordinary fashion for Oedipus until one day he hears a provocative outburst from a drunken guest at the home of his parents in Corinth. The guest says that Oedipus is not the child of his Corinthian parents. Oedipus consults an oracle, who warns him of a profound secret: He must beware of a pre-existing curse wherein he will kill his father and marry his mother. Confused, Oedipus sets out on a journey. He will leave Corinth, find out who he is, and avoid the curse with respect to his "parents" in Corinth. Oedipus then comes to the well-known crossroads where he is provocatively ordered to give way by the party that does not identify itself and a fight ensues. Oedipus kills all except one. Unbeknownst to Oedipus, he has killed his father; the one witness to the act who escapes returns to Thebes and remains silent. Oedipus next comes upon the Sphinx who has put a curse

---

* Later, in the third play of the Oedipal trilogy, Sophocles has Oedipus as an old man in Colonus, defending himself bluntly to Creon who comes to rile him with others from Thebes. He involves the image of the three intersecting roads where he was knocked off the pathway. "Just answer me one thing: If someone tried to kill you here and now, You righteous gentleman, what would you do, Inquire first if the stranger is your father? Or would you not first try to defend yourself I think that since you like to be alive You'd treat him as the threat required . . ." (Fitzgerald trans, lines 991–96).

on the people of Thebes in the form of a plague. If Oedipus can solve the riddle, the plague will cease. Oedipus solves the riddle with the answer of "man," an achievement that changes the way he walks and by implication his power over the course of his life. The first Theban plague of the drama lifts. Oedipus enters Thebes and is welcomed as a hero who has ended the plague. Since the king of Thebes has recently died, Oedipus is encouraged to be the new leader and, according to custom, he is to take the former king's widow as his own wife.

The play itself opens later in the City of Thebes. Oedipus has ruled successfully for seventeen years but now there is a second plague. The oracle is once again consulted and Oedipus learns that the plague will only cease when another secret is revealed and a mystery resolved. The plague will stop when the murderer of the former king, Laius, is revealed and punished. Oedipus sets about discovering who this person is and eventually comes to learn of his parricide at the crossroads seventeen years earlier and of his incest. The major secret seems revealed.

But there are other aspects to the secret. The city was silent for seventeen years during which Oedipus ruled quite successfully in Thebes. The original witness at the crossroads recounted that the king had been slain by a band of robbers and said no more. Creon, the brother of the king's wife at the time, did not pursue matters further. When Oedipus first arrived in Thebes there was no further inquiry into his origin or possible connection with the event, nor did anyone discuss the coincidence of age of Oedipus and his family resemblance to Laius and Jocasta. These considerations led Steiner (1985) to postulate a Watergate-style cover-up. We also hear of an intergenerational secret that Laius had found out about from the oracle before Oedipus's birth, and we learn about the abandonment, heel-piercing, and rescue of the infant by a shepherd (who later turns up in Thebes in the play), and his adoption in Corinth.

The secrets in this tale are multiple. The ones involving parricide and incest are prominent. But Oedipus is also driven to discover secrets of his origins, his relationships with others, and secrets that undo plagues. Moreover, the audience knows of the intergenerational secrets that preceded Oedipus.

I maintain that the formal property of the secret is that it is knowledge held by some and excluded from others. Although one can have a secret about oneself and never tell anyone else, most secrets involve relationships between two or more people and are looked at from the point of view of a third person. Thus, secrets involve a knowledge about relationships from which one is excluded. At this abstract, formal level, secret knowledge often contains within it a statement of who does what in relation to whom and what is held in awe and what is forbidden. When the secret is revealed, shame results. As Siegler (1983) points out, great myths deal with the tension between revealed and concealed knowledge—between knowing and not knowing, seeing and not seeing, hiding and finding.

This retelling is a quest tale—about significant past events involving others, about one's origins, and about the meaning of life itself. But what makes it different from other quest tales is that the sought-after knowledge is secret. It is kept secret because there is collusion among others who harbor the information. Thus, an additional dimension of conflict is added to the oedipal drama. There is psychological conflict because of the fear of the unknown and of what will be discovered. And there is interpersonal conflict about knowing because of others not wanting the hero to know—because of a jealously guarded secret held by others. The secret is jealously guarded by others for reasons of the special privileges of intimacy. The struggle is of a different kind than in the first two oedipal retellings. The hero is motivated against the odds and the elements to discover more about his life space, its meaning and its possibilities, about his past and his awareness of the present. This kind of quest and its retelling is apt to change one's perception of the world. Freud of course institutionalized this kind of retelling through the practice of psychoanalysis and its later training institutes.

Three Castings of the Oedipus Role

More that two thousand years after Sophocles, another dramatist said:

> All the world's a stage,
> And all the men and women merely players.
> They have their exists and their entrances,
> And one man in his time plays many parts. . . .
> (*As You Like It*, II. 7: 139–43)

In the spirit of Shakespeare, let us look at three castings of the oedipal role. Oedipus as an adult and Oedipus as *co-constructed figure in psychoanalysis* will be staged briefly. We will then move to our main act, Oedipus as *child*.

First, as adult. With the psychoanalytic focus on the childhood origins of the oedipal complex, it is easy to lose sight of the fact that the drama itself is enacted in middle adulthood. The hero, Oedipus, is nearly forty years old and Freud was only a few years older when he "discovered" the Oedipus complex. Moreover, the typical psychoanalytic patient, reworking oedipal repressions, is an adult. Psychoanalytic clinical theory has only recently turned its attention to the obvious fact that oedipal conflicts and retellings are in the context of adult development. The casting of Oedipus as an adult therefore involves dramas of adult dilemmas, of conflicts about adult urges and responsibilities. Putting the "past in its place" with respect to childhood oedipal fantasies involves an orientation to the present in the light of one's future life course as an adult. Interpersonal and intergenerational aspects of pride, shame, anxiety, and guilt have more emphasis, as do intersystemic conflicts involving family, school, work place, and community.

The next modern-day casting I would like to reflect upon is of Oedipus as a co-constructed figure during psychoanalysis. Freud, the solver of dream riddles, once imagined himself to be Oedipus, the hero who solved the Sphinx riddle about life (Jones 1953). Indeed, as we saw in our opening 1900 quote, Freud also put forward the role of Oedipus-as-analyst when he likened the unfolding of the oedipal drama to the work of a psychoanalysis. It is true that the more we know about adult development, the more we will know about Oedipus as analyst and the more we know about countertransference (i.e., the analyst's activated oedipal complex), the more we will know about a helper who guides self-reflective inquiry in another. But in this casting our main interest is not in the role of Oedipus as analyst. It is in the role of Oedipus as a dramatic figure co-constructed between two people in the present-day context of transferential work. The staging is current. The action of the story is played out in the interpersonal and intersubjective mode. Moreover, the Oedipus personage and the configurations of the plot change as the story is made and remade. The burgeoning literature about narrative truth in psychoanalysis elaborates this co-constructed role (Stolorow, Atwood, and Lachmann 1981).

This brings us to our main billing—the casting of Oedipus as child. As a result of Freud's own self-analysis and his reconstructions from adults whom he analyzed, a theory of Oedipus as child was created. The theory became the centerpiece of Freud's theory of infantile sexuality, and told of natural impulses appearing in early childhood and then becoming repressed in the course of continued development. The original formulation of the child's Oedipus complex held closely to Freud's retelling of the Sophoclean drama. There were three postulates. The first was that the preschool child normally experienced sexual desires toward the parent of the opposite sex (at the extreme, a desire for sexual possession). The second postulate was that the child naturally had feelings of competitive rivalry with the parent of the same sex (at the extreme, a murderous rage). A third postulate was that the child encountered fear of retaliation from the parent of the same sex for such wishes. Fears of this kind involved fantasies of bodily harm and castration. Freud understood the latter as the psychological version of the Talion Law as experienced by the child at this age.

What initiated the Oedipus complex was a maturation of naturally occurring psychosexual urges. By implication, mental development, including the child's increasing curiosity, was also seen to have an influence. The usual outcome of the Oedipus complex was thought to include an identification with a parent of the same sex and the formation of the basic structure for morality, the superego. Both outcomes could be expected between five to seven years of age.

Other features of Freud's basic Oedipus complex were implicit. It was considered a universal feature of development and important from the standpoint of the child's motivations. Many of the features of the Oedipus complex in the young child would be manifest in behavioral enactments and interpersonal interactions; increasingly, however, the forces of repression occasioned by fear and guilt would make oedipal wishes unconscious. Finally, the Oedipus complex was an organizational construct. According to Freud's theory of psychosexual development, earlier-appearing components of libidinal instincts were organized by the Oedipus complex with a major reorganization taking place during puberty.

Oedipus as Child—Later Psychoanalytic Elaborations in a Current Relationship-Motivational View

The story of Oedipus as child that became the theory of the Oedipus complex has in turn itself become increasingly complex as a result of clinical experience and research. I will briefly review this complexity in order to indicate how it has accumulated to such a degree that there is an enormous uncertainty in today's psychoanalytic world. Freud's early story of Oedipus (his road taken)—so incomplete—has led to a theory that is now so full of exceptions and variations that it cries out for modification. The modification, I will conclude, must take account of the three viewpoints of the drama and supplement the individual/intrapsychic pathways to understanding with the interpersonal and intersystemic pathways. Freud and the early psychoanalysts soon found it necessary to make additions. Originally modeled for boys, the Oedipus complex became elaborated for girls, with the patterns of object choice and emotions adding further complexity. Other editions resulted from the appreciation of ambivalence (for example, both love and hate) in human relationship ties where a "negative Oedipus patterning" often generated still other conflicting emotions. Although prime emphasis was put on intrinsically generated drives, the environment was seen as increasingly influential in causing variations in the complex. Parental overstimulation became a concern and Freud came to think of a complemental series between drive development and the experienced environment as the child wrestles with oedipal conflicts (Freud 1926).

Post-Freudian psychoanalysis has documented extensive variations on the Oedipus complex. But more importantly, clinical experience with children and research have resulted in a number of modifications. First, a superego or conscience formation is not an outcome of the resolved Oedipus complex as Freud thought, since clinical examples show that superego formation can occur without oedipal resolution (Sandler 1960). Moreover, there's considerable moral development prior to age three and prior to oedipal conflict (Emde, Johnson, and Easterbrooks 1988). Second, research has shown that gender identity is not an outcome of the Oedipus complex, since core gender identity is established earlier, usually in the child's second and third years. Third, variations in the family environment are strongly determinative of the course of the child's oedipal conflicts. Since Fenichel's 1945 review on this point, we have come to appreciate the widespread existence of child maltreatment by parents (Kempe 1980; Mrazek and Mrazek 1985) and the circumstances under which there are repetitions of maladaptive oedipal conflict across generations (Fraiberg 1980; Stoller 1980). Correspondingly, the British Object Relations School of Psychoanalysis and Kohut's Self Psychology School have influenced clinicians to be more outward-oriented rather than inward drive-oriented in their views of early childhood conflicts. Bowlby (1973) following Winnicott (1965) theorized about a splitting of self-experience during early childhood based on the harsh realities presented by many abusing families.

We have also come to the view that Freud's portrayal of the child's experience during the family oedipal drama is oversimplified in other ways. Fathers do not appear later on the stage to interrupt an earlier affectionate relationship with mother when the child becomes three or four. Research has clearly shown that fathers under normative conditions have earlier and qualitatively separate affectionate relationships with both young boys and girls (Lamb, Hwang, Frodi, and Frodi 1982).

Where does this leave our view of the child's oedipal story? There is clearly a need for a fresh look. Elsewhere I have described a relationship-motivational view of the child's early development (Emde 1988, Emde in press). A set of basic motives are strongly biologically prepared by our evolution and organized during early caregiving. These motives consist of activity, self-regulation, social fittedness, affective monitoring, and cognitive assimilation. With an emotionally available caregiver, the infant comes to develop an affective core of self and a core sense of early morality. The latter includes a sense of reciprocity, rules, empathy, and the internalization of standards concerning how things should be. The relationship-motivational view also describes how infants and toddlers are motivated to keep up interactions with caregivers because of many procedural involvements that are expectable and "feel good" as well as because of the satisfaction of biological needs. Qualitatively separate relationships with mother, father, and others result from internalized aspects of shared meaning from separate experiences with significant others. Moreover, each child has more regulatory emotions that are activated within the context of interactions with each parent.

The new element that is proposed during the child's Oedipus complex, from the relationship-motivational point of view is an acquired sense of exclusion. The sense of exclusion has a different quality during the oedipal period when the child begins to understand that two other people whom he or she cares about are involved in an intimate way. Because of advances in the child's understanding there is now a new kind of painful exclusion. The child realizes that two others are committed to each other and enjoy themselves when the child is not present. There are other features of the child's understanding concerning the earlier history of relationships and power dynamics. But suffice it to say here that in our psychoanalytic retellings of the oedipal drama the three levels of action we highlighted can be used in our new formulation. In addition to the individual intra-psychic level of the child's understanding we bring in the interpersonal/intergenerational level. This introduces the connected idea of "triangulation," an interpersonal construct with motivational properties that involves the influence of three interpersonal relationships on each other, wherein one person is excluded, while two others are involved in a coalition. Thus, during given interactions of this sort there is asymmetry.

Clinical experience has shown us that it is when there are failures in asymmetric parental responsibility that oedipal conflicts persist in painful variations. There's no way therefore of understanding the child's developing oedipal conflicts and their resolution without including the interpersonal view. Intergenerational boundaries of responsibility are also important. Parents must not substitute for intimacy in the spousal relationship by means of intense and inclusive intimacy with the child. It is appropriate for the child to be excluded during some time of parental intimacy and clear boundaries are necessary for the child to come to grips with this.

The version of the oedipal story with the hero as seeker of secret knowledge emphasized an intersystemic view. Family and community influences operated in such a way as to keep secrets and perpetuate what we might regard as a maladaptive scenario. Intersystemic approaches to understanding are also important in our relationship-motivational view. All too often families, after language development, can use words to overlay the child's experience in such a way that reality is portrayed in ways other than that which the child feels or knows to be true (Bowlby 1973; Stern 1985). Similarly, beginning in the second year the family comes to introduce a level of awareness for the child according to what actions should be put out of mind or not, or are "nice" or "nasty." In problematic variations family secrets, with networks of collusions, can introduce a devastating common censorship that functions to preserve triangulations and violate it into generational boundaries; families can become isolated from the community and find inadvertent support from maintaining enmeshed family styles.

In concluding, I would like to say that the three views of the psychoanalytic story of Oedipus, what I have referred to metaphorically as the three roads of understanding, while perhaps interesting in their own right can only be considered useful if they lead to research that generates and tests new knowledge. We believe some research of this sort is now under way. It seeks the child's story of desires, dilemmas, and conflicts within the family during the three to seven year age period. It is collaborative research, linking several projects and populations. Moreover, according to the metaphor of using three roads to understanding, the research uses approaches from the disciplines of social cognition, psycholinguistics, and today's dynamic psychiatry in order to see what may be a new synthetic version of the oedipal story. Questions will undoubtedly remain, but at least three roads are intersecting.

REFERENCES

Bowlby, J. 1973. *Attachment and loss,* vol. 2. New York: Basic Books.

Devereux, G. 1953. Why Oedipus killed Laius: A note on the complementary Oedipus complex in Greek drama. *Int. J. Psycho-anal.* 34: 132–41.

Emde, R. N. 1988. Development terminable and interminable: I. Innate and motivational factors from infancy. *Int. J. Psycho-anal.* 69: 23–42.

————. In press. Mobilizing fundamental modes of development: An essay on empathic availability and therapeutic action. *J. Am. Psychoanal. Assn.*

Emde, R. N., Johnson, W. F., and Easterbrooks, M. A. 1988. The do's and don'ts of early moral development: Psychoanalytic tradition and current research. In *The emergence of morality,* edited by J. Kagan and S. Lamb, 245–77. Chicago: University of Chicago Press.

Fenichel, O. 1945. *The psychoanalytic theory of neurosis.* New York: Norton.

Fraiberg, S. (1980). *Clinical studies in infant mental health.* New York: Basic Books.

Freud, S. 1900. *The interpretation of dreams. S. E.* Vols. 4–5. London: Hogarth Press.

————. 1926. *Inhibitions, symptoms and anxiety. S. E.* Vol. 20. London: Hogarth Press.

Jones, E. 1953. *The life and work of Sigmund Freud.* Vol. 1. New York: Basic Books.

Kanzer, M. 1950. The Oedipus trilogy. *Psychoanalytic Quarterly* 19: 561–72.

Kempe, C. H. 1980. Incest and other forms of sexual abuse. In *The battered child,* 3d ed., edited by C. H. Kempe and R. E. Holfer. Chicago: University of Chicago Press.

Lamb, M. E.; Hwang, C. P.; Frodi, A.; and Frodi, M. 1982. Security of mother- and father-infant attachment and its relation of sociability with strangers in traditional and non-traditional Swedish families. *Infant Behavior and Development* 5: 355–67.

Mrazek, D. and Mrazek, O. 1985. Child maltreatment. In *Child and adolescent psychiatry*. Oxford: Blackwell Scientific Publications.

Pollock, G. H., and Ross, J. M., eds. 1988. *The Oedipus papers* (Classics in Psychoanalysis Monograph Series, no. 6). Madison, Conn.: International Universities Press.

Rascovsky, A., and Rascovsky, M. 1968. On the genesis of acting out a psychopathic behavior in Sophocles' Oedipus: Notes on filicide. *Int. J. Psycho-anal.* 49: 390–94.

Ross, J. M. 1982. Oedipus revisited: Laius and the "Laius complex." *Psychoanal. Study of the Child.* 37: 167–200.

Sandler, J. 1960. On the concept of superego. *Psychoanal. Study of the Child.* 15: 128–62.

Siegler, A. L. 1983. The Oedipus myth and the Oedipus complex: Intersecting realms, shared structures. *Int. J. Psycho-anal.* 10: 205–14.

Steiner, J. 1985. Turning a blind eye: The cover up for Oedipus. *International Review of Psychoanalysis* 12: 161–72.

Stern, D. N. 1985. *The interpersonal world of the infant*. New York: Basic Books.

Stoller, R. J. 1980. A different view of oedipal conflict. In *The course of life*. Vol. 1 *Infancy and early childhood*, edited by S. Greenspan and G. Pollock, 589–602. Adelphi, Md.: Mental Health Study Center.

Stolorow, R. D.; Atwood, G.; and Lachmann, F. 1981. Transference and countertransference in the analysis of developmental arrests. *Bulletin-Menninger Clinic* 45: 20–28.

Winnicott, D. W. 1965. Ego distortion in terms of true and false self. In *The maturational processes and the facilitating environment*. New York: International Universities Press.

7

Genres as Mental Models

Carol Fleisher Feldman

What kinds of things do human beings know? And how do they come by them and use them? This is the domain of cognitive psychology—a psychology that attempts to discover the forms of human thought. Until recently, cognitive psychologists have largely concentrated their attention on intellectual domains that could be given an algorithmic description modeled by a computer simulation—mathematics and chess, for example, though even in these domains human processes, particularly those of experts, have been found to deviate markedly from the idealized description by including quick intuitive leaps not in the model (Simon and Simon 1978). Notwithstanding these complexities, algorithmic processes are good candidates for computer modeling because one can, in principle, state explicitly the steps in a solution path, whether honored or not by actual human subjects. Thus, in such domains, when actually observed human reasoning falls short of the ideal algorithmic pattern through inexpertise or irrational impulses holding sway, it is often possible nonetheless to give the observed patterns a clear formal description. For one can understand them as patterned deviations from the algorithmic form. Kahneman et al. (1982), for example, have given such a description of human decision making. The format description has the virtue that it is easily converted to a computer program, which can then be used, in principle, to make further discoveries about the intellectual effects of having such an algorithm or algorithm-plus-deviations in mind. This has given cognitive psychology a useful instrumental relationship with the digital computer of today, but it has sometimes suffered from an excess of enthusiasm by suggesting that anything really cognitive about the human mind must have an algorithmic description that lends to its exploration through computer or mathematical models.

But human beings know about many things, and some of them are not well conceived as either algorithmic procedures or deviations from them. For procedures of thought vary across different domains of knowledge, as Gardner (1983) and Sternberg (1985) have noted. And, indeed, some important domains of human knowledge simply may not lend themselves to algorithmic description at all. One such domain, for example, is knowledge relating to the *intentional states* of human agents, whether in life or in story.

Typically, idealized descriptions of the domain of human agency are anything but algorithmic—interpretive rather than causal, associative rather than derivational, thematic rather than categorical, and descriptive rather than predictive. Its goal is to give the existing events meaning or a new construal that makes them more intelligible. And it usually accomplishes this by giving them a narrative frame.

Our way of thinking about intentional states is *interpretive* in the sense in which literary criticism is an interpretation of text. Indeed, just as a text must be taken as given for the purposes of subsequent interpretation, so the actions of human agents are taken as given. And just as the literary interpretation consists of proposals about the *meaning* of the text, so does the interpretation of human action consist of proposals about its *meaning*. Moreover, in both cases, meaning is referable to the intentional states of a human agent—a writer, narrator, character, or actor; and intentional states are composed of beliefs or desires (see Searle 1983) that give acts their meaning. Finally, but in a distinctive sense of the term, in both cases, the interpretation is undertaken in order to *explain* human action, a matter that we will return to in a moment.

And when, moreover, we construct the desires and beliefs that may lie behind human action we tend to tell or retell a story; that is, we interpret human action by framing it in narrative. We tell stories about why someone did what they did when they did it in a certain setting, and the form of story gives these interpretations their form. In any story, certain things have already happened, are given, when we begin: they are the setting. An agent enters this setting, like a character on stage. He (or she) does whatever he does. We want to know what his action means, and we try to find out by invoking his desires, beliefs—whatever intentional states we can attribute to him. This account of its meaning inevitably takes the form of a little story all on its own, a story that places the naked act into a scene and relates it to the intentional states of protagonists. The naked act: say, host at a dinner party fails to offer anyone a drink. The story: the reason the husband was so rude was that he believed his wife was having an affair with one of the guests and wanted to drive everyone away to bring the party to an end.

The fact that interpretations take a narrative form tells us a good deal about the rules for interpretive accounts. They do not simply fail to be algorithmic, but rather strive to meet an entirely different set of criteria of well-formedness. They attempt to make a plausible story, a story that assigns a meaning to action. And in striving to do this, the constraints that they strive to meet are the distinctive constraints on well-formed explanations of human action.

A moment ago, I proposed that interpretations "explain why" or give an explanation for an action, and promised to return to this point. The difficulty is that the kind of explanation given in interpretation is of a fundamentally different kind from the better understood kind of explanation given in, say, scientific accounts. One may well hesitate to consider both of them as explanations, or to call them both by the same name. Von Wright (1971) was the first analyst to give a clear account of the possibility of these two genuinely different kinds of account as equally having a claim to explain, though they do so in a very different way, and of each form of explanation being suitable and optimal for the domain where it operates. Elsewhere, in a different context (Feldman 1987), I have tried to show that any time a domain is explained it is first encoded in a symbolic manner. The particular form of symbolic encoding varies (in that case, developmentally; here, by domain). The form of explanation must be one that can operate over the form of symbolism of the domain to be explained. In view of these considerations, logical or scientific explanation can be seen not as an optimal form of explanation but rather as the one best fitted to account for a (physical) world described in the scientific symbolism of propositions about classes and transformations, while interpretation is the form of explanation that can range over a description of the human world given in terms of intentional states.

On this view, then, the reason for the deep differences between scientific and interpretive explanations lies in the way we conceive of the inanimate versus the human world that they, respectively, explain. Perhaps the fundamental difference between these domains derives from our culturally conventional belief that the inanimate world is inherently determined while the human world is essentially free. This is perhaps only true of the modern, Western worldview. But given our view, the forms of explanation must differ. We do not give scientific, causal accounts of human agency, not because we cannot think about it clearly that way, but because we believe human agents are essentially free and see their actions as chosen rather than caused, chosen for reasons that consist of desires and beliefs. This does not mean that human action is unexplainable—quite to the contrary.

Consider a bit more fully the differences between algorithmic, predictive accounts of the inanimate world and interpretive, narrativized accounts of the human world. Underlying both is a common core—the inquiring mind of the human observer seeking to make sense of experience. In that fundamental sense, both narrative interpretations and causal explanations are expressions of human cognition. Now, if the rule-governed pattern of one of them can be helpfully understood as a "mental model" (Johnson-Laird 1983), so perhaps can rule-governed patterns of the other—even if the form of the rules found in the two forms of explanation is different.

In what sense are interpretive, narrativized accounts rule-governed? We know they are not rule-governed in the same manner as the algorithmic, predictive accounts of science. We need not consider here the myriad technical issues that arise in comparing rule-governed systems. But in terms of their function in cognition, virtually all rule-governed systems have some important things in common. For example, insofar as it makes sense to think of the rules of scientific explanation as prescriptive, so too are those of interpretive accounts. And all "explanations" are probably best understood as systems of constitutive rules that are used to construct the forms of explanation to which they belong. If a rule-governed system is any good, moreover, whatever its kind, it should be generative rather that "one shot." It is on this last aspect of such systems—their generativity—that I would like to dwell.

As a rough gloss, one can put the generativity question by asking whether the rule-governed pattern of explanation is one that can, in general, be applied fruitfully to new situations; for example, can it accept new cases as input, can it create new outputs? Generativity, seen in this way, is a matter of explanatory power or generality—a finite and therefore learnable system that can do a very large, perhaps infinite, set of (similar) jobs. Generative systems then can give a stamp to the cognitive acts in a person's life by virtue of their pervasiveness, their wide spread across many superficially different domains. In this central respect, the system of interpretative explanation is fully of as much cognitive importance, because fully as generative, as the forms of scientific explanation. Scientific reasoning applies equally to the derivational facts about the parts of the molecule, billiard balls, and galactic systems; interpretive explanation applies to the broad range of human action—of oneself and others, now and at other times, in life and in text, here and elsewhere.

One measurable effect of generativity in rule-governed systems is that it leads to performances that go beyond the information that is supplied. For generativity to exist, rules that apply in novel situations must have a generality that lets them go beyond the particulars of any given situation, and therefore to make inferences beyond the information given. In this sense any generative pattern of thought is creative and constitutive. It is an instrument for *making* new accounts. In this respect, too, our two systems seem to be on an equal footing. (Later I will show something of the forms of interpretive thinking that our subjects use to go beyond the [human] information given.)

In real life, one finds these two modes of thought sometimes separate, but often mixed in a variety of ways—nested in one another, sequenced, and even blended. When Primo Levi interrupts his narrative account of the dehumanization of life in the concentration camp to tell us about the manufacture of graphite wicks, or in *The Periodic Table* discourses on the defective chemistry of old paint—what he describes as "half chemistry, half police work" (153), a scientific discourse is nested inside an interpretive one. Or when Richard Feynman tells his life as a series of scientific problems solved one sees an interpretation composed of scientific accounts. And in what mode is George Miller's lovely little book about the excitements and disappointments in the search for psychological reality in Chomskian theory, *Spontaneous Apprentices*?

These are cases of what might be called "blurred genres." And they are as common in life as in text. The mathematics teacher who after showing the pure arithmetic for adding 5 and 8, then turns to stories of apples given and received blurs genres. So does the minister who after an opening discourse on the abstractions involved in "love thy neighbor as thyself," then goes on about the neighborly help being performed by the church's own soup kitchen. He might have kept the mode purer by continuing with a reading from Rawls. So why do we blur?

Plainly there is power in both forms of explanation, and the forms are more complementary than they are substitutable for one another. Each of them is designed to do one kind of explanatory job. But when giving a meaningful account of a complex pattern like Feynman's life, both may need to be invoked to tell the whole story. The *whole* story of Feynman's life or of Primo Levi's experiences in Auschwitz includes interpretations of people's acts in terms of their intentional states, as well as the solving of intellectual problems in the scientific domain.

Genre is a term most commonly found in literary criticism where, traditionally, it referred to essentially different kinds of literary forms. We are all familiar with common lay genres of literature: mystery, science fiction, adventure, romance, and so on. They are used not only to organize the shelves of public libraries, but for deeper reasons as well. Students of literature from Aristotle until now have sought to find mutually exclusive and exhaustive schemes for organizing genres according to deeper principles. In the *Poetics,* for example, Aristotle proposes to organize literature into two fundamental types, comedy and tragedy, on the basis of their forms of necessity, The major genre theorist of this century, Northrop Frye (1957), offers a scheme derived from deeper underlying polarities (introvert-extrovert and intellectual-nonintellectual) consisting of four main genres: romance, confession, (realistic) novel, and a fourth category called "anatomy" that includes systematic nonfiction treatises such as Burton's (1977) *Anatomy of Melancholy* along with narrative satire.[1] More modern students of genre have tended to abandon the taxonomic, foundational enterprise for a variety of reasons. Perhaps the most important of these is the suspicion that there can be no single way of grouping types that is independent of the purposes for which one sets up the grouping, and that there are many such purposes. Taken to its logical conclusion this modern view of the subjectiveness of genre leads to the proposal, often associated with Wolfgang Iser (1978), that, leaving aside problems about a scheme of genres, even single genres are not to be found in text itself, but rather are brought to the text by the reader.

Note that Frye's scheme includes, without distinguishing it, what might be considered a form of scientific writing. For the *Anatomy of*

Melancholy is just that, even if it arises from an earlier, and in some sense prescientific, era. Fowler (1982) says: "Frye . . . considers the formal differences between fiction and nonfiction relatively superficial—as also those between the narrative, didactic, and other presentational modes. With this I have not felt able to agree. The difference between fictional and nonfictional contracts with the reader seems to be fundamental" (118). Despite differences between them on whether such writing constitutes a unique and separate genre, both Frye and Fowler agree in supposing that at least some kinds of didactic and scientific, nonfictional writing are also genres.

I have suggested that scientific text and story text are forms of expression, or genres, that apply respectively to two main forms of cognitive life, scientific thinking about the inanimate world and interpretive thinking about human action. The important aspect of the proposal for our present purposes is that genres are epistemic forms as well as literary forms; that the pattern of their expression gives pattern to the thoughts expressed in them. It is not the controversial claim that scientific discourse is just another form of expression, a point whose defense would take us too far from the main message of this chapter.

For what I am principally concerned to show here is that various kinds of nonscientific interpretation, what might be considered as narrative or fictional genres, constitute (various) modes of thought. For example, an interpretation that construes the intentional states of a protagonist in a short story about a young man about to enter a seminary is different from an interpretation of the same tale that is less interested in the psychology of the young man and focuses on his action, and when it searches for intention, on authorial intention. These two kinds of genre, of which we will hear more later, exist, if they exist anywhere, in the minds of our readers. They may or may not correspond to any conventional genre distinction found in literary criticism. Rather they are integral patterns of explanation that are evoked by stories and attributed to the stories themselves by subjects who have them as part of the tool kit of culturally acquired explanatory models that they bring to the task.

Over the past three years we have done a small series of studies on how people interpret real (literary) short stories that we read out loud to them. I manipulated the amount of content about the protagonist's conscious states. I also manipulated the subjects' mental set to expect such psychological material, as well as the voice (first or third person) in which the same story is told.

Let me turn now to the studies. In the first study, reported in Feldman et al. (1990), we explored the interpretive thinking of sophisticated urban adults by reading short stories to them and asking questions about them. The stories used were written by Heinrich Böll and Brendan Gill, and surely had qualities that the Russian Formalists would call *literaturnost*— the use of tropes, the metaphoric compression of meaning, and a good deal of presupposition and implication. In general we were interested in the thinking about the stories—the rules and patterns by means of which they created new material beyond the information given. We wanted to create two contrasting versions of each story, one that highlighted the intentional states of the protagonist, the other that minimized them.

I proposed above that human action is explained by means of interpretation in terms of intentional states. As a first step, we wanted to vary the richness and explicitness of intentional states in stories, to see if these variants would evoke different patterns of explanation. We constructed, therefore, a "consciousness-reduced" version of each story by deleting mental state language that made explicit the protagonists' thoughts and feelings, leaving subjects with the full set of tropes to infer from but no explicit mental descriptions. They were read both stories, the Böll and Gill—one in its original written version, what we called the "conscious version," the other in its consciousness-reduced version, in a counterbalanced design. Would the versions evoke different kinds of interpretation?

There were twenty-four subjects averaging thirty-two years of age. We interrupted our reading of the story twice to ask, first: What is the most important thing I've told you so far; why? And, then, What are the directions this could be going; what way do you think it will go; why? After the reading was over, we asked them: "Tell me some things about the character that I haven't told you; what's he like?" Then we asked them to tell the story again in their own words.

In simple summary, reactions to the original conscious version, compared with responses to the consciousness-reduced version, contained far more "information beyond the given," particularly about the protagonist's psychological states. They were more psychological, more developmental, and for that reason, more diachronic. This result held for the various questions we asked, but perhaps it is not surprising. After all, had we not told them more about the protagonists's psychology in the first place? Perhaps they had just been more oriented by the story material to psychological matters. We looked at frequency of use of a long list of words that might reveal the speaker's stance toward the story. Three of them appeared significantly more often in responses to conscious versions than to reduced versions and suggest differences in stance. They are the words "conscious," "feel," and "wouldn't." An examination of their actual usage in context shows that they were used to describe the protagonist's psychological stage, rather than subject's own. Plainly, the conscious version makes the psychology of the protagonist more vivid.

If the responses to the reduced versions were merely less psychological, we could stop now, but other things were happening in the responses to the reduced versions. At times, the absent psychology was replaced by invented action as if subjects had endowed these versions with a generative logic of another kind. And when we asked them our most direct question about the underlying logic of the story's progression (why do you think it will go that way), there was a tendency to appeal to the logic of writing style or authorial obligation. The protagonist's motives were replaced by another's motives. If the protagonist was less vivid as a person in his own right, the story plan that gave him life had a greater vividness.

This interpretation—that responses to less conscious versions focus more on the story as an artifact—is supported by a look at stance markers used in responses to the two versions. The words "we" and "why" are used significantly more often in response to the reduced version. The word "we" is used principally to talk about what "we" know and what "we" have been told—that is, what is given in the story as told, and what a generalized reader would think or feel. It is used, then, to reify the story itself as an object of analysis and to present it to the interviewer as an object of joint attention. The usage of the word "why" was equally revealing. It was often used to talk about what we don't know—that is, we don't know why. And it appeared as the subject struggled with and repeated the interviewer's "why?" questions. This pattern, though it suggests on the one hand a greater distance from the characters as psychological agents, equally suggests a greater awareness of the story itself as a nontransparent vehicle that requires analysis in its own right.

The results of this first study suggest that our subjects came into the experiment with two different interpretive patterns in mind, patterns that might be conceived as roughly analogous to genres—a less consciousness-oriented one corresponding to a genre of action or adventure tales where well-formedness consists of the unfolding of the tale's action, and a conscious version with an interpretation roughly corresponding to the genre of more modern psychological fiction. We can suppose that our readers are familiar with exemplars of both these genres, sufficiently so to have internalized them as mental models. In this view, when subjects are presented with a story, they look for signs of its genre and interpret it accordingly—as an action tale or as a psychological one.[2]

The great worry about this study is that the reduced versions were not actual literary products but created by our nonliterary pruning of psychological language. They were, in fact, distorted versions of the originals. Had we driven our subjects to a heightened attentiveness to story itself by giving them such queer stuff?

NOTES

1. I am indebted to Alastair Fowler for his helpful summary of Frye's work in his book cited below.
2. We learned one more thing about the two genres viewed as cognitive models from this study. When we examined frequency of usage of important mental state terms, three of them—"know," "believe," and "realize"—appeared not less but more often in response to the action label. The two versions of the story had given the opposite result—more for the conscious than the consciousness-reduced version. There the great majority of uses were to describe the subject's own mental state rather than the protagonist's. The conscious protagonist made a more conscious interpreter. In this the label is different from version to version. Evidently, when given the action label is used, subjects have to work harder to make sense of what's going on. Somehow, with no change in the story itself, the motivations of the character have been rendered more opaque. It is as if these motivations are *hidden* behind a veil consisting of the narrated story—the *szujet* rather than the *fabula,* which is very salient with this action label. If we had ever supposed that the action narrative was easier to understand, we were talked out of it by this finding. For an action label evokes even more cognitive effort after meaning.

REFERENCES

Bruner, J. In press. *Acts of meaning.* Cambridge: Harvard University Press.
Burton, R., ed. [1621] 1977. *Anatomy of melancholy.* New York: Random House.
Feldman, C. 1987. Thought from language: The linguistic construction of cogni-

tive representations. In *Making sense: The child's construction of the world*, edited by J. Bruner and H. Haste. London: Methuen.

Feldman, C.; Bruner, J.; Renderer, B.; and Spitzer, S. 1990. Narrative comprehension. In *Narrative thought and narrative language*, edited by B. Britton and A. Pellegrini. Hillsdale, N.J.: Erlbaum.

Fowler, A. 1982. *Kinds of literature: An introduction to the theory of genres and modes*. Cambridge: Harvard University Press.

Frye, N. 1957. *Anatomy of criticism*. Princeton: Princeton University Press.

Gardner, H. 1983. *Frames of mind*. New York: Basic Books.

Iser, W. 1978. *The act of reading*. Baltimore: Johns Hopkins University Press.

Johnson-Laird, P. 1983. *Mental models*. Cambridge: Harvard University Press.

Kahneman, D.; Slovic, P.; and Tversky, A. 1982. *Judgment under uncertainty*. Cambridge: Cambridge University Press.

Searle, John. 1983. *Intentionality*. Cambridge: Cambridge University Press.

Simon, D. P., and Simon, H. A. 1978. Individual differences in solving physics problems. In *Children's thinking: What develops*, edited by R. S. Siegler. Hillsdale, N.J.: Erlbaum.

Sternberg, R. J. 1985. *Beyond I.Q.* Cambridge: Cambridge University Press.

Von Wright, G. H. 1971. *Explanation and understanding*. Ithaca: Cornell University Press.

8

Representability and Narrativity of the Self in Development

Adele Nunziante Cesaro

Freud's elaborations on the theme of representation have already been touched upon in the course of this book.

My contribution shall take its impetus from Freud's distinction between the two levels of representation, that is, the word and the thing, in order to try to understand the relationship between the representation and the object world, and their limits. As we shall see, these are both limits to the representation of the self and of the object and of the narrativity of both of them.

In *The Unconscious* (1915), Freud assigns a fundamental value to the two levels of representation: the "thing presentation," that characterizes the subconscious system, holds a more immediate relationship with the object; in primary hallucination the "thing presentation" would be considered by the child as being tantamount to the lost object and would be cathected in its absence. In fact, Freud writes that the thing presentation consists of a cathexis, if not of direct mnemic images of the thing, then at least of more distant mnemic-traces derived from them. This means not only that the representation is sharply distinct from the mnemic-trace (transcription of the event), but also that the thing presentation must not be considered as the mental analogue of the whole thing. The thing can be found in different associative systems or complexes depending on its different aspects. Instead, word representations are introduced by a conception that binds together verbalization and consciousness. Again in his 1915 essay, Freud stresses that: "conscious representation" includes the thing presentation plus the corresponding word representation (secondary process), while the unconscious presentation is the only thing representation (primary process). Funari, in his brilliant work on "Nature and Destiny of Representation" (1985) going back to Freud, emphasizes that representation, considered as a mental event, arises as the prototype of any possible psychic event, as the filter and film into which the origins of signification and its subsequent articulations precipitate.

Representation, then, as the fundamental category of psychism, is the necessary condition for any knowledge of the self and of the object, it is what can be represented "in the immediacy of experience, as a 'place' that, so to speak, cannot be reduced either to the internal world of the body, or to the external world" (Funari 1985, 5).

The link between representation and word originates from the fact that representation, in order to be enunciated, needs the word that enriches and dilates it, but at the same time word is precisely what sets the often deforming limit to the significance of representation. The perception-representation word process gives rise to interrelated transformative events and the earlier the stage of development the more important such a process becomes. If we think of the very beginning of life, of the newborn, we may safely state that what it perceives and represents of itself and of the world of objects is halfway between the sensations and perceptions coming from its own body and the induced ones coming from outside. What the infant perceives in its somatic life, with its sensations of pleasure and displeasure, of tension and relaxation, along with the earliest object perceptions, gives rise to representations in which it is difficult to distinguish sensations from the formal aspects. Then the concept of phantasy arises, very much like Freud's primary hallucination, and its meaning coincides with a world in which objects are part-objects that are undefined,quite blurred and fading the one into the other. Then phantasy is probably the earliest form of representation itself and also a possible modality of representation.

Sandler and Rosenblatt in their essay on "The Concept of Representational World" (1962) define the representational world as a function of the ego viewed as a structure or organized series of functions. It "contains much more than the mere thing or object representations: starting from the sensations coming from the child's body itself in its interactions with the environment, a representation of the body (body scheme) is reached and instinctual impulses find their psychical representative in the form of representations of needs and affects." Representation differs from image because it includes a "set" of images. For example, the child's representation of his or her mother is obtained from a multiplicity of impressions and images of the mother, the mother who feeds, who holds, who lulls, who speaks, who is absent-minded and so on, which overlap, thus giving rise to the maternal representation.

The emergence of differentiated representations of oneself and of the representational world objects takes place gradually, starting from Rougher primal representations of pleasure and displeasure and only little by little does the infant learn how to distinguish the self from the nonself or the self from the object. Then Sandler and Rosenblatt define the representation of the self as a representation which is much more than a body representation; it "includes all those aspects of the child's experience and activity that he/she progressively feels (either consciously or unconsciously) as his/her own. Its "status" is perfectly parallel to that of object representations, save the fact that it refers to the child himself. . . . The construction of the representational world is a product of the Ego functions and the representations of the Self and of the object form a part of the representational world" (1962, 134).

A very suggestive metaphor is used by the authors to describe the representational world: it is like the stage of a theater. The characters on the stage represent the different objects and the child himself is the drama's hero. The theater should correspond to the ego structure and to the various functions (such as those of changing the scene, raising and dropping the curtain), and all the machines that can be used for the performance should correspond to those ego functions we normally know of. In this model the characters on stage stand for self and object representations; whereas their particular aspects or expressions at this or that moment during the performance should correspond to the images of the self and of the object. Nevertheless, this effective representational metaphor does not cover the affective-cognitive relationship that permeates the representation and causes the multiplication, in real life as in the audience of our metaphoric theater, of self and object representations dependent upon the phantasies that direct cognitive modalities and elicit or are elicited by this or that image. The self and object representability itself is questioned and the object emerges as a multiplicity not of images, but of possible representations that we experience in the intricate series of human relations halfway between narcissism and object relation. But there is another issue I would like to address concerning the subject of my contribution that is becoming increasingly polarized by the dialectic between representation and representability and secondly between account and accountability.

In the two or three first months of life, we can speak of perceptions or, in the terms redefined by Funari, of phantasies, rather than true self and object representations. Stern, who has the merit of having brought to the attention of psychoanalysis, by his fascinating and accurate experimental studies, the infant's extraordinary neonatal competencies, formulates for this stage of development the construct of amodal perception. Stern (1985) assumes that children possess a general innate capacity, that he defines as amodal perception, for receiving information in a sensorial modality and translating it somehow into another sensorial modality. How they do it is not yet clear. Stern thinks that probably information is not received in a particular sensorial modality, but transcends the modality or the channel and takes on some unknown supramodal form. So it is not simply a problem of direct translation from one modality to the other. It is more likely that we are faced with a codification in a still mysterious amodal representation that can be subsequently recognized in each sensorial modality. Stern argues that the need and the capacity for creating abstract representations of the primary qualities of perception and for acting accordingly begin with mental life; they are not the peak or a milestone of development that is reached during the second year of life. That is to say, children do not need repeated experiences to start developing some emerging pieces of the self and of the object; they are predisposed to build certain integrations. Then children, we may say, have immediate self and object perceptions, or rather of parts of the self and of the object, parts that, as such, are not integrated yet, but the child is predisposed to integrate them. And at this point the problem of self and object representation as a pathway of development or as a datum of primitive neonatal experience comes up again.

In order to have a self and object representation it is necessary to start perceiving them as distinct. This does not mean that in the earliest months of life there is no self or object perception whatsoever, but rather that it partakes of a sort of all-embracing sensation that, if everything is all right, includes the object into the self providing a magically unified experience. I am talking of Winnicott's construct of illusion, or Gaddini's construct of the self, defined also as primitive mind or basic mental organization. I would like to dwell on this concept. Basic mental organization—described by Gaddini in his *Writings* (1989)—is developed as:

> a result of the mental learning of the body, that is to say of the sensorial experiences related to certain body functions. . . . Sensorial activity is unrelated to perceptions, it uses sensations and therefore implies an imitative functioning. The chief sensation of imitative functioning is that of contact, due to the original importance of physical contact with respect to the sense of self, to one's own existence. We may say that all the sensorial organs . . . originally function as contact organs. . . . Mental presentation of a given sensorial experience at this stage merely provides evidence of one's own presence—of one's own existence. We should add that such an existence of oneself, for the infant's mind, is magically produced by oneself. Each time such an experience is made—for example[,] the rhythmically repeated sensorial experience of nutrition—the mental sense of oneself created by oneself is also experienced again. If experience is lacking and is magically reactivated by phantasy, its mental sense is not altered for that reason at this stage. That is to say[,] experience activated in phantasy is not distinguishable from real experience. When the Self, in the course of the first three months, is developed steadily enough, the newborn acquires the capacity for getting in touch with the surrounding world. (569)

In order to fulfill this task, writes Gaddini, "a more differentiated mental structure must be developed, but the basic mental organization conceives of it primarily as a function of the Self's needs" (569).

Then mental experiences of the body—undistinguished from the object—consist of sensations connected to a specific body function. Phantasy development itself seems to get started by phantasies expressed by means of the body functioning that Gaddini labels as *phantasies in the body*; they are followed by visual phantasies, which seem to be the early mental representations of the bodily self, and are defined by the author as phantasies on the body. In order to reach a rudimentary form of self and object representation, a separation, an initial recognition of self and non-self, of self and object must be attained. For such authors as Winnicott and Gaddini, this can only be achieved after the first two to three months of life, for representability itself is guaranteed by the separation process that goes beyond the magic omnipotence of the sensorial area which characterizes the earliest stage of human life. Within an experience of fullness and contact, of fulfillment of primary needs, we may speak as Winnicott does, of the experience of the continuity of existence, a continuous experiential flow constituting the early self, rather than of representation; in order for representation to be there, a distinction, a gap, a gradual absence of the environment that meets the infant's need are needed; in other words, need must make some room for desire. Such theoretical constructs as the primal scene, the phantasy, phantasies in the body, and continuity of existence help to describe the early development of the infantile self, the early sensorial and perceptive forms of the infant's relational world, the basic conditions for the construction of the representational world. The more the infantile self develops adequately in its relation with the environment, and the events of differentiation and separation from the object respect the infant's individual growth rate and his or her natural tendency to integration and independence, the more the representational world develops harmoniously, thus reducing the risk of distortions that might thwart and deform it significantly in the course of early development. Within this contest, Winnicott's clinical and developmental distinction between the use of an object and getting in touch with the object by way of identifications (1971) takes on a particular meaning. In describing this sequence Winnicott maintains

> that getting in touch with the object comes first, whereas the use of the object comes last: nevertheless in between there is maybe the most difficult thing in human development, or at least the most troublesome early failure and the most difficult to heal. In between getting in touch and using it, there is the object displacement made by the subject out the area of omnipotent control by the subject itself, that is the perception of the object as an external phenomenon, not as a projective entity: actually, a recognition of it as an entity. (189)

As is well known, according to Winnicott the use of the object is related both to the possibility that the subject may destroy the object, and that the object survives destruction and contributes to the subject depending on its characteristics. In other words, until the object forms a part of the self, the other forms a part of the self, coincides with the subject's self, and is a subjective object. Until then, according to Winnicott, there is a getting in touch with the object, but in order to acquire a capacity to use the other, and, I would say, to represent the object to oneself as separate, aggressiveness must come into play in the form of the potential destruction of the object that allows it to fit into the outside world, but on condition that the object survives and is not retaliatory. We may say also, in a different way, that in order to represent the object outside the subject's projective area, and this affects the infant's affective and instinctual life, besides the cognitive one, the object must necessarily always be destroyed in phantasy and survive in reality, for only in this way can it be used.

If, as Sandler writes, it is possible to define the process by which representations are formed as "internalization," it is also true that the internalization process is driven by the movement by which the primary object is placed in the outside world or rather is recognized as external to the self. In many human relationships, starting from early infantile relationships, the use of the object never seems to be attained or is attained incompletely, intermittently. I am referring to those relationships in which the narcissistic personality is such that it forbids a nondistorted representation of the object, its placement in the exterior reality, and its use: the other, the object continues to be a part of oneself, a bundle of projections, compelled by the subject's omnipotent control not to exist in its own right, but only as an undifferentiated nourishment of one's own self. From sensation to perception, representation and language, with all the affective and instinctual correlates of such processes of human development, there is no linear progress, and distortions and deformations make some human relations difficult and painful. Finally language, as a means that conveys representation (with all its affective corollaries), is the last step in human communication; it is what makes it enunciable, but also, as I said before, potentially subject to deformation. I would like to move at least apparently away from the development of the self and from the conditions for representation, to resort to an effective metaphor that, as Sandler's and Rosenblatt's metaphor on theater, would allow me to express better the problems of development and in particular the dual character of narration. I am referring to *Six Characters in Search of an Author* by Pirandello. The text is well known; we have a stage, a group of actors, a director and six characters searching for an author who stages their family tragedy: the father, the mother, the stepdaughter, the son, the boy, the little girl. The narrating ego is chiefly represented by the stepdaughter, the father, and the mother, and is often interrupted by the timely curiosity of the director, apparently not in unison with the protagonists' performance. The actors, in their turn, try to reproduce by fits and starts the story that is dramatically staged by the protagonists but they look faded like colorless, sham copies: it is a performance within the performance, the rebounding of deformed specularities. One narrates one's own life, the tragedy that traversed it, and each narration spins a yarn and a story again, reconstitutes a story which is not only one family story but as many stories as the six characters and there are still other stories, small fragments of which the actors play out. It is a story that cannot be narrated, what is narrated is what cannot be seen. Children, being almost dumb protagonists, do not narrate by language, but action narrates for them, in the same way that the mother's cry reweaves the painful thread of her own existence. Narration and action alternate and each of them unravels the individual thread of what the character is for himself and for the others. The risk, underlying the whole text, lies in what is actually performed and seems to be expressed, all of a sudden, by the father's sorrowful words:

> That's where the tragedy lies in my view, sir: in the consciousness I have, that each of us—you see—believes to be "one," but this is not true: we are "many" sir, as "many" as all the possibilities of being that rest with us: "one" with this one, "one" with that one—very different! And with the illusion, meanwhile, of being always "one for all" and always "this one" that we believe we are in each of our acts. It is not true!
> We get very well aware of it, when in some of our acts all of a sudden by a very unlucky chance we feel as if we were hooked in and suspended: I mean we get aware that we are not completely exhausted by that act, and therefore it would be a dreadful injustice to judge us on that only, to keep us hooked in and suspended, to the pillory, for a whole life, as if that act were the compendium of that life!

This problem is related to that of self and object accountability, the possibility to communicate one's own self to others and to be understood in one's hundred thousand of representations, and the possibility to understand what the object tells about himself through the language and the action. In relational dynamics the identification together with empathy acts as a carrier of knowledge, whereas a massive reverberation of projections hampers knowledge. The necessary condition for accountability through language is a mental representation which already is a mental elaboration of raw percepts, bodily sensations, "phantasies in the body." When from raw percepts, from "phantasies in the body," no mental representations evolve, then action as privileged narrative modality or the psychosomatic symptom emerges. What cannot be represented cannot be narrated either, except sometimes by means of the body which plays an action instead of using a symbol. The limits of our understanding of cognitive processes are, I am well aware, still rather limited and for this reason I feel inclined to conclude my chapter remembering the illusory ambition of Borges's Imperial Cartographers who, after drawing up a map as big as the territory they wanted to chart, in the end realized it was useless.

REFERENCES

Freud, S. 1915. *The Unconscious. S. E.* Vol. 14. London: Hogarth Press and The Institute of Psycho-analysis.

Funari, E. 1985. *Natura e destino della rappresentazione.* Milan: Raffaello Cortina Editore.

Gaddini, E. 1989. *Scritti.* Milano: Raffaello Cortina Editore.

Sandler, J., and Rosenblatt, B. 1962. The concept of the representational world. *Psychoanal. Study of the Child* 17:128-45.

Stern, D. 1985. *The interpersonal world of the infant.* New York: Basic Books.

Winnicott, D. W. 1971. *Playing and reality.* London: Tavistock.

9

Narration and Discursive Thought in Infancy

Clotilde Pontecorvo

Introduction

In recent times story narration in infancy has been the focus of attention in so many research fields and been approached from so many theoretical perspectives that it is difficult to quantify all of its interesting academic aspects. Indeed, this chapter will only be able to examine a few of these theoretical approaches.

From a developmental point of view it is well known that small children start to explore the domain of narration and discursive thought from early infancy and they are very quick to develop a narrative perspective. During book reading, particularly with the mother, at around two years of age they are able to intervene in dialogue using a narrative type of discourse, which becomes more autonomous as the child explicitly takes on the role of narrator.

The study of the use and progressive acquisition of complex linguistic structures during narration is thus particularly interesting. The famous study carried out by several authors (Nelson 1989) on the language of Emily in her presleep monologues from twenty-two to thirty-seven months not only shows her considerable linguistic competence, but also how narrative discourse referring to what has happened, what is about to happen, and what usually happens is prevalent in her monologues. Quite apart from the exceptional nature of such linguistically articulate data, it is interesting to note in Bruner and Lucariello's analysis (1989) how the child uses narration as a means of giving meaning to events and to her own experience and emotions. In doing this she uses various means (used as analysis categories by the authors), such as sequential organization of events, distinction between what is normal and abnormal, explicitation of intention and expression of a perspective/point of view (uncertain, emotional, epistemic, etc.). Using linguistic instruments that are in continual evolution, Emily orders, qualifies, evaluates, and underlines what happens so as to "give meaning" to her life. In other words, from an emotional point of view, "narrating to herself" is of primary importance in organizing her internal world.

There is no doubt that the results of this study alone are sufficient to reveal the importance of narration and narrative competence for the development of the child. To this should be added children's interest in reading and storytelling from a very early age, and the cognitive and linguistic importance of the reading, comprehension, retelling, and discussion of stories.

The rest of this chapter will deal with the latter. They will be analyzed from a psychopedagogic perspective and particular attention will be paid to the ways in which these early skills can be improved and how they can be stimulated by adult intervention.

Narration and Literacy

Interest in the development of child narration evolved from studies comparing procedures used by different types of parent and teacher in reading and storytelling with their effects on narrative production skills such as comprehension and explanation. In comparing different types of adult strategy it emerged that these strategies produced different infant skills (Heath 1982) and that some of them facilitate literacy in school—for some children the acquisition of written language is easier (Sulzby 1985). Research has shown that training parents to this end can have positive effects because they tend to be more in tune with and sensitive to their children's interests. Storytelling and story reading to and with children is a strong factor in the development of their linguistic abilities because it both teaches them to construct and extract meaning from a text (which includes images) and leads them to associate story reading and comprehension with positive emotions: Wells (1989) suggests that we "learn to read," that is, become familiar with the cognitive acts of reading, "in our parents' arms" in a warm, reassuring, and pleasant situation. The long-term positive effects of this early family-based process of familiarization with reading (and therefore with narration) are that children learn to read more easily, are more motivated, and show greater enthusiasm for books, narrative invention, and writing.

This line of research tends to highlight the importance of story reading in the family and in nursery school for *literacy* purposes, that is, for the acquisition of further skills in using written language. It is clearly a particular kind of perspective which focuses on special features of "written culture" but does not cover all the developmental and educational implications of child narration by any means.

Indeed, narration has its own particular collocation and has a dual nature. On the one hand it is an oral form of discourse organization (typified by such ancient cultural forms as the epic, legend, myth, and popular fable) since its characteristic sequencing forms facilitate the processes of memorizing and transmission in primarily oral contexts. On the other hand it tends to appear as a "frozen" oral form built around conventional structures and expressions. This enables both a spoken discourse with characteristics similar to those of writing, in as much as it is a text relatively independent of context (Chafe 1982), and of monologues, that is, production not linked to dialogue and conversation (Bereiter and Scardamalia 1987), to be produced. From a psychopedagogic point of view this process of acquisition of the ability to produce a monologue, that is, autonomous discourse from a familiar text, has been described by Sulzby (1991) in a comparison with storybook reading with the adult. This coincides with the results of the study of Emily cited above: her monologues before going to sleep were mainly in the form of narrative discourse. Narration as an early cultural form and progressive acquisition is thus a form of discourse playing an intermediate role between specific oral forms (conversation, dialogues, the various face-to-face modes of communication) and specific written forms (the scientific, philosophical, or historical essay, judicial sentences, the short story, and the modern novel).

Although the role of narration and the consequent acquisition of narrative ability in the development of literacy will not be discussed below (see instead Orsolini 1991; Orsolini, Devescovi, and Fabbretti 1991, for a specific treatment), the fact that any narrative activity is a key motivating context for introducing the child to the peculiarities of written culture from the age of two, and from the moment he enters the nursery school in particular, is of particular importance for the psychopedagogical perspective adopted here.

Interactive Contexts and Production Variables

Using the theoretical framework described above this study will deal with several aspects of specific educational interest:

1. Narration, in as much as it provides a context for the use and development of linguistic abilities in the written language, is an important element in starting off the process of early literacy (Orsolini and Pontecorvo 1991).

2. Narration within social interaction (with two or more speakers) provides an arena for practicing the complex cognitive skills of narrative (Bruner 1986) and argumentative thought (Orsolini and Pontecorvo 1989b). Infant narrative skills from four to nine years of age can thus be developed in *social interaction contexts* which facilitate their explicitation and practice.

3. During narration and interactive discourse aimed at narration, children compare interpretations of the natural world, the social world, and the "narrative" world of the story. In so doing they use special linguistic, cognitive, and emotional modes which vary in relation to the various aspects of the situation being talked about.

A basic premise of this study is the child's early narrative competence regarding stories in the strict sense of the word, that is, tales and fables. This has been widely researched (see Orsolini 1987, for a review in Italian). Children have already mastered the essential structure of the story (Stein and Glenn 1979) by the age of four and use the main components of the story (the setting, the initial event, attempts at a solution, the conclusion) in comprehension and production. They remember its central elements, that is, those elements which have more connections with others, more easily and are able to produce "good" stories from the age of four to five years. They are also able to produce stories with characteristics that are different in relation to different stimuli: miniature toys, visual or verbal cues, a request to retell an already known story.

These different procedures or story production requests can be linked to two other procedural aspects:

1. The first is the degree of approximation to the written language situation. In addition to the story "telling" and before directly requesting "story writing," we generally adopted a "dictation" procedure: the child dictates a story to the adult who acts as a scribe; the story itself tends to be different from a story which would only have been "told" and to be closer to a written story (cf. Orsolini, Devescovi, and Fabbretti 1991; Pontecorvo and Zucchermaglio 1989, 1990).

2. The second aspect is variation of interactive context. This might be an adult-child or child-child dyad (both have been used in "dictation") or a small group situation led by an adult who stimulates and gathers children's suggestions, writes them down, and reads them back to the group. The latter technique is already being used by the more aware teachers in nursery schools. It was pioneered in the United States by Vivian Paley (cf. Paley 1981) and has been used by Ludovica Muntoni (1992) in Rome and many other teachers all over Italy.

This study involves a particular group situation in state nursery school classes (part of a wider piece of research carried out with Margherita Orsolini and Maria Amoni: cf. Orsolini, Pontecorvo, and Amoni 1989). In this situation there are three groups with four children in each group. The teacher reads the story to each of these groups separately, interrupting the reading about four or five times to ask the children to predict what is going to happen. At the end there is a discussion comparing children's predictions with what really happened in the story. This discussion first takes place in the small group and then with the whole class of twelve children. This scenario not only activates and stimulates children's narration skills, that is, their ability to produce discourse organized along narrative lines, but at the same time helps them to make explicit and compare their ideas about the world and people's behavior, their knowledge of stories and how they work, and their expectations regarding fictitious events. It might be termed a collective problem-solving situation, as Carol Fleisher Feldman claims in her analysis of Emily's monologues (1989), in which she uses "talk about herself" to resolve the problem of something she does not know or does not understand. In our own case the linguistic instruments required by discursive interaction (cf. Orsolini, Pontecorvo, and Amoni 1989) are used to achieve the cognitive objectives of interpretation and explanation. These cognitive objectives, however, have strong social connotations due to the unavoidable competition that is set up between different speakers, the adult-controlled situation, and the authoritarian school setting.

Story Discussion in School: What Is the Adult's Role and What Does the Child Acquire?

The social interaction context used in this research is the discussion and it takes place at school (a nursery school in a Rome suburb). The interactive characteristics of class discussion have been discussed elsewhere (Pontecorvo 1985). It is a discourse event aimed at sharing and constructing knowledge among pupils, and follows rules which are different from those that operate in normal school lessons.

The role of the adult teacher is different in discussion. It is not the usual teacher's role of the teacher questioning, the pupil answering, and the teacher evaluating (Sinclair and Coulthard 1975) that has already been internalized by children from the first year of primary school (Mehan 1979); the teacher's role is more as a facilitator of communication between the children themselves. As will be seen in the examples below, the teacher has to follow different rules of communication. He or she does not control speaking turns rigidly but "mirrors" (to use Rogers's term, subsequently adapted to the educational context by Lumbelli 1982) and/ or reformulates the child's utterance in a selective way, by focusing on aspects relevant to his or her aims. The teacher "quotes" children's discourse in reformulations and questions, avoids comment or direct evaluation, and does not even use approval to reinforce. He or she stimulates comparison between opinions and refrains from intervening in the more lively phases of disagreement among children.

When this teaching strategy is adopted and children are guided toward using the above reading procedure, they come progressively closer to knowledge of the object under discussion. As has been previously shown (Orsolini and Pontecorvo 1989b), children take part in the narration game by forging links with each other, often in dramatic form, and by continuing or varying the original story; they refer to other stories and to world knowledge in their comments; above all they have disputes, often very lively ones, about alternative interpretations and different ways of explaining characters' behavior, and are thus able to practice modes of argument and therefore thought. It is this aspect which in our view is one of the most important effects of discussion (Pontecorvo 1987).

Children also progressively master the narrative genre and its particular linguistic forms (locution, internal expression of verb tenses, anaphoric reference, cohesive forms), the general characteristics of structure and content of stories, the literary skills of prediction/anticipation of content, comparing expectations with the text itself, trying to give a reason for the events in a story and the choices and feelings of its characters. Modes of analysis of conversation, which have been dealt with elsewhere (cf. Orsolini and Pontecorvo 1989b), will not be discussed here although it is worth remembering that it has enabled us to study the extent to which the adult regulates modes of discourse linking and to identify the various frames of interaction (Bateson 1955; Goffman 1981) between teacher and children, for example, guessing, remembering, taking a position, and disputing.

This study uses a psychological perspective aimed at describing and interpreting the knowledge and forms of thought shown by children in the interactive situation in the following spheres: the world of stories; the real, physical world; and the social, interpersonal, and mental worlds.

Forms of Reasoning Linked to Narration in Four- to Five-year-old Children

(a) The World of Stories

The educational interaction situation described above, which children have experienced several times in nursery school under the guidance of their two teachers, is particularly suited to the activation and use of knowledge of the world of stories and fables; even though these children are not middle class, this world is already available to them.

For example, in the story of "Mascia and the Bear," when the reading is stopped at the point when Mascia is lost in the wood and spies a little cottage, children frequently predict the arrival of a wolf, as in the story of

Little Red Riding Hood. The wolf is more frequent in our culture than the bear, as the following examples show:

(1)

FRANCESCO: Or else the wolf had eaten them all up, all the people in the house

(2)

FAUSTO: And then, and then the wolf'll go away with a big heavy tummy
FEDERICA: Then the hunters come along and they shoot him

(3)

FAUSTO: and Mascia was inside and she saw the wolf was in the bed so she ran off
FEDERICA: hush, hush and nobody heard her.

The reason for getting lost in the wood activates the memory of the classic ways of finding the way home as a stories like *Tom Thumb*:

(4)

FAUSTO: N . . . no I haven't finished yet, . . . because well the birdies they found some bread when they were coming along and so they dropped the crumbs and so they w . . . went back home . . . and the crumbs were all the way along to Mascia's home, and so she followed them.

During the discussion phase, when the children know the whole story and attempt to compare it with their predictions by retelling it in their own way, they use locutions which are typical of traditional storytelling (for example, "he went on and on") but which were not in the original text. More importantly, the child who remembers the story by retelling it might also supply alternative solutions of the "what he would have done if he had been the main character" type. Fausto develops these hypotheses at length, despite the teacher's requests for details of the story as it really was:

(5)

TEACHER: But Fausto could have said so? Francesco said he couldn't.
FEDERICA: Well he thought . . .
FRANCESCO: He'd have been in the story otherwise
TEACHER: Because, you see, Francesco says otherwise you would be in the story yourself and you could have told him.
FAUSTO: Well think wallow! And that, d'you think you'd say that, Miss . . . , cause well in stories you can say you were in the story and so you could say that's that and that's that. Well!

The stories may contain dramatic elements but these should always be credible: Federica hypothesizes that the grandparents get eaten up (cf. 6), but Fausto objects that if people get eaten up their bones are left behind (see 7):

(6)
FEDERICA: But then she started to flap her wings and she got home, and she says: "Where's Grandad? The wolf ate him up." And so she was so sad, she went off to bed and she started to cry.
(7)
FAUSTO: No no, because then you'd have seen his bones, wouldn't you?

(b) The Physical World

A predominant aspect of children's proposed solutions or alternatives to the story which has been narrated, anticipated and discussed is their reference to its credibility and to whether it is true to life. It seems that the children easily master the principle that a story, that is, narrative invention analogous to what is found in short stories, novels, and all literary production, must follow a "true to life" criterion. As Bruner has stressed (1986), stories are convincing by their "lifelikeness" rather than their truthfulness; the credibility of a story is quite different from the credibility of a scientific hypothesis.

Indeed the children in this study made widespread use of the credibility criterion as a basis for their claims for possible alternatives for the development of the story (during the prediction stage) and in order to object to the claims of others (during the discussion stage). As regards the latter, previous research has clearly shown that reference to physical credibility is used as a further argumentative wealth during the more heated moments of discussion, i.e those disputes in which the validity of the claim of one or the other is questioned in order to reinforce the speaker's social "school" image; it is true that disputes take place with little or irrelevant intervention from the teacher but children are already aware that what is in question at school is knowledge and "truth."

There are frequent examples of this questioning of others' claims based on the above principles during children's discussions of the way in which Mascia managed to escape from the bear:

(8)
(This is about how Mascia managed to hide inside the basket with a plateful of scones on her head, and about how later the bear took her to her grandparents' house.)

ALESSIO: The plate's on her head, she's not holding it in her hands!
FEDERICA: Well (ironically) Fancy that so the plate will fall down!
ALESSIO: But it couldn't fall down with the blanket on top? And besides she's holding it with her hands isn't she?
FEDERICA: No, it's like this (and she pretends she's holding a plate on her head) not like this (holding the plate down below) otherwise she'll squash 'em, won't she?
ALESSIO: What's wrong, she holds 'em with her hands, can't she?
PIETRO: Rubbish, she holds 'em w'th her hands, then she'll fall down herself!

The following example is about the children discussing whether Mascia could escape by making herself a pair of wings. Of course, it's a borrowing from the myth of Icarus, but the conjecture is analyzed according to what five-year-old children may consider physically possible:

(9)
FABIANA: Um, when she stuck on the wings and then she started to fly, the wings could also fall off.
TEACHER: D'you see (speaking to Francesco whose mind is wandering)?
FAUSTO: If they're stuck! they're stuck!
FEDERICA: But if, but if she put too little glue on, they'd fall off because it's cold!
FAUSTO: No, not 'cause it's cold! If she used wax, wax would melt in the sun and she'd fall down.
TEACHER: So Francesco, d'you see what Fabiana says?
FEDERICA: But the rainbow, it's just colors! It's just color, it's not like it's a bit of thing here, like a bit of cloth and it'll hold it up!
TEACHER: It's not made of cloth so it can't hold things up.
FAUSTO: It's just colors, just colors

This subject is taken up again by the same group and elaborated further: the idea that the wings can't come off and that she will have to tear them off with the dress they are attached to leads to controversy on the grounds that Mascia can easily put on a new one, considering that according to the story she managed to get home in the end.

Children thus make use of rules of the physical world in their arguments—the way glue works, the effect of heat, what a rainbow is made of—which are generally referred to using the present tense, the "impersonal you," and the use of "have to" conveying the idea of necessity. Yet they also make use of events in the story itself and refer to the text as written (and therefore not modifiable).

(c) The Human and Interpersonal Situation: Acts, Intentions, States of Mind

We have already shown how the dispute situation in which all available arguments are used is, at least as far as our data are concerned, the most typical context in which children are really motivated to refer to "world rules" and thereby to make their theories about the way it works explicit. A typical "argumentative flow" starts from a claim relative to some story event which then leads to more general claims that bring world rules into play. Sometimes there is going back to the world of the story as a "that's the way it is" situation (it has been written in that way and read aloud by the teacher in that way (cf 11) and it is referred to as supporting (cf. Toulmin 1958; Pontecorvo 1985) the plausibility of the arguments that have been produced.

An interesting example of the "social rule" occurs in the discussion of the "the fox and the crow," in which the fox tricks his way into eating two baby crows. Walter's suggestion that the crow can have other babies prompts children to make some general comparisons with their own mothers:

(10)
SABRINA: Well 'cause you see, our Mum, she's had us, and if somebody takes us away, she can't have more.
WALTER: Well, what about Auntie, ain't she got three?! She's got a little one and two older ones. Why can't the crow have two more?
ALESSIO: It's my turn now, shut up! She could have. . . . She had us, didn't she? Then she had another and then no more.
(. . . .)
WALTER: But if my Auntie had three!
ALESSIO: Then that's because your Auntie's a bit funny. She's had three!
FAUSTO: Um that's why. . . .
PIETRO: D'you know why she can't have more birdies, our Mums have more babies, because then they'll have to marry somebody else! (All the children start talking together.)
WALTER: But if she doesn't marry somebody else, she can't have babies. And if she marries again . . .

It would seem that in order to reassure themselves that their mothers cannot have any more children, the children extend the "rule" to the crow world. The only way to have another child is to marry another man. Even Walter, who is the most realistic of the children, is prepared to accept that getting married to someone else, hinting perhaps at a sexual relationship, is a necessary and sufficient condition for having another child.

Reference to world rules are also frequent in discussion of Mascia and the bear. In the following extract there is a discussion of whether Mascia is already "big" (i.e. more than five years old) or little (three or four years old). Walter claims that Mascia cannot be little:

(11)
WALTER: If Mascia was three, how could she be intelligent if she's little? She hasn't got any ideas yet, her granny has to tell her.
FABIOLA: There, what d'you know about it, she goes to school.
WALTER: She's a big girl . . . if she's big then I . . .
FABIOLA: What d'you know about it . . . she went to school in the story?
SABRINA: How do you know how old she is? It's not even written.
WALTER: What d'you mean how old? D'you know how old she is? Let's hear.
FABIOLA: She's five!
WALTER: Tell me how old she is.
SABRINA: If it was written, the teacher would have read it out!

In his first claim Walter takes Mascia's intelligence for granted (perhaps because she managed to deceive the bear): the relation between age and intelligence is a rule of the human world and is expressed in the present tense. Fabiola and Sabrina cleverly shift the question to "how can you know" her exact age by insisting that the text and the reading are the source of their knowledge. Children extend their role both to the interpretation of characters' intentions and feelings, which are often implicit in the text, and to the evaluation of their mental states. In the first of the two examples given below, children give a series of answers to the teacher's request for explanation and they suggest various possible states of mind for Mascia:

(12)
TEACHER: But why do you think Mascia wanted to run away? Not . . .
ALESSIO: Because she didn't like going inside.
PIETRO: Because she wanted to see her granny and grandpa again.
TEACHER: She wanted to see her granny and grandpa again.
FEDERICA: And 'cause she didn't want to live with that animal.
ALESSIO: She didn't like that cottage 'cause she knew the bear lived there and so she didn't want to live there anymore.
PIETRO: Do you know why, miss ? 'cause she didn't want to get *tired* out.

The teacher's request is for information which is not very explicit in the text. The children's discourse is directed at making the type of information which has been focused by the teacher's request explicit. The teacher has brought the reasons behind Mascia's "wish" to the center of the discourse and the children accept this focus by suggesting various possible mental states: "liking doing something," "wanting," "knowing." What the children are trying to explain is in fact the reason for Mascia's feeling that she did *want* to run away. The second example involves the bear's thinking: what he thought, what he noticed, and what he did not notice. In one group Walter claims that "if the bear was clever he would have known that Mascia would have tried to run away" and he should have noticed the trick: "he should have realized it . . . he should have realized that she was inside the basket." In another group (13), Pietro accepts the way in which the bear fell into the trap, claiming that you cannot now say that he should have noticed the trick:

(13)
PIETRO: No, Mascia's clever, 'cause Mascia Mascia has more ideas than the bear ! 'Cause . . .
ALESSIO: She gets ideas and the bear doesn't get ideas.
PIETRO: Because she said I'll climb up in that tree but then she hid inside the basket.
FEDERICA: Instead the bear gets ideas too because he saw her. . . . The bear saw Mascia getting out so, he could eat her up. And instead the basket arrives instead . . .
PIETRO: But didn't he see her? How can he see her now?
FEDERICA: When he went to that rock he opened the basket straightaway and saw that lovely dish. He lifted it up and sees Mascia and says: "Ah yes. You've come along with me then!"
PIETRO: I know but . . . how do they see . . . ? If he saw it now, how could they see it before [meaning: later]! How could he think about it before [meaning: later], if he saw it before?

Conclusions

It is quite clear that reading and discussing stories is of immense educational importance for the three- to six-year-old children involved in this study. Interpretation and analysis of the material that has been collected over the years reveals the extraordinary ease with which, when carefully "guided" by the teacher, these types of collective narrative discourse produce important results at a *metacognitive* and metacommunicative level. When the above texts are compared to stories which have been made up and retold by children of the same age in *individual* interviews they show a striking superiority in inventiveness, in suggesting, justifying, and comparing complex inferences, and in providing alternative solutions to story development. Not only does the activity involve an interactive context with lively group discussion, but the stimulation, comparison, and discussion of alternative continuations of the story facilitate the development and acquisition of the above-mentioned skills. Although these results are due to the interactive context and the prediction-discussion sequence, as has also been found in discussions of scientific knowledge (Pontecorvo 1987), it should be stressed that the narrative content gives particular scope for the cognitive development of children of this age.

Narrative provides a type of discourse in which children can easily insert and articulate their own points of view. The emotional closeness of narrative to children's worlds, particularly in the more traditional forms (fable, legend, fairy tales, etc.) has been widely shown in the psychoanalytic literature (cf. Bettelheim 1975). Similarly, the cognitive relevance and early mastery of the "grammar of stories" has been underlined by cognitive developmental psychology (Stein and Glenn 1979).

Although both these aspects are shown in our data, the most important aspect is the metacognitive one. In discussing stories children think about events, make complex alternative hypotheses, make inferences about what the story says and does not say, and make lengthy attempts to interpret the characters' states of mind at the various stages of the story. It is for this reason that narration and discussion are a powerful instrument for the development of discursive thought and for learning to "give meaning" to human life.

REFERENCES

Bateson, G. 1955. A theory of play and fantasy. In *Steps to an ecology of mind*. New York: Chandler, 1972.

Bereiter, C., and Scardamalia, M. 1987. *The psychology of written composition*. New York: Academic Press.

Bettelheim, B. 1975. *Il mondo incantato delle fiabe*. Milan: Feltrinelli.

Bruner, J. S. 1986. *Actual minds, possible worlds.* Cambridge: Harvard University Press.

Bruner, J. S., and Lucariello, J. 1989. Monologue as narrative recreation of the world. In *Narratives from the crib,* edited by K. Nelson, 73–97. Cambridge: Harvard University Press.

Chafe, W. 1982. Integration and involvement in speaking, writing and oral literature. In *Spoken and written language,* edited by D. Tannen. Norwood, N.J.: Ablex.

Feldman, C. F. 1989. Monologue as problem-solving narrative. In *Narratives from the crib,* edited by K. Nelson, 98–119. Cambridge: Harvard University Press.

Goffman, E. 1981. *Forms of talk.* Philadelphia: University of Pennsylvania Press.

Heath, B. S. 1982. What no bedtime story means: Narrative skills at home and school. *Language in Society* 11: 49–76.

Lumbelli, L. 1985. *Psicologia dell'educazione. Comunicare à scuola.* Bologna: Il Mulino.

Mehan, M. 1979. *Learning lessons.* Cambridge: Harvard University Press.

Muntoni, L. 1992. Le domande giuste. *Cooperazione Educativa* 16, no. 11: 4–8.

Nelson, K., ed. 1989. *Narratives from the crib.* Cambridge: Harvard University Press.

Orsolini, M. 1987. *Narrare, conversare, discutere: un intervento sperimentale nella scuola dell'infanzia.* Ph.D. dissertation in Experimental Research in Education. University of Rome "La Sapienza."

———. 1991. Oralità e scrittura nella costruzione del testo. In *La costruzione del testo scritto nei bambini,* edited by M. Orsolini and C. Pontecorvo, 14–28. Florence: La Nuova Italia.

Orsolini, M.; Devescovi, A.; and Fabbretti, D. 1991. Dettare una storia: che cosa cambia tra i 5 e gli 8 anni. In *La costruzione del testo scritto nei bambini,* edited by M. Orsolini and C. Pontecorvo, 99–118. Florence: La Nuova Italia.

Orsolini, M., and Pontecorvo, C. 1989a. Arguing versus co-constructing in children's verbal interaction. *Dossiers de Psycologie* 37, (September): 53–60.

———. 1989b. La genesi della spiegazione nella discussione in classe. In *La spiegazione nell'interazione sociale,* edited by M. S. Barbieri, 161–89. Turin: Loescher.

———, eds. 1991. *La costruzione del testo scritto nei bambini.* Florence: La Nuova Italia.

———. 1992. Children's talk in classroom discussion. Accepted for publication in *Cognition and Instruction* 9, no. 2: 113–36.

Orsolini, M.; Pontecorvo, C.; and Amoni, M. 1989. Discutere in classe: interazione sociale e attivita cognitiva. *Giornale Italiano di Psicologia* 16, no. 2: 156–78.

Paley, V. 1981. *Wally's stories.* Cambridge: Harvard University Press.

Pontecorvo, C. 1985. Discutere per ragionare: la costruzione della conoscenza come argomentazione. *Rassegna de Psicologia* 1–2: 23–45.

———. 1987. Discussing for reasoning: The role of argument in knowledge construction. In *Learning and instruction,* edited by E. De Corte et al. Oxford: Pergamon Press.

Pontecorvo, C. and Zucchermaglio, C. 1989. From oral to written language: Preschool children dictating stories. *Journal of Reading Behavior* 21, 2: 109–26.

———. 1990. A passage to literacy: Learning in a social context. In *How children construct literacy: Piagetian perspectives,* edited by Y. M. Goodman, 59–98. Newark, Del.: International Reading Association.

Sinclair, J. M., and Coulthard, R. M. 1975. *Towards an analysis of discourse.* Oxford: Oxford University Press.

Snow, C. E., and Goldfield, B. A. 1982. Building stories: The emergence of information structures from conversation. In *Analyzing discourse: Text and talk,* edited by D. Tannen. Washington, D.C.: Georgetown University Press.

Stein, N. L., and Glenn, C. G. 1979. An analysis of story comprehension in elementary school children. In *New directions in discourse processing,* Vol. 2, *Advances in discourse processes,* edited by R. O. Freedle, 53–120. Norwood, N.J.: Ablex.

Sulzby, E. 1985. Kindergarteners as writers and readers. In *Children's early writing development,* edited by M. Farr, 127–200. Norwood, N.J.: Ablex.

———. 1991. Oralità e scrittura nel percorso verso la lingua scritta. In *La costruzione del testo scritto nei bambini,* edited by M. Orsolini and C. Pontecorvo, 57–75. Florence: La Nuova Italia.

Teberosky, A. 1988. La dictée et la rédaction de contes entre enfants du même âge. *European Journal of Psychology of Education* 3, no. 4: 399–414.

Toulmin, S. 1958. *The uses of argument.* Cambridge: Cambridge University Press.

Wells, G. 1989. Communications by electronic mail. From the XLCHC Network of the Laboratory for Comparative Human Cognition, University of California at San Diego, La Jolla.

Zucchermaglio, C. 1987. *Alfabetizzazione e continuità educativa tra i 5 e i 7 anni: una ricerca sperimentale sui processi di acquisizione della lingua scritta.* Ph.D. dissertation in Experimental Research in Education. University of Rome "La Sapienza."

III

REPRESENTATIONS AND NARRATIVES IN CLINICAL WORK

10

The Place of the Psychoanalyst

Christopher Bollas

Perhaps it was St. Augustine, in his *Confessions,* who discovered a theological form through which to fashion a particular psychological representation. Prompted by his spiritual crisis he reflected on his inner life, in a very particular sort of way. His introspection was, of course, licensed by the Christian model of conflict, between the forces of Christ and anti-Christ, but the literary form derived from Augustine's practice was, as Abrams maintains, the "first distinctively Christian spiritual autobiography. (p. 48)"

Men had always looked to themselves in one way or another. Augustine did not invent introspection, but he may well have been the first person to construct a form for its adequate representation. So although we do marvel at the depth to which Shakespeare knew man, we do not have the privilege of Shakespeare addressing himself, an act of singular difficulty.

Although we do see the effort of Montaigne in his *Essays,* or of Pascal in his *Pensées* to objectify the self, it is perhaps only in the seventeenth century Puritan diary—such as that by Michael Wigglesworth—that looking into oneself achieves a certain depth, although Wigglesworth's is a diary and confession driven by a desire to reveal himself to a highly discerning and shrewd deity who is not fooled by bad faith. Wigglesworth, like so many Puritan writers, practically took his soul out of its habitual incarnation to confess every nook and cranny of evil's doings to his God.

What one can see in his literature that is absent from Augustine is a new depth of self-disclosure that is driven by unconscious efforts to convince this God to vote the believer into the world of the elect and therefore to an afterlife. This placed the subject in the clearly unhappy task of confessing every devious personality feature in the hope that some such self revealing would win him grace, even though this was meant to be an arbitrary and predetermined choice of the God.

Rousseau, of course, aimed to confess himself, although the urge to confess others virtually overwhelmed his enterprise. Nonetheless, his work is an obviously distinct hallmark of autobiography. The first writing of this specific literary form belongs to W. P. Scargill whose book *The Autobiography of a Dissenting Minister* was published in 1834 (Olney 1980, 5). The word "autobiography" was invented at the end of the eighteenth century when "three Greek elements meaning 'self—life—writing' " were brought together: an act that subsumed confessions, diaries, and memoirs (p. 6).

In *The Prelude* Wordsworth saw a poetic structure not simply for the reflective representation on the self—as a figure of action and event that has moved through history—but for the evocation of that figure, or of those former selves, in and through the act of recollective mediation from which *The Prelude* was to spring. *The Prelude* is subtitled "Growth of a Poet's Mind; An Autobiographical Poem." "Oh there is blessing in this gentle breeze / that blows from the green fields and from the clouds / and from the sky: it beats against my cheek, / and seems half conscious of the joy it gives." So he opens his *Prelude* announcing the refreshing arrival of memories of his childhood. "I breathe again," he writes. "Trances of thought and mountings of the mind / come fast upon me," he thrills as the movement of imagery (of recollection) imposes itself upon him, displacing his "own unnatural self" that seems the outcome of a false self that he ascribes to the "heavy weight of many a weary day / not mine, and such as it were not made for me. (l 18–22)"

There is romance here. And liberty as the poet is freed by the mnemic object's capacity to transport the self into a reexperiencing of a prior state of being. Wordsworth takes autobiography to its next evolutionary stage; it is to be an evocation of the former selves, called up into rebeing, a special act of mind, sustained by the structure of poetry.

Ninety years later Freud would move autobiography to a new place as he wrestled to analyze himself, an act never attempted in such rigorous terms before. "I am gripped and pulled through ancient times in quick association of thoughts," he wrote to Fliess on 27 October 1897, in terms not dissimilar to Wordsworth's account of being evoked by the imagery of his past.

Like Wordsworth, Freud had invented a particular form—in this case rigorous analysis of the dream and associations to it—to establish a new depth to the autobiographical idiom. Not just the past came rushing to him via the dream associations, but his sexual urges that had been repressed, his competitive tendencies, his rivalries and so forth. In short, in this place his drumming raised the person Sigmund from the tombs of repression to a live presence before his very eyes.

What Freud did with his own autoanalysis, however, is really quite curious, though well known to all of us by now. It was out of this internal dialogue that he enriched the psychoanalytical situation, as now the patient was to be the tormented inhabitant of such recollections, leaving Freud, or the doctor, to be the cool, dispassionate, deconstructor of its meanings. "My moods changed like the landscapes seen by a traveller from a train," he wrote to Fliess (27 October 1897) describing his self-analysis. Some years later, when telling his analysands how to free associate he would encourage them to pretend that they were in a train and to report to Freud the landscape that they saw in front of them.

Now prior to this, in the circuit of self-analysis, the train (the unconscious) and its passenger (consciousness) were both in Freud. If his train took him to new landscapes then he would try to sight them and report them, in phenomenological detail that metapsychologically would certainly have to assign to this landscape its status as the visual representation of the train's desire.

As long as Freud was both the train and the passenger he could, in the best of times, link the psychic representation (the landscape) with an inner movement that his ego train took, thus linking himself up, or retaining the link, between his urges, his affects, his thing presentations and his word presentations. But the moment he broke up the train service, he divided up affects, ideas, words, and images in a particular way, something he was (perhaps correctly) to see in his obsessional patients who did the same.

My point is, that what was gained in his self-analysis—as an evolution in the performance of autobiography—was lost in his splitting it up to form psychoanalysis: a failure from which we have, ironically enough, been the beneficiaries. This is not an occasion for apology, however, as, at the very least, Freud tried to share that autobiographical discovery with the other. Consciously or not he may well have relied upon Fliess as a transference figure, thus implicitly acknowledging the possibility of being the subject engaged in the process speaking to a dispassionate other who would, as it were, hear of it. That may have been the origin of the psychoanalytical division of labor. But if so, then Freud equally recognized, again perhaps unknowingly, that the auditory other (a Fliess) was a bit of a dummy, hardly instrumental, at an empathic interpretive level in the comprehension of Freud's trains of thought.

But did Fliess's position, then, form the basis of a naive listener, who from afar made his occasional interpretations such as they be? And although Freud's place as train driver, passenger, and witness was not present in the presentations to Fliess, did Freud give up this particular axis of the mental, affective, and memorial, to a distant, remote, and rather psychically removed psychoanalyst when he passed on this function to the person who would listen to the patient? In other words, did Freud pass on Fliess to the analytical community as the model of the psychoanalyst, a model of dissociated detachment, whilst retaining for himself the memoirs of the heart of the matter?

Certainly, by 1921 Ferenczi and Rank were alarmed by the type of technicians emerging in psychoanalysis who would practice this art from a position of extreme detachment. And at this time Freud removed himself from a certain conquistadorial enthusiasm to a growing pessimism about the therapeutic effectiveness of psychoanalysis, in sharp contrast to the years 1897–98, when through his self-analysis he drew true personal and visceral inspiration.

Is it not possible then that his pessimism drew in part from his personal crucifixion: he gave himself (his self-analysis) to mankind, so that men might, in part, benefit from the sacramental host, to be found in the ritual practice of psychoanalysis? Well, who knows.

The point is, Freud disowned a very particular form of representation, drawn from a long history in Western culture, but unique to himself. He could speak to himself, but at the same time the voice that spoke back constantly undermined the rationalist enquirer, who found the premises of his prior resolutions ultimately usurped by a new series of unconscious expressions. We may certainly ask ourselves what was the original Freudian analysis, referring now to that circuit of ideas that moved in his self-analysis. To pose this question, in light of the limitation of time, is daunting and mildly insulting to that integrity of effort undertaken by Freud, but ask it in a limited way I shall.

To begin with he lives in a personal context—the near death of his father, his complex relation with Fliess, an increasing delibidinalized relation to a woman he loves—that is background to a personal crisis. These are the aleatory movements of events, each of which is charged with evocative potential. From this environment come his dreams, which take him everywhere: back to his childhood, to scenes of contemporary professional life, to Rome—the city of imagined but thwarted desires—in other words, to the world of Freud's former and present selves, all disturbed by his present context. As always the dream performs its ahistorical mixture function: it will bring it together. It is left to the awakened dreamer to decide upon its value as a source of self-questioning, but Freud allowed the dream this place, and, over time he both licensed its voice and added his own associations, to which he brought his reasoned effort to make sense of it all.

The sheer power of this self-evocation—or should I say its vulnerability—is almost fearsome. Freud took the autobiographical venture certainly to its limits: after all, he could only just bear it. Fliess, of course, though a "classical analyst" minimalist—who did not interpret, but only ever listened, did help, but the capacity to live in the place of continuous self-evocation through the dream, seemed too much to bear. The task was then split: the patient would bear the dream and Freud would, from a considerable distance, listen to it and make his interpretations. He was no Fliess of course. But his occupation of Fliess's place, that location Fliess originally held in relation to Freud, he now transferred to the practicing analyst. This split has been maintained for over one hundred years now in the practice of psychoanalysis and even though the division of analytical labor has been an essential step in the practice of psychoanalysis, it has nonetheless been a flight from the stringencies of self-analysis. Indeed, Freud's increasingly dispassionate invocation to the patient to be the object of a surgical calm on the Freudian part suggests that by 1926 he had moved a very long way from this impassioned participation in the power of the unconscious to unseat the sanest of minds.

Nonetheless, a unique splitting of the autobiographical, or self-analytical, act was achieved by Freud who now insisted that the bearer of memory, instinct, pain, and trauma, be the patient—leaving the analyst free to think about these matters from an unbiased (that is mentally

unmoved) place. But as time would tell, the patient's transference intentions seemed to be aimed at forcing this dispassionate observer into a less
than objective place, indeed, slightly back to the heart of the patient's
inner turmoil. Initially this appeared as a form of transference love which
may well have been the analysand's effort to love this distant figure back
into involvement. Freud viewed it as a resistance to his split-off function,
but we may wonder if it was the patient's effort to undo the split and to
force the analyst back into a union of minds, affects, and associations that
Freud abandoned with his renunciation of self-analysis.

The psychoanalytical literature is replete with articles which argue that
the patient's courtly love bears an aggressive demand that the analyst not
only feel the analysand's love, but that even if he will not return it, he
nonetheless empathize with it. By now, however, the patient had become
the object of Freud's intensive study, out of which he constructed his
metapsychology and his clinical theory. Theorizing, then, the Freudian
blank page became a third object in the analytical situation, one to which
Freud increasingly would refer himself for dispassionate life. His curiosity, his wish to know what was true, had taken him like Faust into
troubled waters, a reason perhaps why he quoted Goethe in the letter of
October 27:

> And the shades of loved ones appear;
> With them, like an old,
> Half-forgotten myth,
> First love and friendship.

Freud's self-analysis had taken him to a place of "fright and discord." He
wrote: "Many a sad secret of life is here followed back to its first roots;
many a pride and privilege are made aware of their humble origins." He
well understood, now, what it is like to occupy the place of the analysand:
"All of what I experience with my patients, as a third [person] I find again
here," referring to the pain of self-analysis.

To achieve the *classical place,* of dispassionate living and of scientific
study, is respite indeed from the place of pain and suffering. As I have
suggested, however, Freud never really allowed himself to study the true
implications of a patient's transference, precisely because he had disowned
that experience of psychic pain that any emotional participant (including
the psychoanalyst) feels in the analytical location. Transference was at first
a resistance to the semiautonomous function of psychoanalysis, or later, it

was the force of a repetition of early childhood scenes which were placed on to the figure of the doctor, scenes which were fairly coherent and could be reconstructed and referred back to childhood.

Is it possible that those transferences that got under his skin, that compelled him to psychic pain, were ascribed to the dark forces of the death instinct? Indeed, how many analysts to this day, who refuse to be emotionally and psychologically aroused by the patient's transferences, unknowingly attribute this refusal to dark forces acting in the patient?

In any event, evenly hovering attentiveness, neutrality, and benign remove have become the standards of analytical presence in the analytical situation, and though I shall not review them here, I think it fair to say that such positions are indeed essential to the psychoanalytical process which partly rests on the analysand's freedom to speak to the analyst without fear of the clinician encroaching on this privilege with his own prejudices, passing points of view, or wild interpretations.

There are moments in the analysis of most individuals, however, that call upon a different analytical disposition than the classical one, and these occur when the patient "speaks" to the analyst through the moods, images, self-states, and ideas that are called up in the analyst. This, the countertransference, is an effect of transference actions on the patient's part which, amongst other things, cause distress to the analyst. In the early years of psychoanalysis, this countertransference was objectified by the clinician as an obstruction to the task of analysis, as it prevented the analyst from listening with evenly hovering attentiveness, so it had to be either privately self-analyzed or overcome (presumably by invocation of a powerful psychoanalytical superego) so that the analyst could resume his special place. In time, however, many psychoanalysts—particularly those in the British school of psychoanalysis—understood, indeed valued, the movement of feelings, ideas, and self-states evoked by patients as a valuable source of information conveyed by the analysand.

The analyst came to regard himself as a kind of "host" for the psychic inhabitation of different parts of the patient—some unwanted, some valued—which were projectively identified into the analyst. If the analyst, for example, found that he entertained a harsh view of the analysand, he would mull this over internally, and when appropriate indicate how a patient was aiming to put the harsh, disapproving parts of the patient's self into the analyst, as it was too unbearable to bear themselves. If we imagine a patient describing promiscuous relations with lovers, and who is then cast aside, a narrative not characterized by any self-reproach, the analyst might come to feel reproach within himself and the analytical task might then be to point out to the patient how unbearable it must feel to harbor reproachful feelings and how, therefore, the patient was aiming to instill such feelings in the analyst.

With the introduction of this concept of the relation between transference and countertransference, an important if hazardous move was accomplished in the psychoanalytical theory of representation. Heretofore unconscious representations were to be found in the movement of signifiers that bore through word representations the logic of unconscious ideas. Crucial words would contain "inscriptions" of events that wrote themselves into the symbolic order. A patient has a rat phobia and seeks analysis to overcome her near debilitating fear of this loathsome object. The analyst discovers that the patient first obtained this fear as a child lying in bed listening to the sound of rats scurrying about in the attic. Later, when discovering the interesting if puzzling behavior of her mother, she described her as "erratic," thus attributing this symbolism to the word "rat," by signifying its historical link to its place of origin "atic," but ultimately representing the fear of the mother's behavior.

Unconscious representations were also to be found in the ego's moves to negotiate its relations to the id and the superego, so, by watching the ego's state (its impulses, its despairs, its rigidities, etc.) the analyst could speak to it like addressing a beleaguered hero on a pilgrim's progress toward adaptation, thus modestly helping this hero to follow the paths of sane judgment toward the good enough life of which he was capable.

Psychoanalysts also regarded affects, defense constellations, actings out, repetitions, and linguistic idioms as further forms of representing the unconscious, and each of these forms is well considered within the psychoanalytical literature.

The theory of the patient's transference communication and its corresponding effect upon the psychoanalyst brings us to a new, and I should say, radical view of human representation. For this theory argues that significant psychic parts of one person are unconsciously passed into another person who is now in possession of them. This theory is, of course, not entirely free of precedent. The Old Testament describes how God spoke inside the body and mind of the other, who would have a special capacity to hear from this most effective voice. The hallucinating hysterics of the Middle Ages heard the voice of the devil speak in their ears and by the nineteenth-century salons were cropping up in which imposing female spiritualists acted as mediums for the voice of the departed. This is hardly an epistemology from which practitioners of transference and countertransference theory can take heart; indeed, it is rather worrying. Is the analyst imagining the entire representation?

Let us return to Freud, at least for a moment's safety, and for recovery. I have argued that Freud's self-analysis, built around the arrival of dreams usually sponsored by events from the day before, constituted a unique and important step in the autobiographical form, a slight move beyond a Wordsworth because Freud's sexual strivings, murderous impulses, and selfish preoccupations were presenting themselves to him, in a shocking but intriguing manner, because through free association and his theory of the unconscious (particularly of the chain of word presentations) he know he had founded a new form for being addressed by the self and therein had advanced the course of human understanding.

However, by splitting this unique person discovery into a two-person relation—which benefited the neurotic—Freud abandoned full recognition of the value of what Hannah Arendt terms "the two in one dialogue." In psychoanalysis, what happened to that internal dialogue that seemed both to evoke prior selves and urges and to emotionally inform the interpreting subject with a full range of essential information crucial to a good interpretation? By converting the two in one into one in two, Freud seemed to divest psychoanalysis of its very soul.

This is why I regard the revival of interest in the countertransference as such an important part of the psychoanalytic movement, because ultimately, it is an act which restores the heart of the matter, in that the analyst who receives the transferences willingly, and who quietly notes the many moods, self states, wild ideas, credible theories, and so on, that occur inside him, is gradually, then, coming to *the place* of two in one— in one shared "psyche"—where the analyst will feel the pain of joy, experience the confusion of fast moving ideas, or the doldrums of mental inertness.

Much has been written about the necessity of at least a theoretical blank screen upon which the patient projects, or of an evenly hovering attentiveness valued precisely because transference acts punctuate and disturb this evenness, so we need to value the classical attitude as a crucial basis for analytical listening, just as Freud needed Fliess who knew little. Gradually, however, the analyst feels himself mentally occupied by the patient's associations, moved to different self-states by the analysand's transference actions, and sometimes this shaping of oneself by the patient makes the sort of sense that lends itself to interpretation. A patient who acted out repeatedly brought out in my internal self-state a type of worry, as I assumed that all the misdeeds committed at the hospital were his fault. As the patient was talking about how his mother was always intruding into his space with her worries about him, I could use these two sets of data (his report and my inner state) to say that I thought he was unconsciously aiming to bring out in me the worrying mother whom he now enjoyed teasing and controlling by his actings-out. Another patient, who began the analysis as a very engaging and reflective participant soon had a love affair which absorbed all of his energy. The analysis caused self-reflection, and in my countertransference I first felt angry at this loss of analytical rapport and work and then, over time, I felt rather superfluous. In a few months he told me that as a small child his mother deserted him by passing him to the nanny and she totally withdrew from him, leaving him feeling full of hate toward her and deadened by it. Using his narrative account of his life history and my countertransference, I could now point out how his actings out showed me what it was like to have an alive beginning followed by a sudden abrupt absence and a determined refusal to remain alive to a relationship.

Such moments are not so frequent as to be everyday in an analysis; indeed, they are more like epiphanies which emerge out of a kind of two-in-one moment, when both patient and analyst are speaking and experiencing the same phenomenon. These episodes are notable, however, because the patient is usually narrating life events or historical scenes in a dispassionate way whilst the analyst is feeling them, often in a most intensive manner. What a curious reversal this is of the classical model, built as it is around the patient's passion and the analyst's dispassion!

Nonetheless, such two-in-one moments constitute important psychic occasions when the analyst brings to the analytical encounter—and therefore back to the patient's psyche—split-off portions of the analysand's scenes or objects.

But what about the long periods in between these epiphanies? This is the heart of my essay which I have deferred until now.

Freud's self-analysis, like Wordsworth's evocative relivings and Augustine's reflective rememberings, is an act of intelligence, living in a place of constantly used, hence familiar, solitude. I speak of man's inevitable relations to and with himself in that two-in-one dialogue. To be sure, this inner speech is unreproducible if for no other reason than, as Vygotski claims, such inner speech is a condensation of elements not speakable. Perhaps if we could utter speech, music, visual imagery, mood movements, and so on, in one simultaneous moment we could represent this inner dialogue. We know this, however, to be an impossibility.

So we may sympathize with Freud who tried to represent this inner happening, and we can see how the dream, with its somewhat neat story content, lent itself to representations whilst the opera of inner speech is so beyond telling. So too, however, must we extend our compassion to the working psychoanalyst, who, I shall argue, is there working with his patient in a place exceptionally similar to the space occupied by Freud once he undertook to hear his voices speak.

When I meet a new patient I see a stranger. Usually I know nothing of him. In the seconds following my first shake of his hand I nonetheless gain my first impression. It is there inside me. A representation of this person who stands before me. To spare us the exhaustive list of evidential registrations (i.e., clothing worn, facial expression, body gait, etc.), I simply say that each person has his or her idiom and that "it" begins to impress me right from the beginning.

So what do I do with these gradually unfolding impressions? I have no Fliess, although there is my notebook in which, now and then, I write to some "other." But as with Freud's relation to Sigmund, so too with each analyst's relation to his own patient, this is to be a relationship incrementally unfolding fundamentally inside the psychoanalyst. Our technique correctly insists that we remain silent, allowing the analysand to maintain unintruded the momentum of free associations. Their silences are usually not resistances, but "shifters" to their deeper levels of self speaking, and they use silence for its ballast and support. All this while, however, in a place elsewhere, this patient is forming a world inside his analyst, a world largely kept to the self, yet essential for the analyst to know, if he is to be of help to the analysand.

As the analysand presents fragments of his life history, endless cameo shots of the mother, the father, brothers, and sisters, episodes from his present-day life, dream after dream after dream, layers of subtle silence upon layers of silence, I find that a condensation of these stories, pictures, abstractions, and so forth, builds up inside me to form a very particular ongoing object: the patient in me.

In a manner akin to Freud's attempt to analyze his dreams, in order to liberate himself from psychic pain and to find sufficient truth around which to live, I think at certain points I form interpretations to process this internal object—this patient—partly to be relieved of the pain caused by their confusion in myself. However, my custom is to keep this inner object and my struggle with it to myself, remaining silent as my patient occupies the analytical space. I wish to stress the singular solitude of the analyst's work, of his private struggle with his patient's internal objects and their evocative capacity. I think back to a particularly distressed patient who possessed the gift of a remarkable narrative ability. He could and did describe his father's personality in painstaking detail. In an attempt to fulfill my analytical obligation, I struggled internally to see this father as a metaphor of unwanted parts of my patient. When I interpreted this to the analysand, linking it to my view of this transference to myself, I felt marginally relieved. But the accounts of the father's incredible small-mindedness continued, in contrast to my patient, who shared with me some strange relief in thinking of his descriptions as a metaphor of his own internal world. It was as if we were both asserting the omniscience of projection, despite the force of a reality well beyond our control. The memories continued. One night I dreamed of my patient's father. It was a "good" dream. He corresponded to my theory of him as a good man, abused by my patient. Then in the closing frames of the dream I saw what looked like a wrinkle under his chin, a crease, which upon further inspection I knew to be a mask. When I saw my patient the next day, my "attitude" toward his father had changed. I no longer attempted to see the father as a container, a projection, as I just listened and mulled over my patient's memories. These recollections took me into the family home, to their kitchen with its small cooker and refrigerator barely able to contain a daily meal, to the somber living room with its gas fire heater to warm the place at precisely specified hours, to the toolroom where the father worked to fix objects in the house, allowing the son to watch but never to touch the objects.

This is not meant to be a case illustration. It is only given to represent some sense of what it is like to live as a psychoanalyst, to inhabit a patients' world, to be carried by his narrations into his life.

A patient tells me a dream in which he travels by bus to the seaside. He glimpses the blue sea and is momentarily elated, but is lost in a crowd of people. He walks along a hillside and a bottle rolls down the embankment, breaks, and fragments of glass pierce his skin. He has been in analysis for five years and as he tells me this dream I am there as a participant. I ride the bus. I glimpse the sea. I feel the annoyance of the crowd, but when the bottle rolls down the hill, although I "see" it, I associate: "just as he is about to reach the sea (i.e., to see) he loses his bottle (English slang for the loss of courage.)" The patient is as usual silent, awaiting the chain of ideas that emerge. I am carried back in my mind to a dream he reported some four years before, when he walked down a boat slip near a childhood holiday resort and saw the sea that graced his childhood: a sea of simplicity. The patient's associations are to his recent journey abroad, its crowded city, and to an abscess on his leg. He is quiet. I ask, "And the bottle?" He replies, "Nothing really, only a sense of its breaking up." "To lose one's bottle?" "You mean to lose one's courage?" A long pause. I say, "It brings to my mind your recent journey across the sea where I think you have high hopes of business success. The sea is wonderful because it has no obstacles on it; you can see as far as you like, but you must deal with the crowds of businessmen before you can reach such a place and I think you are afraid you will lose the courage necessary to cope."

The correctness or not of this interpretation is immaterial to my essay here. Each of my patient's dreams become my dream. They arise in me, each time a novelty even though conveyed in its unmistakable fictive form, and so I am, in some respects, in the place of the dreamer who is dreamt by it. The telling of it moves me from place to place, through adventures, to the bizarre, and each step of the way it evokes associations within me. Occasionally it is the affective register as I am moved like a cinemagoer at a "Hollywood" film. Sometimes the visual order is so compelling that I simply travel on an internal train through marvelous landscapes. At times the density of plotting pushes me back to a more literary remove as I concentrate intensely, aiming to remember the characters, their actions, the strange twist of events. Always I am tapped by Lacan's wand, as a clear word presentation pops out of the imagery to its place as subtitle formation, and there it rests until joined by another signifier that begins to speak its meaning within the symbolic order. Often I wander back to previous dreams that seem evoked by present dreams, wondering why the dreamer returns to the same landscape, wondering what he now chooses to do there.

Here I am, then, with my patient, who takes me from the social surfaces of his life to the puzzling yet moving depths of his dream, who presents again and again like now familiar cinema heros (or baddies) his father and his mother, who transports me through the subtly graded time zones of his past, as I attend his school with him, play on the cricket field, join in his erotic experiences, bear the breakdown of his marriage.

Each session is like a fifty-minute evocation. Somewhere between dream and reality, and yet distinctively characteristic; each patient's idiom is such that living through his life is to live myself in new places, with new objects, calling me to my "other" lives.

This is the life of the psychoanalyst. It is where we live. And our comments are a minute fraction of our total experience, which is the object of this study. For I shall say that it is in *this place* of solitude and surprise, that we sit in Freud's chair as he analyzed himself. For that is exactly what we do, all the time, day in and day out, as a precondition for our comments and whatever theories we develop about mankind. In the Wordsworthian sense we travel a sometimes "pleasant loitering journey," but one often densely exacting of one's self-exploration ("When, as becomes a man who would prepare / for such a glorious work, I through myself / make rigorous inquisition"), as the place we occupy as an analyst, like that of the poet, is an evocative one, where memories seem to come to us with urgent claims. When I recall patients' dreams, former sessions, or "see" the mother or father, I feel I am called to a place of intense work and responsibility. As Wordsworth expressed it:

> Dust as we are, the immortal spirit grows
> Like harmony in music; there is dark
> Inscrutable workmanship that reconciles
> Discordant elements, makes them cling together
> In one society (23)

But if there is this ego aesthetic (Bollas 1987) that inspires us to intensely meaningful condensations of the discordant elements of a life, a place I occupy with my patients at my work, traveling through categories (affects, things, presentations, word presentations)and time (spans of the analysand's life), there is the unheralded Freud-chair—of Christopher Bollas at Mount View Road—where the associations that come to mind (and some to body) are often those of "fright and discord," although like Freud I could say that there are also "days when I drag myself about dejected because I have understood nothing of the dream, of the fantasy, of the mood of the day" (October 27) conveyed by my patient.

So too there is a British chair, carved by Melanie Klein and W. Fairbairn, warmed to familiarity by Winnicott, when I am not simply unconsciously moved, as in the Freudian chair, but subtly molded into being other than myself, into being an unwanted part of my patient's mind that I now feel to be my mind or into feeling myself the particular mother of my patient coming now into being, not simply listening to stories about her.

These occupations, places of the inhabitation of the self, are the seats of the psychoanalyst who, in the quiet of his room, is engaged in an often intense self-analytical enterprise. The outcome may be simply sustained silence, or an association, or an interpretation, but such analytical acts are mere derivatives of an intense internal process of being moved, shaken, bewildered, bored to near narcoleptic inertness, puzzled by the word: in short, put through the first Freudian place, that of self-analysis.

If we think that our patients are ignorant of this our personal struggle, we not only do them a disservice, we discredit our understanding of the unconscious. But I find that, except for the occasional enquiry (i.e., "What are you thinking?"), my patients leave me to my psychoanalytical chair and the task of analyzing myself as I live through, am evoked by, and inhabited by their childhoods and their personal idioms. They will only rarely know where I have been, and so it should be: my gift, as is any psychoanalyst's, is my silence which supports the verbal priority of the analysand, and also ensures the boundary of my own privacy essential to the task of sustaining the patient and myself through this long process.

This tacit understanding on the psychoanalyst's part of the function of solitude and the two-in-one dialogue for the analyst is not properly subsumed under the title of object relations theory. It is a form, instead, of subject relations, by which I mean a dynamic mutuality of intereffective solitudes, in which one moves the other, in turn to be the object of evocation, the essence of which dialectic is to sponsor deep private internal states that are, again privately and slowly, partly worked into a limited but shared discourse. I wish to stress, however, that subject relations is part of the heart of our lived lives, as in all of our intimate relations, as we turn the other into ourself, hence to a representational place where representer and receiver become one and the same: two in one.

Our brief comments, our jokes, our gestural affections signify to our friends that we live in a place of no representation, but sad as this loss of communicative reserve might be, we each live life under the same terms, and subject relations respects this privacy of our being, whilst object relations optimizes the derivative possibility of the play of subjectivities that have found an intermediate area for a limited dialectic.

Finally, just as all psychoanalysts sit in an undistinguished Freudian chair, traveling in their trains to nowhere, they embody and personify for the analysand that generativity intrinsic to the two-in-one dialogue, which they know drives their analyst's attentive presence, and this secret work they too take with them upon leaving the analytic space, after their "spot in time" as object of the generative Freudian split.

SELECTED REFERENCES

Abrams. M. H. 1971. *Natural supernaturalisn*. New York: Norton.

Bollas, Christopher. 1987. *The shadow of the object*. London: Free Association.

Ferenczi, Sandor, and Rank, Otto. [1922] 1986. *The Development of Psychoanalysis*. Madison, Wis.: International Universities Press.

Freud, Sigmund. 1985. *The complete letters of Sigmund Freud to Wilhelm Fliess, 1887–1904*. Cambridge, Mass.: Harvard University Press.

Olney, James. 1980. *Autobiography*. Princeton: Princeton University Press.

Wigglesworth, Michael. 1965. *The diary of Michael Wigglesworth, 1653–1657*. New York: Harper & Row.

Wordsworth, William. [1850] 1968. *The prelude*. Oxford: Oxford University Press.

11

Memory and Narration in Clinical Psychoanalysis

Anna Maria Galdo

Whenever we start writing a new paper or undertaking new research we try to be backed by the thought of other authors. We feel that we move within ambiguous dimensions, the boundaries and antecedents of which escape us, while we are captured by projects and configurations that may even seem hostile and unstructured: as if we were afraid not to be able to keep a dual representation or to lose the relationship of the self with oneself. Donald Meltzer (1984) reminds us that it is difficult to penetrate into our innermost imaginative thinking without making inroads into other people's imaginative world and thinking.

The support or the criticism of an interlocutor seems indispensable to us in order to maintain the permanence of what we mean to say. Our assumptions open up new perspectives that by their endless interactions foreshadow such a complexity and such a mutable and piecemeal scenario, that we may possibly be induced to give up. It looks as if we were spellbound but also at the same time wanting to escape; nevertheless, on that particular occasion there is a precise possibility to approach and describe a reality that cannot be circumscribed by the boundaries of images, but acquires its natural extension thanks to words. Bion calls this state "the uncertainty cloud" and compares it to Pirandello's play *Six characters in search of an author,*[1] as in a cluster, fragments of a potential thought encircle and surround an emotional experience.

This introduction, characterized by a doubtlessly subjective tone, intends to exemplify by way of analogy a situation analysts respond to in their daily work. It also aims to introduce the dynamics of the analytical relationship which is buttressed by the validity of a method still capable of further developments.

The analytical situation is, as we all know, a twosome situation, of interchange between two subjects who within the "relation" turn into temporary and partial loci of resistance and otherness (De Renzis 1987). Thanks to a constant dialogue, our mind's functions become better defined by their representation of themselves and bestow a sense on the analytical relationship.

Exposed to emotional vicissitudes, we are traversed by new productions that cannot be easily or painlessly integrated into our previous convictions. Furthermore, in the analytical relation it is not possible, if we consider it as a single dynamic field, to ascribe to the analyst or to the patient separately the transformations of significant elements, even though individually each of them defines and distinguishes the transformations.

From a more abstract viewpoint, we may consider such a relationship as a systemic unit, sustained by an invariance of the basic organization, that is, of the relations between parts. Nevertheless, this relationship is subject to a continuous destabilization of its "dynamic equilibrium" (Cargnelutti and Muratori 1988), that is, open to alterations of its structures which are all linked relationally in an amalgam of dreams, memories, narrations. As in an oneiric functioning of "dream life," emotions and meanings gather in internal spaces to be modified in a circular reciprocity and in a continuous process of multiple images and reinscriptions.

Unconscious phantasies are particular thinking processes, from which meanings originate. In *Leonardo da Vinci*, Freud wrote: "This is often the way in which childhood memories originate. Quite unlike conscious memories from the time of maturity, they are not fixed at the moment of being experienced and afterward repeated, but are only elicited at a later age when childhood is already past; in the process they are altered and falsified, and are put into the service of later trends, so that generally speaking they cannot be sharply distinguished from the phantasies" (Freud 1910, 83). Therefore "resignification" processes are marked by temporalities that are different from the linear ones. Both the present and the past would bear the stamp of propulsive wishes or disappointments, the explicit meanings of which are not the deepest ones, since their deep sense is enveloped by the unconscious and curled by "a posteriori" trends. So our remembered times or more simply our memories, albeit marked by discontinuity, underlie syncretic logic and a continuity typical of the unconscious. In the passage quoted above, Freud stresses that the conscious memories of maturity are a different thing. Since he wanted to identify in the memory an area in which unconscious interferences diminish, he hypothesized a system that takes note of all the data coming from the outer reality, periodically explored by the conscious activity of attention (1911). Nevertheless, we may say that his model of memory is characterized by the close connection between memory and the unconscious: in 1900 he writes that our memories, including the most deeply impressed ones, are unconscious.

Melanie Klein (1957) speaks of a memory of emotions, a primary memory that links phantasies and proverbial images having their own symbolization modalities. In fact, being emotions, they keep their specific force as signals and emerge again as such in the analysis[2] with puzzling modalities that are refractory to speech, and with unpredictable breakaways from ordinary patterns. Remembering is not equal to reproducing, but rather to experiencing that particular emotional relation that memory interprets and comments upon. In remembering we miss the virtual coexistence of present and past, by which an old context cannot be separated from the present emotion, and differences and repetitions in the end oppose each other only apparently. On the contrary, there is a true antagonism and complementariness between active and contemplative life, the potentialities of which are unfurled just by memory.

In *Reflection, Repetition and Working Through* 1914 Freud places great emphasis on the strife between these two ways of being and specifies that acting is a way of remembering under the influence of the compulsion to repeat. He then adds:

> The first step in overcoming the resistance is made, as we know, by the analyst's discovering the resistance, which is never recognized by the patient, and acquainting him with it. . . . From the repetition-reactions which are exhibited in transference the familiar paths lead back to the awakening of memories, which yield themselves without difficulty after the resistances have been overcome. (153–54)

In fact action, being a direct energetic discharge, interrupts or slows down the working through processes. Only through a complex working out can new associative connections and repressed meanings emerge. Nevertheless we may equally maintain that the more the sense of an action preserves its original proximity with the body the more its communicative relevance becomes effective (Mathieu 1980); in the same way we also know that in the place of a repressed word a perturbing act may arise.[3]

There are intensely repeated memories that look like split and incongruous acts. They remain unaltered, out of any circularity, we may consider them as strongly resistive points, as signals of traumatic events that should have been forgotten.[4] They are images that, albeit linked to a suffering and motionless discontinuity, still try, by the repetition of memory, to meet the inalienable demand for continuity.

Resistances in analysis must necessarily be considered as resistances in the relational area too, as unconscious collusions sustained by projective and crossed identifications that tend to immobilize the dynamics of the patient-analyst relation.[5] From a different angle, on the contrary, some of these resistances may be considered as points of invariance indispensable for supporting the system organization. In the same way the heterogeneity of the essential characters, preserved and expressed in different languages, such as the verbal and emotional bodily language, is also essential to the mind's activity. There exists a multiplicity of levels, expressed by verbal language in the plurality of its meanings. The variety of codes in any semiotic system has a common origin in the early organization of the experienced and phantasied body. Nevertheless, as Didier Anzieu points out, the order of language, always subject to strict and stringent laws, is not the order of nature, let alone that of phantasy.[6] Language is a code that transcends the individual even though those who speak it transform it according to their own perspective (Anzieu 1980). Thanks to these personal modulations in analysis we are able to approach different functional levels.

If the use of the word requires compliance with a regulating order, only by way of a subjective style can we take an individual position in the discourse. In fact style[7] is the modality by which we try to recreate the functional space for a personalized communication which at the same time contains an optimum distance and allows us to be understood (Anzieu 1980). Word must foster an intermediate area where the intimate emotional experience can pass and be turned into a communicative experience. But we are often caught by a double antagonistic movement: the desire to let us be understood complying with an agreed code and the narcissistic need to remain impenetrable (Galdo 1985). So most of the material that the patient brings to us in analysis remains hardly decipherable and not only due to the incomplete and uncertain nature of memories. Freud (1914) noticed that it often happens that something is not remembered "which never could have been forgotten because it was never at any time noticed as conscious" (149), so it cannot be recalled; having been experienced without being understood, it has been realized and interpreted a posteriori only. There are voids of meaning that can be taken up only by paying special attention to transference and to the compulsion to repeat. In fact, from specific movements in the transference it is possible to infer clues that reveal dynamics of the patient's inner world and object relations. Nevertheless, in this reconstruction of events which has anyhow the character of a narrative performance, by which verbal expression is given to an entanglement of timing and emotional experiences, the unity and consistency that characterize the unfolding of narration are never achieved. Francis Pasche (1988) writes on this subject: "Our individual stories are so full of contingencies, regression, stagnations, conflicts that they make me really doubt the truth of a coherent presentation of our reconstructions" (23).

Certainly through the analysis of his own projection, phantasies, and defense mechanisms, the patient rediscovers his reality and, along with extremely troublesome voids, partly rediscovers his own past. The analyst accompanies him or her in this research, but the story and the reconstructions[8] that are formulated did not exist before the analytical relation and discourse; they are obtained by dislocating logic and meanings that marked out safer horizons in a presumed completeness. Our statements stand out on perpetually changing backgrounds that reveal or conceal them under precipitating images and emotions.

The interpretive moment is for the analyst the moment of maximum distinction. His interpretations certainly provide confirmations of the identity and of the individualized structures of each member of the couple. At the same time they are also an expression of the analyst's direct participation in and maximum commitment to clarifying the emotional quality and meaning of the analytical tie. Furthermore, the interpretation is almost always punctual, and even though it fits into a *hic et nunc,* it addresses at the same time the defenses and resistances structured by the patient to deny or to cope with past traumatic events. So in repetitions, psychic knots tied up with stories of several traumatic events come to the surface again. In their treading the paths of inner conflicts, the contents of interpretations and psychoanalytical reconstructions are based on the possibility of keeping intensely experienced events at a distance. Making a story implies the capacity to look at the event and to feel at ease in remaining detached from it. Bion thinks it is fundamental to evolve from the "learning-from-experience" matrix to the "learning-around-an-experience" matrix,[9] thus developing the capacity to work out symbolic languages and to make use of abstractive resignification and reflection processes. Such a trend prevents the accumulation of information and finds its representation in a structural change by which the search for the object is felt as a need for a "similar" image. The peculiar characters of these dynamics are a permanent expectation for new comprehensions and an openness to newly emerging meanings, typical of transformative and ever-changing dynamics. The transformations we mainly address are those which in a verbal inscription render unconscious phantasies accessible to the levels of conscience. Serge Viederman (1979) writes that archaic experiences possess no structure. It is the discourse that provides a de-nomination, unifies them, and makes them concrete in a totally original fashion, inducing into the analytical space a "semantic halo" that will evoke contents of emotional and narrative truth. So the narrative tradition, with its needs for continuity, consistency, and completeness, comes into play as soon as the patient speaks and the analyst understands. But if we acknowledge that in order to understand we need a context, in analysis this does not mean, as Loch argued (1977), that the context is organized "to build truth put at the service of the coherence of the Self for the present and the future on the basis of a mutual agreement" (238), nor does it mean that "the missing ring in the complex picture of events will tend to be kept in place by the general framework or, vice versa, will serve to hold together the whole picture" (Loch 1977, 245).

Freud (1937), with regard to the reconstruction work in analysis and the archaeological model, states that, if we have a right to reconstruct by means of integrations and recompositions, such constructions, for analysis, are nothing but preliminary work. Preliminary in the sense that each piece of the construction will produce its effects on the analysand and only from the newly emerging material will it be possible to proceed further. Nonetheless, in the discourse names organize, classify, change, and control affects; the narrative context possesses its own formal structure and coherence, for exhaustiveness and exactness criteria must be met somehow. An excessive richness of meanings may render the discourse less incisive and hamper comprehension.

A story is based upon the planning capacities of thought; events are temporalized and ordered; memories are made understandable in such temporally distinct areas as the past and the future; discontinuities emerge where irreconcilable continuities should arise. But all these constructions are incomplete even though huge truthful contents are evoked by sometimes metaphorical and oblique expressions.

Analytical reconstructions, as Deleuze (1964) points out for signs differentiating them from the sense, cannot be developed or explained without a symbolical response, without intersecting each other, without forming complex combinations that constitute the system of truth. In analysis such complex combinations are the knots of ambivalence, splitting, and perplexity through which the anxieties of fundamental conflicts—signs of a system of truth—manifest themselves. Spence (1982), who nevertheless argues that narrative truth per se has a significant impact upon the clinical process, reminds that it would not hold if all the fragments of narration were invented, that is to say, if the historical truth amounted to zero.

Our emotions are always intertwined and it is not possible to satisfy them separately; by the same token they are all subject to their own negative qualities. At the levels of passion, of desire, and concern for knowledge, pleasure and pain are always inextricably intertwined. Consistency is only one possibility in life, and the universe of words is the attempt to establish a relation among its infinite potentialities. Freud (1909) insists that the "phantastic covering" of analytical stories be unravelled "thread by thread." Deconstruction forms an integral part of his method: the threads that weave emotion must be loosened and recovered one after the other in order to be tied up again in a different pattern, reconstructed by the same materials, and nevertheless apparently characterized by a latency, a sort of possibility of meaning inscribed in the basic text (Lavagetto 1985).

This possibility of meaning is by its very nature an interminable process because it proceeds by repressions, repetitions, and the return of the repressed. And the accepted sense—the preliminary construction—has its own explanation provided by an explicative theory and by a relationship among laws that allow it to highlight otherwise hidden connections (Hempel 1962). In *Moses and Monotheism,* Freud stresses that he is ready

to use each individual possibility offered to him by the material as a
point of support to fill gaps and affirms he will give preference to those
assumptions that can be considered as having the maximum verisimilitude. But he adds also:

> The greater the importance of the views arrived at this way, the more
> strongly one feels the need to beware of exposing them with a secure basis
> to the critical assaults of the world around one . . . not even the most
> tempting probability is a protection against error; even of all parts of
> problem seem to fit together like the pieces of a jigsaw puzzle, one must
> reflect that what is probable is not necessarily the truth and that the truth is
> not always probable. (1938, 17)

NOTES

1. See D. Meltzer, "Dream Life."
2. S. C. Soavi in "Are Emotions Thoughts?" writes: "Emotions cut out a specific
   area within the organization of experience that outstrips and differs from the
   area covered by other symbolization modalities. Such area is particularly evident in mystical, cosmic and fusion experience, but it also manifests itself at an
   everyday level relating to the experiences of ties as Heiman points out" ("On
   countertransference," *Int. J. Psycho-Anal.* 32 [1950]: 81–84).
3. Cargnelutti and Muratori (1988) write that we must suppose that unconscious
   communication, as well as communicative interchange at the conscious level,
   retains its informative potentiality even by destructuring and disorganizing,
   for the purpose of redelivering the system.
4. In 1895 Freud expresses that the traumatic moment comes when the ego finds
   itself confronted with the contradiction and denies it.
5. M. and W. Baranger define such areas of resistance in the analytical field as
   "ramparts" that oppose the working-out process (M. and W. Baranger, "Process and Nonprocess in Analysis," *Int. J. Psycho-Anal.* [1983]: 1–16).
6. Anzieu (1980) also says that each of these productions constitutes a distinct
   reality with its own laws, and such realities can be completely dissociated, as
   we find in some pathological cases, or can concur to the same plan.
7. It can be interesting to quote from the headword "Method" (Gilles and Gaston
   Granger, *Enciclopedia Einaudi* [1980]): "We won't say then anymore that it is
   a question of method but rather of *style*, in the sense that a style, speaking in
   very general terms, is the organization and the performance of what, in individual experience, escapes the network woven by concepts to grasp the generic
   fact by a method. A posteriori we can certainly describe style as a *strategy*, but
   there can be no recipe for such a description" (251).
8. I choose the expression "reconstruction" rather than "construction" because
   the transformations of psychic structures are included into an invariant equilib-

rium of the system organization. Furthermore, on the basis of Aristotle's distinction between praxis and poiesis (in *Metaphysics*), I agree with F. Pasche who considers the analytical relationship as the meeting of two praxes, that is, two actions having no other purpose than that of perfecting the "agents." Construction would be instead the equivalent of poiesis, that is, an action upon the world in the attempt to create a work external to the agent.

9. See D. Meltzer in *The Apprehension of Beauty* (London: Lunie Press, 1988).

REFERENCES

Anzieu, D., ed. 1980. *Psychanalyse et langage*. Paris: Bordas.

Cargnelutti, E., and Muratori, A. M. 1988. Trasformazioni in psicoanalisi. *Riv. Psicoanal.* (1988): 455–73.

Deleuze, G. 1964. *Marcel Proust et les signes*. Paris: Presses Universitaires de France.

De Renzis, G. 1987. Soggetto e relazione. In *Soggetto, relazione, trasformazione, Methods*. Rome: Borla.

Freud, S. 1900. *The interpretation of dreams*. S. E. Vols. 5–6. London: Hogarth Press.

———. 1909. *Notes upon a case of obsessive neurosis*. S. E. Vol. 10. London: Hogarth Press.

———. 1910. *Leonardo da Vinci: Memory of his childhood*. S. E. Vol. 11. London: Hogarth Press.

———. 1911. *Formulations of the two principles of mental functioning*. S.E. Vol. 12. London: Hogarth Press.

———. 1914. *Reflection, repetition and working through*. In *Collected papers*, Vol. 2. London: Hogarth Press.

———. 1937. *Constructions in analysis*. S. E. Vol. 23. London: Hogarth Press.

———. 1937–38. *Moses and monotheism: Three essays*. S. E. Vol. 23. London: Hogarth Press.

Galdo, A. M. 1985. La parola, una connessione di continuo e discreto. *Riv. Psicoanal.* (1985): 188–96.

Hempel, G. G. 1962. Spiegazione scientifica e spiegazione storica. In *Filosofia antica e conoscenza storica*, edited by Predeval Magrini. Florence: Nuova Italia.

Klein, M. 1957. *Envy and gratitude*. London: Tavistock.

Lavagetto, M. 1985. *Freud: La letteratura ed altro*. Turin: Einaudi.

Loch, W. 1977. Some comment, on the subject of psychoanalysis and truth. In *Thought, consciousness and reality*, edited by I. Smith. New Haven, Conn.: Yale University Press.

Mathieu, M. 1980. Preso atto. In *Psychanalyse et langage*, edited by D. Anzieu. Paris: Bordas.

Meltzer, D. 1984. Dream life. London: Lunie Press for The Roland Harris Ed. Trust.

Pasche, F. 1988. The work of construction or, if it is preferred, of reconstruction. *Psychoanalysis in Europe* 31 (1988): 15–27.

Spence, D. 1982. *Narrative truth and historical truth.* New York: Norton.

Viederman, S. 1979. The analytic space: Meaning and problems. *Psychoanal. Q.* 48: 257–91.

12

The Problem of Representability

Celestino Genovese

The problem of the relationship between representation and narration in psychoanalysis is the concern of at least two different fields of analysis which, although distinct, share significant common features.

The first of them is, in my view, the clinical-epistemological domain where the discussion focuses on whether the analytical narrative can be characterized as the representation of a historical truth or whether it is independent of such a historical truth insofar as it is a creative act of psychoanalytical hermeneutics. The answer to this question will result, more or less directly, in the identification of what were once called the "therapeutic factors" of analysis, an expression which many view as embarrassing today and which has, therefore, become unpopular.

The second domain has a clinical-developmental nature and tackles the problem from the point of view of developmental theories: the concern, here, is on the relationship between affects, representations, and language, as it is organized in the different stages of life. Since different notions of the object-relationship may result, there are obvious consequences which may have a bearing on the whole conception of the analytical process, affecting its objectives as well as the technical aspects of the clinical work.

Obviously, those who, within the clinical-epistemological approach, choose the hermeneutic solution may apparently disregard the issues raised by the developmental perspective as, for these authors, the psycho-analytical biographies play a role, and have a fate, independently of whether they match the patient's historical truth. I feel, however, that an element which is certainly shared by these two areas of reflection is the revived need to make reference to the notion of "psychical reality" which represents both the subject matter of the analytical experience and that being investigated in developmental processes.

An example of the first approach is given by the advocates of the so-called narrational perspective who are, in a way, urged by the sound need to set themselves free from the "naive realism" that claims that the psychoanalytical interpretation reliably reconstructs the analysand's far and recent past.

Schafer (1983), among others, points out that any psychoanalytical biography is functional to the context generated by a given query; it, therefore, changes whenever in the course of analysis different queries become the focus of attention. Thus, it also follows that analytical approaches based on different theoretical assumptions end up by producing sets of different biographies which tend to support the assumptions themselves.

The focus is, therefore, switched to a notion of the analytical process viewed as a system which is, per se, producing psychoanalytical stories; our concern is no longer focused on their reconstructive reliability, but on their being a second reality, generated by the analysis itself and representing the very object of the analysis.

It is clear that, by so doing, one seriously questions (provided it were necessary) a simplistic notion of the reconstruction work meant as a puzzle, consisting of fragments of memory which come to the surface as the domain of repression slides back. At the same time, however, other problems arise whose solution is far more difficult.

We can, for example, share Schafer's observation that "the analysand's account of what he or she is talking 'about' must be regarded as merely one version of the story-content to which reference is being made" (252) and that "each account presents a more or less different event" (ibid.). The discourse becomes, on the contrary, more difficult to follow when Schafer states that "the conclusion to draw is that there is no one, final, true, all-purpose account of that event" (ibid.). We may certainly agree on the first two adjectives: no account is, ever, one and final. However, the adjectives are used by the author as if they were complementary to the other two ("true" and "all-purpose") whereas, in my opinion they are completely independent of one another. The very fact that it is impossible to obtain a final account of an event means that the richness of the inner world, with its emotional implications and its symmetrical logic (Matte

Blanco 1975) which also includes contradiction, gives rise to a similar richness of narrative angles. From this there does not follow (at least, not necessarily) that, since there are many versions of one account they are not "true" and "all-purpose." For example, from the point of view of the psychical reality, the statement "I loved my mother" is not invalidated by the opposite statement "I hated my mother," in that both can be, even historically, true and variously interlocked.

In other words, the manifoldness of accounts only explains that it is impossible to translate, into a univocal semantic representation, a truth which, defensively simplified in the analysand's memory, is gradually discovered by him/her in its incredibly complex and contradictory features.

On the other hand, by disregarding or even disavowing a truth, the hermeneutical position comes across the thorny and unsolved problem of interpretative criteria. Namely, if each account is only one of the many feasible ones, what are the unfeasible accounts and how can one differentiate them from the others? In sum, what is the difference between analysis and confabulation, reality testing and delirium?

As others did before him (e.g. Sherwood 1969), Schafer seeks to solve this problem by making sure each account is validated within the system it belongs to and, to be valid, the system must show it possess "the values of coherence, consistency, comprehensiveness" (236). It is quite apparent, however, that for these criteria to be effectively defined they need, in turn, further parameters; the author himself seems to be quite aware of this when he identifies a "refined common sense" as the ultimate referee—a concept which, epistemologically, is even weaker in my view.

Another possibility would be to link the "all-purposefulness" of the account to its transformative effectiveness. This, however, would assign an absolute value to the notion of transformation regardless of its direction, since the link between the patient's historical truth and the psychic economy of change has been removed.

Taken to its extreme, this position would make the very objectives of the analytical process questionable. In fact, if—as advocated by Schafer— the events are a function of the questions posed by the analyst on the basis of "his narrative strategies," the clinical intervention would inevitably reflect manipulative endeavors. Some authors, such as Spence (1982), explicitly theorize, on these grounds, the efficacy of interpretation.

In this way, the critique of the naive and simplistic idea of historical truth escapes control and the conception of the psychoanalytical process results in a sort of pragmatic-operational radicalism.

My contention is that, in spite of its apparent simplicity, the notion of 'historical truth' itself is often used in a polyvalent and basically ambiguous way.

Spence's contribution—referred to above—is a very effective example of such a misunderstanding. His central argument is that, in the course of analysis, the patient continuously finds himself tackling the conflict between what is true but hardly describable—"the pure memory"—and what is describable but somewhat untrue—"the screen memory"(61).

Quoting Barthes (1977), he compares the so-called true memories with the faithful description of a photograph, whilst the screen memories would be more like drawing, in that, by definition, they are more stereotyped and functional to producing a certain type of effect. Now, since the latter would more easily lend themselves to verbal description, as they have already been modified and adapted, the analyst would find himself to be mostly working with this kind of material without, however, being able to discriminate it from what is "true." Spence (1982) infers that "the change in a patient's productions during the course of treatment may have more to do with a change in his descriptive ability than with a change in the memories per se" (61).

This contrast between a hypothetical truthful representation of reality (photograph) and a narrational, virtually artistic, representation (drawing) can hardly be proved. In fact, it would imply that the assumption be made of a representation only erratically related to affects, an assumption which has become impracticable since Freud showed that the traumatic theory of neuroses was unreliable. All memories are the result of a psychical working out and can always be considered, though to a varying degree, more like drawings than photographs. Thus, since the early stages of the individual's life, they make up that second reality that Schafer considers, instead, a peculiar construction of the analytical work alone. In this sense, when we speak of "psychical reality" we do not only mean to designate that domain of psychology that has an order of reality of its own, which may be scientifically investigated, but what for the person, in his or her own inner world, takes up the value of reality (Laplanche and Pontalis 1967)

In addition, in any analytical reconstruction work it is unimportant whether the psychical reality of the subject is, or is not, equivalent to a truthful representation of events that have actually occurred. Freud himself stressed that "up to the present we have not succeeded in pointing to any difference in the consequences, whether phantasy or reality has had the greater share in these events of childhood" (Freud 1915–17, 370).

However, not only this view does not diminish the importance of the historical truth, but it stresses and enhances its peculiarities as a history of subjectivity and of its phantasies, as these have become sedimented in time from as far away as a very distant past.

There is no doubt that the narrative truth, which concerns the *hic et nunc,* alters and continuously transforms the account of the past; however, no account, in all its versions, would be feasible and to a certain extent analyzable save as today's landing place of the complex past history of the analysand's subjectivity, whose traces must not be searched for in the "true" memory or in the reliable representation. They are, instead, actual and tangible traces expressed by the compulsion to repeat and the power of transference as well as by the peculiar features of defenses that tenaciously survive any semantic change and any query raised by the analyst.

The same need for clarity as to what is meant by "psychical reality" is also found in the critique that Spence himself makes of the analysis of dreams made in the clinical practice.

According to Spence, the method of free associations is mistakenly considered a favored way to gain access to the meanings of the dream. It would, instead, lead to an arbitrary breakup of the pure dream image, of the visual representation of the scene, into fragments. In other words, since the process of association is oriented and conditioned by language needs, it would end up by inevitably eroding "the visual plot of the original dream" (Spence, 64). The role of interpretation, therefore, would not be that of decoding—as this is not feasible—but would lie in the aesthetic experience that interpretation itself represents. As is apparent, the complexity of the association activity which is viewed as misleading is once again opposed by the idea of a pure and original image, a truthful perception of something that has the nature of an unattainable elementary unit. And this becomes the very basis of a narrative option which allows one to be relieved from the dramatic responsibility of any correspondence.

As a matter of fact, we know that this phantasied pure and original image of the dream is the result of a complex work which uses, as its ingredients and instruments, the ancient representations differently loaded with affects and ancient affects differently represented by residues of wakefulness. They are combined together through displacements and condensations, following the modes of operation of that very psychical reality which is produced in the association activity. In sum, what Freud calls "the condition of representability" in visual dream images is laboriously acquired through the translation of the ideational contents into other more representable language forms, based exactly on the same mechanisms as also regulate the reverse process of free associations (Freud 1900). It suffices to recall, as a mere example, the dream of the high tower placed at the center of the stalls in the Opera House, on top of which the orchestra director stands. Freud shows how the scene translates the ideational contents of the man's grandeur in the language form of 'towering' on the other members of the orchestra, thus constructing the condition of the visual representability. This Freudian intuition has been recently validated by the cognitivist assumption that—as M. Mancia puts it—"the system organizing one's own awareness of the dream (in its narrational and representational aspects) is the same as the one which organizes language (in its syntactic and semantic aspects) (Foulkes 1985)" (Mancia 1987, 102). This would, among other things, be supported by Epstein and Simmons's observations (1983) on the absence of dreams in aphasic subjects.

Of course, there are sufficient chances that the two processes will not overlap; it is now acknowledged, however, that the clinical usefulness of the construction or reconstruction work on dreams does not lie in the accurate and detailed decoding of a repressed plot. In this case too, the historical truth must be understood as the history of the patient's truths, brought to the present and reexperienced not in the account, but in today's relational experience. In this regard, Mancia's definition of the dream as a "hierofany" proves to be quite effective, that is, as the expression of one feature of the sacred at one time of its history, which represents those internal objects that have a theological meaning for the individual. In the course of analysis, therefore, the dreams allow us "to recover the emotions once experienced, that have characterized the developmental path of the mind and that allow the childish traits of the patient's personality to become manifest in the transference" which is meant in all its relational manifestations, "including the use that the patient makes of the analyst, beyond what he/she can communicate with words" (Mancia, 127).

The latter is an important qualification as it extends the domain of the relationship to mental contents which, while expressed in the analytical setting, cannot be represented verbally and, therefore, go beyond psychoanalytical narratives.

The experience of any analyst can only confirm this observation (Genovese 1986) which, however, simultaneously introduces many other problems in different domains. Let us try and indicate some of them.

First, since, as stressed earlier, there is a close link between dream representation and language, is it legitimate to conclude that—in order to be dreamed of—the mental nonverbalized contents must lack the "condition of representability?"

And if we accept an exclusively presentational unconscious activity (Gori 1988), lacking the requirements to gain access to a true representation, what is—if any—its protopattern in childhood development?

With respect to this, one could also embark on the endless discussion as to whether the infant has true dream activity, but there is a great risk that we would be confronted with an unanswerable question: in fact, the only data we could make reference to are those produced by the neurophysiology of sleep which can tell us nothing on the quality and meaning of a purely mental activity. What we know in this area is that, while even at birth it is possible to discriminate active from quiet sleep, the more or less final organization of sleep with a one-phase trend and a desynchronized tracing is not obtained before the sixth month of life.

This, per se, does not allow us to draw any conclusion concerning the psychic domain. However, we can but observe that it is fully homogeneous with the assumption frequently made in the psychoanalytical literature that, apart from all theoretical models, this stage of development is crucial to the maturation process: the creation of the internal object in Melanie Klein (1952); the early signs of differentiation in Margaret Mahler (1968); the onset of transitional phenomena in Winnicott (1951).

Even Stern, who has indeed devoted most of his studies to reject the developmental model worked out by these authors, does acknowledge that the first sense of Self, which he defines as "nuclear," needs a maturation time which in the child ranges from the third to the sixth month of life. Before this age, the infant's experience would be the emergence of progressively integrating networks. He qualifies, however, that the integrated networks which are formed are not embodied yet into a single organizing subjective perspective. This task will, instead, be fulfilled in the subsequent developmental stage (Stern 1985).

We may disregard, here, the lively debate introduced by Stern's surveys on the richness of the infant's early interactive abilities. I will confine myself to observe that, where the experiences cannot yet be organized by a unifying subjectivity, the infant's feeling of himself can only be fragmentary and may be confined to the single experience that he is, from time to time, living through (Gaddini 1982). Thus, since he lacks the sense of continuity of self (Winnicott 1956) he will also lack, at least in his early months of life, the comparative and discriminative function that represents a presupposition of representability. This initial condition experienced by the newborn has a huge emotional value. In fact, with his vulnerability, he may be exposed to a massive mobilization of anxiety which, mind you, does not depend on the intensity of the stimulus, no matter whether endogenous or exogenous, nor is it only a quantitative problem. The experience can, instead, be anxious because of the disrupting mental sense it takes insofar as it does not have the discrete character it could have were it representable.

For example, the desperate cry of the infant whose mother is only a few minutes late on scheduled meals, is certainly disproportionate to the presumable intensity of the hunger stimulus. It is more likely to be the consequence of the inability to indicate the presentation of the frustrating experience by means of a range of representations, from those related to space and time to those related to the actions specifically targeted to getting satisfaction. In other words, the distress that the infant experiences in this condition has no mental space-time limits and, most importantly, has neither a "why" nor a "solution." The feeling that he has of himself coincides tout court with his distressing experience; hence, a nameless anxiety pervades all his precarious balance and threatens its wholesomeness. Only the ultradian rhythms of repetition, in the rich pattern of interactions with his mother and with the activation of memory, will gradually allow the infant to scale down the sense and scope of the experience, for example, to assess its appropriate dimension. If the developmental conditions are satisfactory, this will be the early basis of representability. If not, in the subsequent periods of life, the primary anxiety can be mobilized also in an advanced representational setting to which it may link in order to seek, a posteriori, a narrative expression.

Let's consider, for example, the agoraphobic symptom or anxious dreams of falling in the vacuum. In both cases, the open spaces or the act of falling down, in the dream scene, are semantic expedients that seek to explain to the conscience affective presentations which, otherwise, would not be mentally recordable and thus be disruptive.

Here, however, the mechanism is not—as in Freud's formula described earlier—to translate one form of representation into another language form. What occurs, instead, is a de novo construction of a link between the primary affect lacking representation and a representation which is conveniently selected: in this way, the attempt is made to give a semantic form to contents whose emotional peculiarity remains however, as indicated earlier, the inability of being represented.

I think that this paradox explains the agoraphobic patients' insistence in seeking to describe in detail their anxiety episodes ("I wish you could be in my place, even for one instant, so you would be able to understand!"). This anxiety seems to affect all the levels of mental organization which are close to the somatic domain; thus, the feared "rupture of self" (Bertolini 1984; Gaddini 1984) is experienced as a threat of being physically crushed.

There are major clinical implications stemming from this problem, as they lead us to tackle, among other things, the issue of psychoanalytical narratives in a reversed perspective relative to that chosen by the authors mentioned earlier. The question that we are posing, in fact, concerns the fate that these prerepresentational—I would say prehistorical—elements have in the psychoanalytical setting, in that they cannot become part of the autobiography, but preserve their disruptive potential for the individual's mental distress and throughout his or her life.

In other works I have tried to stress that in the analytical setting, along with the verbal relation a silent relational experience develops which embodies various ingredients, among them the physical person of the analyst, with his attention capacity, his style, his voice modulations, etc. It is an interactive, indeed prerepresentational, level which is expressed in the actual physical attributes of the consulting room made up of penumbra, of scents, of tactile peculiarities to which the most primitive and ineffable aspects of the patient's personality are related. Only gradually, through rhythmic repetition, the setting constants acquire for the analysand both a sense and a value in terms of intersubjectivity and make up a double rhythm which is the very presupposition that makes the world of representations develop into a dialogical realm in which meanings can be shared (Genovese 1986, 1990).

A reductive interpretation of these issues could result in the analyst's encoding a precept of the kind "speaking less and paying more attention to the setting." Although this warning would often be appropriate, this is not what concerns me here. What I mean to say is that the failure to understand the ongoing process involving the unspoken level of the relation can sometimes lead to a pseudo-working through of the representational contents, at times to a "negative therapeutic reaction," and still at other times to a possibly interminable analysis.

It is, indeed, clear that when the primary anxiety of the loss of the self is underlying the psychic distress, the whole autobiographic account may play a defensive role: it lends an apparently meaningful form to emotional contents that, by their own nature, are not representable and assigns them more clear-cut boundaries, a time frame and, most importantly, the possibility of thinking of them so as to dilute the dramatic power.

There are, for example, patients who, in the course of the analysis, remain for a long time hanging on not more than five or six pivot-events of their childhood. They evoke them again and again, regularly, with a lot of pathos, every time with the same details, and assign them an unreplaceable and ineffable documentary value that explains their current distress. I think of a young analysand who, through these accounts, effectively represents his condition of unwanted child, abortively expelled from the mother's mind since the very beginning. The narrative plot of his memories resembles some of Dickens's novels where the child character is a powerless victim of the most dreadful cruelties. He shows, in this way, to have a very poor and fragile sense of self, to experience the condition of being a forsaken wretch without reference points and without resources whatsoever. Even in his dreams, the patient represents himself as a deportee in a concentration camp, being hardly able to survive and dispossessed not only of his capacity to react but of his capacity to desire.

In the course of the session the associations follow a predictable course, in that they unfailingly lead to one of the events of the patient's personal myth (Kris 1956).

Under these circumstances, the crucial point is that the narrative truth of the myth is the screen (in its twofold meaning of representation and concealment) which defensively historicizes a dramatically present truth, as it is a timeless truth. By proposing his myth, the patient calls us into the play of his tragedy but, at the same time, puts us at a distance lest the tragic elements should become too evident.

This is, actually, what we are coping with.We can certainly determine to act on the myth, by relieving it—if we can—from its hypostatic motionlessness and by making its metaphor dynamic from the intrapsychic point of view. This is the narrational hypothesis which aims at fostering the production of new narrative horizons.

However, the risk is that of not recognizing the tragic and actual dimension of the anxiety "of one's own insubstantiality" which is desperately exorcised by searching for a story which makes sense.

In this case, although each account of the same story may make the world of representations problematic and richer, it may at the same time end up by perpetuating the screening of despair for the still impending catastrophe.

Translated by Silvana Siciliano

REFERENCES

Barthes R. 1977. *Image, music, text*. New York: Hill & Wang.

Bertolini, A. 1984. Fusione, separazione, funzione dei genitori. In *Atti* of the congress *Il trauma della nascita, la nascita del trauma* (Rome, 27–29 January). Rome: IES Mercury.

Epstein, A. W., and Simmons, N. N. 1983. Aphasia with reported loss of dreaming. *Am. J. Psychiat.* 140: 108–9.

Foulkes, D. 1985. *Dreaming: A cognitive-psychological analysis*. London: Lawrence Erlbaum.

Freud, S. 1900. *The interpretation of dreams. S. E.* Vols. 4 and 5.

———. 1915–17. *Introductory lectures on psychoanalysis*, Chapter 23, *S. E.* Vol. 16.

Gaddini, E. 1982. Early defensive fantasies and psychoanalytical process. *Int. J. Psychoanal.* 63: 379–86.

———. [1984] 1989. Trauma della nascita e memoria della nascita. In *Scritti*. Milan: Cortina.

Genovese, C. 1986. La sensorialità e l'ineffabile nella relazione analitica. Paper presented at the *Giornate di Studio sul pensiero di E. Gaddini*, Centro Psicoanalitico di Roma (27–28 September).

———. 1990. Narcissistic repetition and primary creativity in the analytic situation. *Riv. Psicoanal.* 26: 1082–1111.

Gori, E. C. 1988. *Costruzioni Freudiane: la mente*. Rome: Armando.

Klein, M. 1952. Some theoretical conclusions regarding the emotional life of the infant. In *Developments in psychoanalysis,* edited by M. Klein, P. Heimann, S. Isaacs, and J. Riviere. London: Hogarth Press.

Kris, E. 1956. The personal myth. In *The selected papers of Ernst Kris.* New Haven: Yale University Press, 1975.

Laplanche, J., and Pontalis, J. B. 1967. *Vocabulaire de la psychanalyse.* Paris: Presses Universitaires de France.

Mahler, M. 1968. *On human symbiosis and the vicissitudes of individuation, Vol. 1: Infantile Psychosis.* New York: International Universities Press.

Mancia, M. 1987. *Il sogno come religione della mente.* Rome: Laterza.

Matte Blanco, I. 1975. *The unconscious as infinite sets: An essay in bi-logic.* London: Gerald Duckworth.

Ogden, T. H. 1989. Autistic-contiguous Position. *Int. J. Psychoanal.* 70, 1: 127–40.

Rossi, R. 1985. Mito e tragedia: passato e presente nell'interpretazione. *Riv. Psicoanal.* 21, 4: 495–508.

Schafer, R. 1983. *The analytic attitude.* London: Hogarth Press.

Sherwood, M. 1969. *The logic of explanation in psychoanalysis.* New York: Academic Press.

Spence, D. P. 1982. *Narrative truth and historical truth.* New York: Norton.

Stern, D. N. 1985. *The Interpersonal world of the infant.* New York: Basic Books.

Winnicott, D. W. [1951] 1958. Transitional objects and transitional phenomena. In *Collected papers: Through paediatrics to psycho-analysis.* London: Tavistock; New York: Basic Books.

———. 1956. Primary maternal preoccupation. In ibid.

13

Construction and Reconstruction in Transference

Mauro Mancia

In this essay I will examine the construction and reconstruction processes that are liable to develop within transference. Hence I will take construction to mean the comprehension, selection, and organization of the transferential material which emerges into the ongoing relationship, while reconstruction will be understood as an operation which recaptures the (traumatic and untraumatic) events and affective processes of times past, reproduced during the actual time of analysis. Following this principle, construction may be considered a synchronic operation, whereas reconstruction is diachronic; it is founded on an integration of the past and on the capacity—emerging during analysis—to relate in an affectively significant manner to past actions, that is, to the ontogenesis of affective and cognitive processes.

For construction and reconstruction to be integrated in such a manner as to hold a specific meaning for a particular patient, his memory will have to be activated and used as a supporting frame for all possible events connected with the relation. It is, therefore, with memory as the creator of every reconstructive process that I will begin my inquiry.

Memory as a function is a dominant recurrent theme in Freud's works. It is mentioned in his *Project for a Scientific Psychology* (1895) as part of the metaphoric system called ψ, the seat of released drives and repressed desires. In *The Interpretation of Dreams* (1900), it is assigned the task of interconnecting our perceptions; in *Screen Memories* (1899), however, the memory of the first years of childhood is viewed as rather untrustworthy: the recollection of an event might be a *constructed* remembrance of childhood. Freud thought that childhood memories only gain substance in later phases of life, through a process which involves the same kind of remodeling as that exercised by a nation edifying legends about its own origins. It is a historical activity, therefore, which makes it possible to apprehend the past in the contemporary present. In Freud's metapsychological works of 1915–17, memory is introduced as an indefinite storage system of whatever has been repressed, acting as a function related in equal measure to both the conscious and the unconscious. Analogies with *A Note upon the Mystic Writing-Pad* of 1925 decisively bring memory into the sphere of analytical work, because it is in analysis that the patient can "be brought to recollect certain experiences," according to Freud (1937), "and the affective impulses called up by them which he has for the time being forgotten" (257–58). The analytic work in fact addresses the past transposed into the present through transference and through its capacity to promote a return of the affective relationships which are significant to the patient.

We should not forget at this point that Freud had, at the beginning of his career (1914), practiced the method of hypnosis, which was considered "the ideal remembering of what has been forgotten" (151), since under such conditions—that I would call experimental—resistance is constantly discarded. When he renounced hypnosis, Freud was faced with the necessity of finding out, through free associations, what the patient failed to recollect when in a conscious state. Positive transference, according to Freud, allowed the patient to plunge into the sea of his memories, exactly as under hypnosis. If the transference were hostile, on the other hand, remembering would immediately give way to acting-out. Freud will never cease to astonish us, however, with the valuable contradictions which he integrated into his thought and due to which we must constantly reexamine our ideas. The patient's illness, he said (1914), should be treated "not as an event of the past, but as a present-day force" (151). He thus stated in clear terms that, although the patient experiences those elements of his disorder which come into the treatment's field of action in the *present,* the analyst must reconduct such elements to the *past.* Contrary to what happens in hypnosis, then, the analytic treatment allows the patient to conjure up "a piece of real life" (152), an exercise which is not easily tolerated by the patient, and which would at any rate account for any temporary deteriorations of his state. There is always a danger for the patient to be dominated by a compulsion to repeat which would prevent him from recollecting. Transference is the "playground" in which the analyst can help the patient handle this compulsion to repeat, "replacing his ordinary neurosis by a 'transference neurosis'. . . . The transference thus creates"—Freud concludes (1914)—"an intermediate region between illness and real life, through which the transition from the one to the other is made" (154). The obvious obstacle to this process is the state of resistance in which the patient might plunge himself with the aim of reelaborating and surpassing it.

In 1937, Freud reexamined the question of memory and recollection. In *Constructions in Analysis* he affirmed that the task of recollection must be shouldered by the patient, while the analyst must construct "what has been forgotten from the traces which it has left behind" (258–59).

At this point, Freud (1937) coined a metaphor borrowed from archaeology: "His [the analyst's] work of construction or, if it is preferred, of reconstruction, resembles to a great extent an archaeologist's excavation of some dwelling-place that has been destroyed and buried or of some ancient edifice" (259). It seems clear to me at this point that, in Freud's opinion, the work of the archaeologist and that of the analyst are comparable. Both reconstruct a piece of past life through an integration and recomposition of material. Nevertheless, when it comes to the concept of transference that Freud had at this stage of his life, the analyst seems to have an easier time of it than the archaeologist. His working conditions are in fact more propitious because the transference guides him in his search for past events and guarantees the accuracy of his reconstructions, which are based on the historical truth of the patient, that is, on repetitions of his past.

As it was formulated in 1937, Freud's statement might give the impression that the two terms were used interchangeably. This belief stems from the fact that—to Freud—transference recreated a foregone situation highlighted by analysis, in which the patient's past history was reenacted and when what seemed forgotten was revived. The point was, according to Freud, that of contrasting a historical truth with a material or real truth; the historical truth would emerge from the patient's dreams and free associations, possible evidence for events that had really taken place in the patient's mind. It is on the basis of this historical truth that the analyst seeks to produce a construction similar to that of the archaeologist who strives to fit together the different fragments of his finds. In Freud's words (1937): "it is a construction when one lays before the subject of the analysis a piece of his early history that he has forgotten" (261). It is obviously this operation, therefore, that makes the analytical work directly reconstructive. This is exemplified by Freud's following conjecture (1937): "Up to your nth year you regarded yourself as the sole and unlimited possessor of your mother; then came another baby and brought you grave disillusionment. Your mother left you for some time, and even after her reappearance she was never again devoted to you exclusively. Your feelings towards your mother became ambivalent, your father gained a new importance for you" (261). This interpretation, in my opinion, is clearly a reconstructive one.

By keeping the distinction between construction and reconstruction hazy, Freud reflects his conviction that the construction based on the patient's narrations or dreams constitutes his *historical truth,* which may be transformed through analytical work into his *psychic reality* and, as such, be related to the past in the form of a *reconstruction.* As the expression of a process that is so closely linked to historical truth, reconstruction seemed to Freud a valid protection against the charge of suggestion. Construction, on the other hand, might seem rather like a creation which is not necessarily related to the past and might therefore lead to an accusation of suggestion by the patient. Furthermore, construction might be considered arbitrary because it is not based on historical truth. Reconstruction, on the contrary, was more objective in his opinion, and provided him with a guarantee that he was abiding by the scientific method.

The new paradigm proposed by Klein (1932) shifted the main emphasis of analytical observation from repression to the chain of processes that is the groundwork of the internal world. The unconscious thus becomes a "society" of interrelated objects at the heart of which the constructive and reconstructive work carried out by the analytical couple integrates itself. Construction and reconstruction are then subjected to a new conceptualization linked to a transformation of the concept of transference (Etchegoyen 1986). In the postscript to *Fragment of an Analysis of a Case of Hysteria* (1905), Freud reaffirms that the analytical treatment does not create a transference, but simply reveals it and makes it conscious. It is a common phenomenon, a special object-relationship of infantile origin, of an unconscious and therefore irrational nature, which tends to confuse the present with the past due to a "false" connection for which the primary object of childhood is confused with that of the current relation. Hence transference pertains to both psychic reality and phantasy, insofar as it is a product of the unconscious rather than of material reality or facts. The psychic object born through the transference is a consequence of this dialectical interplay between phantasy and reality.

To Klein and her students (Joseph 1985), transference, with its anxieties and defenses, is more than that: it is the reiteration in the present situation of a relationship between internal objects, a procedure which represents, as in a private theater, the relations that the objects which make up the inner world have with each other and with the self. But since the organization of the inner world and its objects is an expression of the affective-cognitive development of the child, beginning from its oldest object relation, it is in transference that the most significant processes underlying the history of the child's relation with its objects (parents in the first place) are represented. This is at least true of some (traumatic and untraumatic) affective events, even if the occurrence of an isomorphic mother/child and analyst/patient relation cannot be demonstrated. Recent inquiries, in fact, have shown that many hypotheses on child development, which were deduced from works on transference in the adult, do not correspond to what may actually be observed in an experimental inquiry (Stern 1985). Nevertheless, analytical observations allow for the creation of a model of infantile mental development with its own clinical importance and heuristic power, independently of experimental observations on the mother/child relation. The child who emerges in the course of analysis is not a real child. He is a mythical child, reconstructed within transference, presenting himself as the model of a sui generis relation activated by transference. Along this line of thought the reconstruction which can be carried out in analysis is not so much connected to a material or real truth as to a historical one—which brings us closer to Freud's theory (Rinaldi 1988)—if, by historical truth, we mean the memory of the (traumatic or untraumatic) affective-cognitive processes which characterize the patient's story and his mental development.

An important contribution to the development of this idea is the concept formulated by Cassirer (1955) that in the most primitive temporal structures, "the whole of consciousness and its contents falls, as it were, into two spheres: a bright sphere, illumined by the light of the present, and another, dark sphere; and between these two basic levels, there are as yet no mediations of transition, no shadings or degrees" (1,

217). It is the analyst, with his work on transference as the word is currently understood, who carries out this mediation by proposing passages and matching shades so as to integrate the two spheres, the illuminated one and the dark one.

The reconstructive work is therefore carried out by the pair in conjunction. The patient shares in it with his memory activated in and by transference. The analyst is thus enabled to infer the affective history of the patient from the transference material as well as from his own countertransferential feelings. As a result, it becomes possible for the patient to write a new biography for himself, and such rewriting is also equivalent to a construction, inasmuch as he gains the ability to represent a new internal world, organized into a new "society," with objects having a different relationship with each other than they had in the past. Construction as a work of comprehension (Riesenberg Malcolm 1988), selection and organization of transferential material, together with its contextual integration in the relationship, are the main duties of the analyst (Mancia 1990). Constructions constitute the liveliest and most creative aspects of analytical work, but they are by definition incomplete and always subject to change and transformation. They are related to partial aspects of the patient's personality, specific relational modalities, and defenses represented or acted out in accordance with the anxieties activated by the analytical relation. The analyst's task is to put into words, that is, to provide a narrative linearity, for the associative sequences and dreams narrated in the analytical context. In his construction, the analyst must be capable of guessing the metaphorical meaning of the patient's associations and the symbolical level of his communications. Only through such construction can he connect the emergent material to the transference and then eventually to the patient's past. "'The logical development' of the link between the present and the past," writes Corradi Fiumara (1980), "seems feasible only through a level of symbolization suitable not only to indicate and constitute external *objects,* but also to construct (internal) relations that in fact express the connections, or links, between the different elements of the internal organization, as between inner and outer, and also between present and past real situations" (translated freely, 96). This idea is obviously related to psychoanalysts like us who, on the strength of the transferential elements which appear during the analytical session, succeed in constructing internal relations and interpreting connections, links, and elements of an internal organization, as it is represented in transference.

The final goal of any construction is, I said, its fitness for narration. The specific narrative modalities of the analytical couple are of the utmost importance because they are part of this "formal" aspect by which the transference/countertransference interplay develops itself. The musicality of the patient's narration, for instance, the tone of his voice, whether it is lively or monotonous, his use of syntax, his choice of words, his rhythmic assemblage of single words and construction of sentences, all this comes under those formal aspects which convey, over and above the words themselves, and beyond their content, such affects that have a deep transferential significance. We know from clinical experience that the manner in which language is used in analysis can represent a real acting-out and that it can be used to threaten the bond rather than to favor insight.

The same holds true of the communications made by the analyst, who can deliver an interpretation in numberless ways, in which the tone of his voice, his choice of words, the syntax and the rhythms he adopts, are all vehicles of intense countertransferential emotions. This is why the role played by the narrations of both patient and analyst in the analytic process has been the subject of remarkable studies by various analysts (Schafer 1983). Let me refer at this point to the ideas formulated by Spence (1982), who underlines the manner in which narrative truth, to Freud, merges with historical truth taken as psychic reality, and the manner in which it is the coherence of the account which inspires belief in the reality of the event in question. Freud's idea that every interpretation, in view of the fact that it is narrative truth, always contains a piece of historical truth, follows from this analogy.

What I wish to emphasize most of all here is the importance of such narrative elements over and above the verbal language. The verbal language is not always the most adequate vehicle for the affective representations that the subject wishes to communicate. Galdo (1990), paraphrasing Anzieu (1958), asserts that language is a code which transcends the individual and that those who speak it update, bend, and modulate it, transgress and pervert it, to express, show, and impose their own subjectivity. She concludes that we are often caught by two opposing desires: the desire to be understood that leads us to comply with an agreed code and the narcissistic desire to remain impenetrable.

Analysis has in fact made us realize that the patient is subjected to a conflict that is as real to him as a piece of life but that he has difficulties in communicating in words; whereas what he is able to describe, on the other hand, might not exactly correspond to his life experience. In reality, however, he can communicate to the analyst even what he is prevented from putting into words by the inadequacy of his language, or because the affects he lives are related to experiences from preverbal epochs, experiences organized into affective representations that fall short of linkage to verbal representations, of coming, that is, under the linguistic system of meanings. In such cases, the patient can use nonverbal modes of communication, dominated by splitting and projective identification, which in the analytical pattern of development correspond to those lived by the child in its primary childhood (I am referring to the paranoid/schizoid position). Such modalities, in fact, exist prior to the formation of language and survive in the mind as emotional memories (the memories in feeling described by Klein). During the analytical session such experiences are not verbally remembered and communicated by the patient, but emotionally reexperienced and reenacted in the relationship by means of the preverbal modalities which are better than words at inducing intense countertransference emotions (Rosenfeld 1987). It is only natural and part of the analytical game that the nonverbal communications of the patient—if properly elaborated—should become precious instruments for us to understand the more subtle aspects of transference or to unearth split parts of the self and construct a hypothesis of specific significance.

All this work—which can be very creative—is made possible by transference, which forces the patient to take in the analyst as one of his internal objects and hence to interact with him through phantasies, anxieties, and defenses characteristic of his relations with the primary objects of his childhood. Construction then develops a new biographical story which takes into account emotions and experiences that had never as yet reached the level of consciousness. The new biography narrated in the course of analysis is new inasmuch as a new meaning is attributed to the affective experiences which are considered keys to the past. It is necessary, at any rate, to remember that both the patient's verbal and nonverbal communications during the hour, and the analyst's constructions and interpretations, serve to constitute hypotheses about the mind of the patient and its operative modalities. Further work might confirm or refute such hypotheses, but they do in any case stimulate the patient to produce more transferential material, and eventually modify his relation with reality: this will give the analyst, as he works on the basis of his own countertransference as well, the possibility to offer other construction hypotheses to his patient. These hypotheses are all the more "true" the closer they get to the emotional and affective reality of the patient, and the greater their capacity to confer specific meanings on this reality. Nevertheless, the truth of a construction or of an interpretation is always relative, and its composition develops in the propositional field delimited by transference and countertransference.

The stand adopted by Spence (1982), when he points out that narrative truth is independent of historical truth and that an interpretation, even an entirely imaginary one, can live its own life and achieve a truthful status of its own, seems exceedingly radical to me. In my opinion, the truthfulness of a construction rests most of all in its capacity to grasp and connect the emerging aspects of transference in that specific fleeting relational instant. Hence I would tend to agree with Viederman (1979), when he asserts that an interpretation does not necessarily have to be linked to the past (the narration is in fact a construction) and that it can acquire a truth of its own as it gradually gets structured in the analytical space; and with Loch (1977) when he says that the analytical material does not provide a truthful image of the past and therefore constructs contemporary truths only. Nevertheless, the patient's affective past is present in the ongoing relationship. Hence, construction can reshape the past, especially as regards preverbal experiences, which remain unacknowledged as long as they are not verbalized. In this form, construction may be confused with reconstruction, which would justify Spence's assertion (1982) that the past is constantly reconstructed during the analytical process. This allows us then to reaffirm that the constructions of the transferential present and the reconstructions of the infantile past are closely interdependent. It may be this interdependence that prevented many authors from making a conceptual distinction between construction and reconstruction, and that justifies Freud's use of the two terms as synonyms in 1937. At any rate, the construction/reconstruction interdependence signifies that, from the point of view of time, the analytical work is circular and not retrospectively unidirectional. We can then also consider analysis as an incentive to "reread," in the present situation, whatever has been stored and codified in the unconscious, and reconstruction an attempt to represent the patient's past history.

This standpoint naturally does away with Freud's archaeological model and makes us analysts feel a greater kinship with historians than with archaeologists (also see Chianese 1990). As with history, in fact, the past events of an individual can be remembered, represented, and relived in the present as well as reconnected to the past through transference. In this sense, they are no longer situated in time, but they in turn become knowledge of the eternal present (Gardiner 1952). Hence, every analytical story has some roots in the past which also stand as contemporary history, on the basis, that is, of the present situation of the relation. We too, like historians, could claim that the past does not really exist, in the sense that we shall never be able to know it in its actual reality, but a replica of it is available in the actuality of transference, that is, in the present. Transference is the key to the past, which allows us to establish connections between the incomplete and shapeless traces of past times and the emergent affects of the present, connections from which we can infer constructions and develop historical hypotheses.

To conclude, I wish to underline the importance of keeping the concept of construction distinct from that of reconstruction, even if the analytical work develops as a journey across the two concepts, which might overlap and intermingle, but must each keep an identity of its own. Construction must remain the expression of an effort of selection and linkage performed by the analyst on the transference material, so that a selected fact might emerge (according to Poincaré, quoted from Bion 1962) as the basis of an interpretation narrated to the patient. Reconstruction is a task that runs parallel to that of construction while being anchored to the past, thus providing an affective continuity for the experiences lived by the patient in the *hic et nunc,* the here and now, of the analytical relationship.

REFERENCES

Anzieu, D., ed. 1980. *Psycanalyse et langage*. Paris: Bordas.
Bion, W. R. 1962. *Learning from experience*. London: Heinemann.
Cassirer, E. 1955. *The philosophy of symbolic forms, Vol. 1: Language*. New Haven: Yale University Press.
Chianese, D. 1990. La conoscenza come trasformazione. In *Psicoanalisi e antropologia*. Rome: Borla.

Corradi Fiumara, G. 1980. *Funzione simbolica e filosofia del linguaggio.* Turin: Boringhieri.

Etchegoyen, R. H. 1986. *Los fundamentos de la tecnica psicoanalitica.* Buenos Aires: Amorrortu Editores.

Freud, S. *Project for a scientific psychology. S. E.* Vol. 1.

————. 1899. *Screen memories. S. E.* Vol. 3.

————. *The interpretation of dreams. S. E.* Vols. 4 and 5.

————. *Fragment of an analysis of a case of hysteria. S. E.* Vol. 7.

————. *Remembering, repeating and working through (Further recommendations on the technique of psychoanalysis, II). S. E.* Vol. 12.

————. *A metapsychological supplement to the theory of dreams. S. E.* Vol. 14.

————. 1925. *A note upon the mystic writing-pad. S. E.* Vol. 19.

————. 1937. *Constructions in analysis. S. E.* Vol. 23.

Galdo, A. M. 1990. Ricordo e narrazione nella clinica psicoanalitica. In *Rappresentazioni e narrazioni,* edited by M. Ammaniti and D. N. Stern. Rome: Laterza, 178–87. See chapter 11 of the present volume.

Gardiner, P. 1952. *The Nature of Historical Explanation.* London: Oxford University Press.

Joseph, B. 1985. Transference: The total situation. *Int. J. Psycho-Anal.* 66: 447–54.

Klein, M. 1932. *The psycho-analysis of children.* London: Hogarth.

Loch, W. 1977. Some comments on the subject of psychoanalysis and truth. In *Thought, consciousness and reality,* edited by J. Smith. New Haven: Yale University Press.

Mancia, M. 1990. *Nello sguardo di Narciso. Saggi su memoria, affetti e creatività.* Rome: Laterza.

Riesenberg Malcolm, R. 1988. Construction as re-living history. *EPF Symposium,* Stockholm (March).

Rinaldi, L. 1988. Verità storica e psicoanalisi. *Riv. Psicoanal.* 3: 561–605.

Rosenfeld, H. A. 1987. The narcissistic omnipotent character structure: A case of chronic hypochondriasis. In *Impasse and interpretation.* London: Tavistock.

Schafer, R. [1983] 1984. *L'atteggiamento analitico.* Milan: Feltrinelli.

Spence, D. P. 1982. *Narrative truth and historical truth.* New York: Norton.

Stern, D. 1985. *The interpersonal world of the infant.* New York: Basic Books.

Viederman, S. 1979. The analytic space: Meaning and problems. *Psychoanal. Q.* 48: 257–91.

Index

Abrams, M. H., 149
Account/accountability dialectic, 125
Accountability: through language, 129
Acting-out, 188, 193
Action: explanation of, 112–13, 117,
118–19; as privileged narrative modality, 129; and working through, 167–68
Action language, 2
Actualization, 73–74, 80
Adult: Oedipus as, 103, 104; role in narration, 131, 132; role in story discussion,
136–37, 144
Adult Attachment Interview (AAI), 84, 88
Affect(s), 175, 178, 180; in mother-infant
interaction, 91–92; and representation,
183
Affect mechanisms: splitting and isolation
of, 91
Affective-cognitive relationship, 124–25
Affective configurations: intergenerational
transmission of, 81–82
Agency: in narrative, 21. *See also* Human
agency
Agent(s), 112–13
Aggression, 68, 71, 127
Agoraphobic symptom, 183
Ainsworth, M., 81, 82, 90
Algorithmic processes, 111–12, 114
Alvarez, A., 91
Ambivalence, 106
American learning theory, 15
Amherst Project, 80
Ammaniti, Massimo, 1–11, 79–96
Amodal perception, 125
Amoni, M., 135, 136

Analysand's account: versions of, 176–77.
See also Patient(s)
Analysis. *See* Psychoanalysis
Analyst(s), 183, 184; communications by,
193–94; effect of transference communications on, 156–57, 158, 160; Fliess as
model of, 152; as internal object of patient, 194; Oedipus as, 104; place of,
149–64; and reconstruction work, 192–
93; role of, 169, 196
Analyst-patient relationship, 46, 159–60,
168
Analytic couple, 44, 193
Analytic field, 46
Analytic setting. *See* Psychoanalytic setting
Analytical transformations, 48
Analytical game, 194
Analytical process, 176–77, 178, 193–94
Analytical relationship, 57–58, 166, 169,
173 n. 7, 196
Analytical situation, 42–43, 151, 166; psychic conflict in, 68; standards of analytical presence in, 154, 155
Analytical stage, 7
Analytical work, 188, 190, 195
Anatomy of Melancholy (Burton), 116–17
Anthropologie (Kant), 56, 57
Anthropology, anthropologists, 19, 31, 32
Antithetical elements, 42
Anxiety, 68, 182, 183
Anzieu, D., 168, 193
Archaeological metaphor/model, 4, 170,
189–90, 196
Archaeology of Knowledge (Foucault), 32
Arendt, Hannah, 157